Cybercrime and Digital Deviance

Cybercrime and Digital Deviance, Second Edition, combines insights from sociology, criminology, psychology, and cybersecurity to explore cybercrimes such as hacking, identity theft, and romance scams, along with forms of digital deviance such as pornography addiction, trolling, and "canceling" people for perceived violations of norms.

Other issues are explored including cybercrime investigations, nation-state cybercrime, the use of algorithms in policing, cybervictimization, and expanded discussion of the theories used to explain cybercrime. Graham and Smith conceptualize the online space as a distinct environment for social interaction, framing their work with assumptions informed by their respective work in urban sociology and spatial criminology, and offering an engaging entry point for understanding what may appear to be a technologically complex course of study. The authors apply a modified version of a typology developed by David Wall: cybertrespass, cyberfraud, cyberviolence, and cyberpornography. This typology is simple enough for students just beginning their inquiry into cybercrime, while its use of legal categories of trespassing, fraud, violent crimes against persons, and moral transgressions provides a solid foundation for deeper study. In this edition each chapter includes a new "Current Events and Critical Thinking" section, using concepts from the chapter to explore a specific event or topic like the effect of disinformation on social cohesion and politics.

Taken together, Graham and Smith's application of a digital environment and Wall's cybercrime typology makes this an ideal upper-level text for students in sociology and criminal justice. It is also an ideal introductory text for students within the emerging disciplines of cybercrime and cybersecurity.

Roderick S. Graham is an Associate Professor of Sociology in the Sociology and Criminal Justice Department at Old Dominion University. He teaches courses on cybercrime, research methods, and racial inequality. He has published research in *Deviant Behavior, First Monday*, and *Youth and Society*.

'Shawn K. Smith is a Criminologist and Associate Professor of Criminal Justice in the Department of Criminal Justice at Radford University. His areas of research and pedagogy include social networking theories in crime, public policy in criminal justice, and advanced research procedures. He has published research in *Sociological Focus, Journal of Race and Ethnicity, Criminal Justice Studies: A Critical Journal of Crime, Law, and Society*, and *African Journal of Criminology and Justice Studies*.

Cybercrime and Digital Deviance

Second Edition

Roderick S. Graham and
'Shawn K. Smith

Routledge
Taylor & Francis Group

NEW YORK AND LONDON

Designed cover image: Shutterstock

Second edition published 2024
by Routledge
605 Third Avenue, New York, NY 10158

and by Routledge
4 Park Square, Milton Park, Abingdon, Oxon, OX14 4RN

Routledge is an imprint of the Taylor & Francis Group, an informa business

© 2024 Roderick S. Graham and 'Shawn K. Smith

The right of Roderick S. Graham and 'Shawn K. Smith to be identified as authors
of this work has been asserted in accordance with sections 77 and 78 of the
Copyright, Designs and Patents Act 1988.

First edition published by Routledge 2019

Library of Congress Cataloging-in-Publication Data
Names: Graham, Roderick, 1975- author. | Smith, Shawn K., author.
Title: Cybercrime and digital deviance/Roderick S. Graham and
'Shawn K. Smith.
Description: Second edition. | New York, NY: Routledge, 2024. |
Includes bibliographical references and index.
Identifiers: LCCN 2023049441 (print) | LCCN 2023049442 (ebook) |
ISBN 9781032254524 (hardback) | ISBN 9781032249193 (paperback) |
ISBN 9781003283256 (ebook)
Subjects: LCSH: Computer crimes. | Deviant behavior. | Internet–Social aspects.
Classification: LCC HV6773 .G7243 2024 (print) | LCC HV6773 (ebook) |
DDC 364.16/8–dc23/eng/20231107
LC record available at https://lccn.loc.gov/2023049441
LC ebook record available at https://lccn.loc.gov/2023049442

ISBN: 9781032254524 (hbk)
ISBN: 9781032249193 (pbk)
ISBN: 9781003283256 (ebk)

DOI: 10.4324/9781003283256

Typeset in Times New Roman
by Deanta Global Publishing Services, Chennai, India

Access the Support Material: www.routledge.com/9781032254524

To Eun Kyoung, Alex, Ella, Johnnie, and Olivia

Roderick Graham

To my family and friends for always showing me joy in life…

To my colleagues and students for always challenging me to grow…

'Shawn Smith

Contents

Figures

Tables

Acknowledgments

I wish to acknowledge the many agencies and colleagues I have come to rely upon extensively for insight and support as this edition and my contributions to it have come to fruition. Most notably, Maureen McClanahan (National White Collar Crime Center) and John Shehan (National Center for Missing and Exploited Children) …you have my deepest gratitude and allegiance.

'Shawn Smith

Understanding Cybercrime and Digital Deviance

Introduction

In this chapter, we introduce some core ideas and concepts that form the foundation for chapters to come. Most fundamentally, we define what we mean by cybercrime and digital deviance. Our definitions and explanations for these two phenomena are common across sociological and criminological texts. Next, we introduce the student to the notion of a "digital environment" and the layered technologies that produce that environment. We suspect the idea of layering will be unique to individuals not familiar with core ideas in the fields of computer science or computer-related disciplines. However, layering, once explained, helps the non-technologically oriented person make sense of the vast array of technologies that work together to produce the Internet. After explaining how layers work to produce the digital environment, we then address the issues that arise in studying cybercrime and digital deviance because of the rapid pace of technological change. We call these issues the five challenges of cybercrime and digital deviance. We prefer the term "challenges" because while rapid technological change increases the difficulty level when grappling with cybercrime and digital deviance, it also makes these topics exciting and fun! We end the chapter by presenting the four broad categories of cybercrime. These categories—cybertrespass, cyberpornography, cyberviolence, and cyberfraud are the heart of this text and, indeed will comprise the next several chapters.

Defining Cybercrime

There are many ways of describing cybercrime. The simplest definition is any crime that involves a computer. That would include crimes where a computer is the target, such as hacking, as well as crimes in which the target is a human, such as cyberstalking. But this definition may be too simple. Consider a street gang that uses smartphones to send text messages to each other. The text messages are helping the gang coordinate their activities,

DOI: 10.4324/9781003283256-1

and police can use these messages as evidence of a crime is being committed. But are smartphones any more than incidental to the gang's criminal activities? Probably not. The mere presence or incidental usage of computer technology when a crime is committed does not mean we should consider the crime "cyber."

This textbook will use a narrower definition. Cybercrime will be defined as (1) *crimes against a computer or computer network*, or (2) *crimes against a person in which the primary means of committing that crime is a computer or computer network*.

Defining Digital Deviance

What is digital deviance, and what makes it different than cybercrime? First, deviance needs to be defined. An everyday definition of deviance is "the undertaking of actions which do not conform to the norms or values that are widely accepted in society" (Giddens & Sutton, 2021, p. 187). A more social scientific definition of deviance would be normative violations that will elicit social control sanctions if detected. Given the importance of the concept of deviance to this text, we will explore the phenomena of deviance in more detail below.

A normative violation is an action or behavior different from either the statistical norm (the most common behavior) or the declared norm by people in power (a teacher declares in class that no cell phones can be used). Social control sanctions are imposed by others to regulate behavior. These sanctions can be formal and informal, positive or negative. Formal sanctions are prescribed by some type of rule or law and are usually administered within societal institutions. Informal sanctions, on the other hand, are not written but negotiated within a community like a neighborhood or a social group. A positive sanction is a reward given for a certain behavior. Formal positive sanctions include a teacher giving a good grade to a student, a corporation promoting someone at work, or the military recognizing someone for bravery. Informal positive sanctions can be a pat on the back by an elder to a young person for a job well done, or nods of approval from one's peers.

Positive and negative sanctions work together to control behavior. However, this text is more concerned with negative social sanctions. A negative social sanction is a punishment or negative stimulus imposed on a person for a certain behavior. Informal negative sanctions can be ostracism, being shot a bad look, or other ways people show a person that their behaviors are not approved of. A formal negative sanction can be being expelled from school or being fired for violating a policy at one's work. Crime is a type of normative violation that is met with a formal negative sanction from a state's law enforcement body. Table 1.1 presents the information above in a table form.

Table 1.1   Types of Sanctions

	Formal	Informal
Positive	Good grade for a student, a corporation promoting someone at work, or the military recognizing someone for bravery	A pat on the back by an elder to a young person for a job well done, or nods of approval from one's peers
Negative	Being expelled from school or being fired for violating a policy at one's work, incarceration, institutionalization	Ostracism, being shot a bad look, or other ways people show a person that their behaviors are not approved of

Deviant behavior is always a possibility in situations where people interact with each other over time. Deviance will be found in all of society's institutions–from prisons to schools to hospitals. These institutions have developed a set of expected behaviors that the individuals within those institutions are expected to follow. However, individuals will, for a variety of reasons, find cause to deviate from these expected behaviors. Deviance is also found in informal spaces where people congregate and socialize—street corners, boardrooms, fast food restaurants, homes, and social media spaces, to name a few. Expected behaviors develop and are enforced in these spaces as well, and individuals will, for a variety of reasons, want to deviate from these expectations. We can now define digital deviance. *Digital deviance refers to normative violations in the digital environment that elicit social control sanctions if detected.*

THE RELATIONSHIP BETWEEN CRIME AND DEVIANCE

We can illustrate the relationship between crime and deviance with an episode from Boston, Massachusetts, in 2010. In that year, the Boston Police received complaints that a person was using his phone to take pictures up women's dresses and skirts as they rode the subway. Police set up a sting operation, caught this person in the act, and arrested him. The person was arrested under the state's "peeping Tom" laws—photographing an unsuspecting nude or partially nude person.

However, the defendant's lawyer argued that the people whose pictures were taken were neither nude or semi-nude, and thus no law was violated. In 2014, a court in the US state of Massachusetts agreed, and the charges were dismissed. Immediately after the court's decision, the governor of that state signed an "upskirting" law making similar actions in the future illegal. And by immediately after, it is meant the next day. After the court's ruling on a Wednesday, legislators drew up and passed a bill that Thursday, which the governor signed into law on that Friday!

How does this episode illustrate the relationship between crime and deviance? First, criminal behavior is a subset of deviant behavior. Crime is a behavior that is met with a negative sanction *by the state*. But an act can be deviant, met with negative sanctions, and not be criminal. There is no doubt that in most contexts, a person taking photos up a woman's skirt will be met with social disapproval. But in prior eras, when cameras were large and bulky, taking such invasive photos without being detected was practically impossible, and no formal law was needed. It took the emergence of digital cameras and smartphones, followed by the public labeling of the act as deviant, in order for the state to take the steps necessary to make it illegal.

A second relationship between crime and deviance is that informal recognitions of deviant behavior may lead to the criminalization of that behavior. Many—if not most—of the cybercrimes discussed in this text were initially recognized as bad behavior. People and groups in society then lobbied for the behavior to be criminalized. This pattern has occurred with hacking, cyberbullying, and revenge porn, phenomena we discuss in later chapters.

LAYERING IN THE DIGITAL ENVIRONMENT

If one aspect of cybercrime is crimes against a computer or computer network, then we should be clear about what we mean by a computer or computer network. Computers include all devices with computer chips—desktops, laptops, smartphones, Internet servers, and "smart" household appliances. It also includes the content stored on those devices—software applications and personal files. All computer software can be understood as a series of files that allow a user to interact with a computer. A person's favorite social media site is ultimately a series of files stored on a social media company's server. Along with software applications, users usually have personal files stored on their computer—family photos, their favorite music, a Word document of a class essay, and so on. Even information stored in "the cloud" is ultimately a series of files stored remotely on a company's computer. A computer network, then, constitutes computers and files connected through the Internet. Through technologies such as underground fiber optic cables, routers, modems, and Wi-Fi hot-spots, devices with computer chips are connected in a "network of networks" and can communicate with each other.

There is a more systematic way of thinking about computers and computer networks. Computer scientists and computer engineers often conceptualize computer systems as layered systems. A layered system divides a large task into smaller tasks organized by layer. Table 1.2 models the interconnected technologies that produce the Internet as a layered system. The first column lists the category of technology (e.g., "application," "transport"). The second column describes the category, and the third column gives one or more examples. If we think of the Internet as a system, then each layer performs a task necessary for the system to work properly.

Two characteristics of layered systems are important here. First, technologies in one layer receive an input from the layer directly below it and use that input to produce an output for technologies directly above it. For example, the transport layer (a router) receives data from the network layer (a modem) and then produces output for the application layer (Netflix on your smart television). Second, technologies can be designed for completing

Table 1.2   Layers of a Computer Network

Type	*Description*	*Examples of Technologies*
Application	Responsible for standardizing data from different sources and provides a user interface	Web browsers, social media applications, video applications, voice applications
Transport	Responsible for the verification of data and the exchanging of data between specific endpoints within a network. The transport layer can also be called the "host to host" layer because the technologies in this layer control direct connections between user computers. The protocol most often used in this is the Transmission Control Protocol (TCP)	Modem
Network Layer	Responsible for the exchanging of data packets across networks (e.g. a user with service from Verizon and a user with service from Sprint). This layer is also called the Internet layer. Most technologies in this layer use the Internet Protocol (IP) developed during the early stages of computer networking	Routers
Link	Responsible for transporting data from one network to another	Wi-Fi, fiber optic cables

Table 1.3 Layers in the Digital Environment

Type of Layer	Description	Examples
Human	The connections between users	Filter bubbles, echo chambers, the "manosphere," organized crime networks
Content	The information that is produced and shared on the Internet	Disinformation, hate speech, products of artificial intelligence, pornography
Application	Programs that allow users to perform operations on a computer	Social media, e-health, websites, search engines, word processing programs, database programs
Operating System	The software that manages the operation of applications on a computer	Windows, Mac OS, Linux, Android
Hardware	The machines that compute and manipulate data	Laptops, tablets, mobile phones, Internet-enabled devices
Infrastructure	The technologies that transmit data between machines	Fiber optic cables, Wi-Fi connections, dial-up

functions in one layer without considering the technologies in another if they use the proper protocol. A company can begin manufacturing modems without needing to design unique modems for each kind of router produced because all routers use the same IP/TCP protocols. Importantly, because these are "open" protocols, and foster "open" communication, it is easier for cybercriminals to create technologies with malicious intent. Also, open protocols make it easier for cybercriminals to access legitimate technologies illegally.

The notion of layering is meant to aid computer scientists, computer engineers, and software designers as they design technologies. However, we can modify it to fit the concerns of social scientists. Table 1.3 shows a layered model of what we will call in this text the digital environment. We discuss each layer in detail.

INFRASTRUCTURE LAYER

The infrastructure layer comprises cables, satellites, cell phone towers, and other data-transmitting technologies. Internet service providers build and maintain many of these networks and sell access to computer users through subscription services. The first electronic message between computers was sent in 1969, from a computer at the University of California at Los Angeles to a computer at Stanford University. From that time through the early 1990s, the military, financial institutions, and academia were using some version of the Internet to exchange messages.

However, the Internet as we know it, where businesses provide Internet service to customers to "go online," began in the early to mid-1990s. During this time, computers were connected through phone lines, on what was called dial-up services. A computer connected to the phone through a modem, and "dialed" the Internet Service Provider. In a simple sense, the computer *was* the phone, and if you were on the Internet, you couldn't use your computer to call anyone else. Dial-up connections had a theoretical maximum data transfer speed of 56 kilobits per second (kbps). Most readers of this textbook will have little conception of an Internet connection at this speed – most Internet users today are connected through high-speed broadband (or a Wi-Fi connection that is then connected to high-speed broadband). However, a piece from 2017 in *Digital Trends* entitled "What's it like to use AOL dial-up internet in 2017?" may help those with no experience with dial-up understand what it was like:

> *It took around 30 seconds to load the search engine to a usable state, and around 45 seconds to load everything, including superficial components like the Google logo. It took a whopping one minute and 15 seconds for Google to carry out a search for 'Digital Trends.'*

(Jones, 2017)

The author concludes:

> *My frustrating step back in time reminded me of how far we've come, and illustrated how important broadband is to everyday life. Imagine trying to apply for a job over dial-up. Or applying to renew your driver's license. Or trying to view your bank account. These commonplace and arguably essentially tasks would prove almost impossible on an old-fashioned 56K modem.*

Can you imagine an Internet search taking 1 minute and 15 seconds? It is not an exaggeration to say that broadband technologies have revolutionized the digital environment. According to one estimate from 2021, mobile broadband speeds today average about 55 Mbps (megabits per second), and fixed broadband averages about 108 Mbps (McKetta, 2021). A speed of 55 Mbps on your phone is 55,000 kbps. Recall from above that dial-up had a maximum of 56 kbps. That is quite a difference!

In simple terms, faster data speeds allow people to do more things. Faster Internet speeds enable real-time streaming and synchronous online classroom meetings. Faster Internet speeds also allow computers to render more realistic images in video games or from video cameras. Or consider a real-time editing service that suggests changes to a text as you write or a service that allows many people to edit a document in "the cloud" simultaneously. Many students are taking full advantage of ChatGPT and other artificial intelligence services to help them with their work. These types of services would not be possible at dial-up data transfer speeds.

Regardless of the infrastructure technology, the data transferred can move seamlessly through other infrastructure technologies and then up to hardware layer technologies. There are several types of broadband connections, as shown in Table 1.4 (p. 7).

In recent years, users in some countries have gained access to gigabit Internet services. Gigabit services provide data speeds in the 1 Gbps (Gigabit per second). These speeds will further improve the quality of Internet activities like gaming, videoconferencing, and streaming.

HARDWARE LAYER

Technologies in the hardware layer are the devices that house some variation of a computer chip. These technologies compute and store data received from the technologies

Table 1.4 Types of Broadband Connections*

Type of Connection	Description
Digital Subscriber Line (DSL)	A wireline transmission technology that transmits data faster over traditional copper telephone lines already installed to homes and businesses.
Cable Modem	Cable modem service enables cable operators to provide broadband using the same coaxial cables that deliver pictures and sound to your TV set.
Fiber	Fiber optic technology converts electrical signals carrying data to light and sends the light through transparent glass fibers about the diameter of a human hair.
Wireless	Wireless broadband connects a home or business to the Internet using a radio link between the customer's location and the service provider's facility. Wireless broadband can be mobile or fixed.
Satellite	Just as satellites orbiting the earth provide necessary links for telephone and television service, they can also provide links for broadband. Satellite broadband is another form of wireless broadband, and is also useful for serving remote or sparsely populated areas.

*"Types of Broadband Connections | Federal Communications Commission"—https://www.fcc.gov/general/types-broadband-connections

in the infrastructure layer. As with data transmission speeds, there has been a rapid and continuous evolution in the power of computer processors. The Hubble Space Telescope is a technological marvel. Launched in 1990, the Hubble Space Telescope orbits the Earth, and allows scientists to take pictures of the universe without interference from clouds or the Earth's atmosphere. According to the United States National Aeronautics and Space Administration (NASA):

> The telescope has tracked interstellar objects as they soared through our solar system, watched a comet collide with Jupiter, and discovered moons around Pluto. It has found dusty disks and stellar nurseries throughout the Milky Way that may one day become fully fledged planetary systems and studied the atmospheres of planets that orbit other stars.
>
> (Belleville, 2019)

The Hubble Space Telescope remains in operation. Its extraordinary accomplishments are done with a computer having about 2 megabytes of memory. By contrast, a smart home device like Amazon's Echo Dot has a memory of 512 megabytes. This is an illustration of how much more powerful computers have become in a few decades. The author of this text is typing on a computer with 32 GB of memory—128,000 times more powerful than the Hubble Space Telescope.

Of more significance for the social scientist is the degree to which computers have become integral to human life. In the 1950s and 1960s, computing was done on large mainframe machines that took up entire rooms. At that time, computers were used to calculate or analyze data for military operations, federal government censuses, and space exploration. They were also used in academia and in companies processing large amounts of data. The social impact of computers was already significant but continued to grow. Computers became smaller and less expensive beginning in the late 1970s and into the

1980s with the boom in PC (personal computer) ownership. Companies began selling personal computers at affordable prices, thus making them available to a wider variety of users—local and state governments, small businesses, and individual families. PCs were used for the same tasks they are used for today—bookkeeping, accounting, word processing, scientific calculations, and gaming.

In the 1990s and into the 21st century, the number and uses of computers grew alongside other technologies. The growth of the modern Internet, starting in the 1990s, increased interest in the utility of computers for businesses and home users alike. E-commerce (Amazon—1994), dating websites (Match.com—1994), pornography, and more became a part of everyday life. The rise of social networking websites in the early 2000s (Myspace—2003, Facebook—2004, Twitter (now called X)—2006) further increased interest in computing. The activities made available by the Internet and the ability to connect and share one's life through social networking sites made owning a computer more attractive to people from all walks of life. The computer was no longer the reserve of privileged or specialized people in business or academia.

Another significant development in connecting people with computers was the marriage of the mobile phone with the computer (smartphone). Mobile phones were common since the late 1990s. Indeed, the best-selling phone—mobile or smart—in history is the Nokia 1100 released in 2003. By the time it was discontinued in 2009, it had sold over 250 million units (Roy, 2023). But with the release of the first smartphone, the iPhone, in 2007, and subsequently other models like the Samsung Galaxy in 2009, more people were using computers in their daily lives even if they did not think of it in that way.

The smartphone could be considered the first "thing" in the Internet of Things (IoT)—everyday objects embedded with computer technology and connected to the Internet. A social scientist exploring the impact of computer technology in society can no longer focus solely on PCs, laptops, tablets, and smartphones. Nor do they need to wait for the development of robots or artificial intelligence. Everyday objects like cars, televisions, refrigerators, coffeemakers, fitness trackers, heating systems, and home alarm systems have computers embedded in them and are connected to the Internet. For the cybercriminologist, this means that crime and deviance can also occur to and through these everyday devices. As an example, the Mirai malware attacks IoT devices, taking them over and using them for denial-of-service attacks (malware, hacking, and denial-of-service attacks are discussed in Chapter 2).

Key here is that the saturation of computer hardware into the lives of people—in offices, in homes, in institutions, and in the pockets of individuals, means that almost everyone is a potential victim of cybercrime. In the simplest sense, the more computers available, the more opportunity for cybercrime.

OPERATING SYSTEMS LAYER

Operating systems were not an aspect of early computers. But as computers became more powerful, could perform multiple operations simultaneously, and everyday people who could not program wanted to use computers, the need arose for an easier way to manage multiple tasks simultaneously. Operating systems are software that helps manage various tasks on a computer. Bill Gates became for a time the richest man in the world because his operating system—Windows, revolutionized the personal computer industry. Using the terms of this text, the Windows operating system formed a link between the application layer and the hardware layer, making it easier for software applications to be written for personal computers.

You can use the "task manager" on your computer to see how many tasks (also called jobs) your computer is currently running. Examples of operating systems for desktops and laptops are Microsoft Windows, Mac OS, and Linux. Operating systems for mobile phones and tablets include Android OS, iPhone OS, and Amazon's Fire OS. We don't tend to think of operating systems as software, because operating systems are usually sold already installed onto the purchased desktop or mobile phone. For many computer users, the Windows operating system and a Dell or Hewlett-Packard PC are one in the same. Or, a MacBook Pro and the MacOS that runs the machine are also seen as the same technology. However, tech-savvy computer users can add an additional operating system to their computers or replace the pre-installed operating system with a new one. One of the authors of this book routinely purchases a computer with Windows installed, removes it, and installs a Linux operating system.

Operating systems make it easier for third parties to write software for computers. A piece of software can be written for one operating system like Windows instead of having to write unique software for a particular manufacturer of a machine (Dell, Asus, HP, Samsung, Sony, etc.). Similarly, an app developer can write a program for the Android operating system and be confident that the application will perform on any device the operating system runs on—from wearable technology like a GPS device to a mobile phone to a tablet.

APPLICATION LAYER

The application layer comprises software that allows users to perform operations or jobs on a computer. The application layer of the digital environment is where we see the most human–computer interaction. People experience a computer through their use of Facebook, for example. Other examples of applications include word-processing programs such as MS Word, web browsers such as Opera, and video-calling programs like Viber.

Application layer technologies make it possible for people to use computers. As a general rule, most people use computers by working through an application of some kind. Before modern computer applications with Graphical User Interfaces (GUIs), most computing was done through users typing in specific instructions using programming languages from Command Line Interfaces. Most people do not have the time or interest to learn command-line computer languages, and it wasn't until the development of applications with GUIs that many people entered the digital environment.

Two historically significant applications are search engines and web browsers. Search engines are programs that index web pages and list those pages when a person searches for a given set of search terms. Google became one of the dominant technology companies because its Google search webpage was powered by the PageRank algorithm (Thelwall, 2003). PageRank was so useful and popular to computer users that the Google search engine became the most dominant search engine in the digital environment. Web browsers, such as Firefox and Chrome, are GUIs that make it easier for a computer user to access web pages on the Internet.

As we write this edition in the Summer of 2023, ChatGPT and other chatbots are major topics of conversation. One of the authors of this textbook uses ChatGPT and asked the application to describe itself. A portion of the answer they received was:

> *ChatGPT is an advanced language model developed by OpenAI...ChatGPT is designed to understand and generate human-like text responses to engage in conversation with users. The model is trained on a massive amount of diverse text data from the internet, enabling it to grasp a wide range of topics and language patterns. It has the ability to generate coherent and contextually relevant responses, making it useful for various applications such as answering questions, providing explanations, offering sugges-tions, and engaging in interactive conversations.*

ChatGPT is selling itself short. Many believe applications like it will revolutionize the way humans use computers. Applications like ChatGPT can complete essays for students and write cover letters for job applicants. According to one story, it responds intelligently enough to prompts that Google could hire it as an entry level programmer (Elias, 2023). ChatGPT and other chatbots are forms of artificial intelligence. Artificial intelligence will be discussed in more detail in Chapter 8.

Another important aspect of technologies in the application layer is that applications create spaces where individuals connect in the digital environment. Imagine a person in Sri Lanka using their smart phone manufactured by Samsung (hardware layer) operating an android operating system (operating system layer) having access to the Internet through their service provider's satellite connection (infrastructure layer). How do they connect with someone in the UK who spends most of their computing time on a Mac in their home office using a landline broadband connection? They most likely connect via an application they both use, such as Snapchat.

CONTENT LAYER

The content layer is composed of what we see or hear in the digital environment. Humans take inputs from the technology layer and produce content. The particular affordances of Twitter enable and constrain the type of content produced by the human user. Consider a TikTok video. The video is a product of a human using the capabilities of the TikTok appli-cation—filters, music, emojis—to produce content others watch. Similarly, the Twitter (now X) application allows a user to write "tweets." On the one hand, one could argue that tweets are not terribly unique. They are, after all, the same words and sentences one would use on other applications. But on the other hand, would a person not using Twitter condense their thoughts down to 280 characters, and use hashtags and emojis to add mean-ing to those thoughts?

The term "content creator" refers to individuals who produce and share original con-tent with an audience. Content creators produce videos, audio-only podcasts, newsletters, and blogs. They use inputs from different applications and combine them to produce con-tent. Consider what can go into the production of a video to be shared online:

- Video editing software like Kdenlive
- Audio editing software like Audacity

- Imagine manipulation software like GIMP
- One or more social media applications to share the edited video like YouTube or Vimeo

Content creators who are independent of traditional institutions have become powerful figures in societies, with some arguing it has been a net positive and others being more critical. On the one hand, content creators can be a powerful voice for people from marginalized groups or with unpopular opinions. On the other hand, they can also gain a massive following and then spread disinformation or incite hatred against groups.

The content layer and the forthcoming human interaction layer are the two layers that are of most interest to social scientists. Psychologists, sociologists, criminologists, scholars in media studies, and other similar disciplines are interested in how the content produced in the digital environment and how humans interact with that content impacts society.

HUMAN LAYER

In the human layer, individual users *interpret and act* upon inputs from the content layer. The human layer is the layer of meaning-making and behavior. When social scientists measure the amount of time someone spends online, their attitudes about technology, or the meanings they attribute to what they see or hear online, they are measuring phenomena in the human layer.

Meaning-making is an important aspect of the human experience and digital environment. In a broad, sociological sense, meaning is made through the interpretation of symbols. We understand our world by communicating with friends and family, navigating institutions like schools and governments, and consuming media. The symbols produced in the content layer—tweets, TikTok videos, direct messages from friends, Instagram posts, and so on become the fuel for meaning-making as they carry cultural markers and signifiers that users interpret. This interpretation is subjective and based on the culture and experiences of the person consuming the content. The content produced by a 20-something male body influencer on Instagram may be interpreted differently by younger males than older males. Specifically, young males may compare himself to the influencer, find themselves wanting, and get depressed or adopt dysfunctional dieting and exercise behaviors. Older males may not be so influenced.

The interpretation of content in the human layer is important for social scientists. Criminals and deviants not only manipulate technology (hacking for example) but also manipulate content. How individuals respond to that contact may determine whether they are victims. Consider cyberbullying. How people respond to taunts, insults, and hate speech online is a matter of interpretation. Some people may ignore the content they see or be indifferent to it. Others can see similar content and have a severely negative reaction leading to depression or suicidal ideation.

Or consider a phenomenon like stochastic terrorism, which can be described as "the incitement of a violent act through public demonization of a group or individual" (Amman & Meloy, 2023, p. 5). Stochastic signifies that the phenomenon is somewhat random, such that an increased likelihood of terrorism can be predicted, but the specific person or methods used for an attack cannot. Instances of stochastic terrorism appear to be "lone wolf" acts of violence, such as the 2019 attacks on Muslims in New Zealand by Brenton Tarrant. Tarrant killed 51 people and injured 40 more. Tarrant shared a manifesto online, where he made frequent references to online white nationalist forums. Using the phraseology introduced in this section, we can say that Tarrant interpreted inputs from the content layer. His experiences in these forums helped him construct a meaning of Islam and Muslims that warranted, in his mind, committing horrific acts of violence against them.

SUMMING UP LAYERING

Recall that we define cybercrime as (1) *crimes against a computer or computer network*, or (2) *crimes against a person in which the primary means of committing that crime is a computer or computer network*. The discussion of layering above was to help the reader make sense of the many technologies associated with computers and computer networks. These layers work together to produce a single digital environment shared by people globally. All the technologies in the infrastructure, hardware, and software layer can be a target of a crime, as well as the means through which a crime is committed. The content and human layers, while they do not compose computer technologies are necessary for crimes to be committed against a person.

The Five Challenges of Cybercrime and Digital Deviance

There are at least five challenges that someone studying cybercrime and digital deviance will repeatedly encounter. These five challenges are (1) defining cybercrimes and digital deviances, (2) understanding new laws and policies pertaining to cyber phenomena, (3) understanding the impact of new police practices, (4) making sense of the social and historical context within which cyber phenomena occur, and (5) conducting and applying research about cyber phenomena. What follows is the "revenge porn" case from 2018 of a former politician from the United States, Nick Sauer. This case illustrates these five challenges.

THE CASE OF NICK SAUER

Nick Sauer, a state representative from the American state of Illinois, resigned from his office in August of 2018 after his ex-girlfriend Kate Kelly filed a "revenge porn" complaint against him. Kelly alleged that Sauer created a fake Instagram account using photos of her. The account, she claimed, used nude pictures of her to bait men into online sexual conversations. The *Huffington Post* reported on August 2, 2018:

> *Kelly's complaint reportedly says a man she did not know reached out to her on July 12 via her personal Instagram account to say he'd "been communicating for 4 months with someone pretending" to be her. After that, Kelly says, she wrote to Instagram,*

who disabled the account, and talked to Sauer about it. Sauer allegedly admitted to everything.

(Amatulli, 2018)

On January 9, 2019, Sauer was charged with 12 felonies. At that time, Sauer was a rising star in Illinois politics. Ironically, he had served on a legislative task force on sexual harassment and had cosponsored legislation that would require sexual harassment training for lawmakers. Sauer resigned from office. Let's connect the details of this case to the five challenges.

CHALLENGE 1: DEFINING CYBERCRIMES

Kelly filed a complaint with the local police under Illinois' revenge porn laws. Revenge porn refers to the public displaying or sharing of sexually explicit photographs of a current or former intimate partner. Images between two adults that are knowingly shared—for example, between two people in an intimate relationship—are legal. It becomes unlawful when those images are shared publicly or with a third party.

The naming of the violation as "revenge porn" derives from the practice of someone sharing previously confidential photos of an intimate partner publicly to humiliate or shame because they have been rejected or jilted. But revenge porn does not need to be about revenge. The key element of revenge porn is nonconsensual sharing of sexualized photos, as Sauer allegedly did by sharing pictures of Kelly on a fake Instagram account he owned.

One of the authors conducted a web search of the media attention placed on the case in 2018. Web results showed that revenge porn was not the phenomenon the media had focused on the most, although it is the crime Sauer was alleged to have done. Instead, media attention had been placed more on the catfishing done by Sauer—using a false online identity to lure people into relationships. One of the authors of this text was even asked to write their opinion for a London newspaper about catfishing—not revenge porn. Catfishing is a form of cyberdeviance that is worthy of study, however it is not illegal, not the violation attached to Sauer, and not why he resigned.

This illustrates one of the challenges in studying and investigating cybercrime. Unlike most traditional crimes, the public does not have an adequate vocabulary and set of definitions to employ when trying to talk about and understand cybercrime-related phenomena. As we move through this text, we will pay close attention to definitional matters.

CHALLENGE 2: LAW AND POLICY

Legal systems have been scrambling to keep up with changes in technology. Kelly's complaints in 2018 to law enforcement would have been interpreted differently had they been made just five years earlier in 2013. In 2013 Illinois did not have specific legislation prohibiting the unauthorized sharing of adult photos. The state did not pass a revenge porn law until 2014. Under the current law in Kelly's jurisdiction, someone convicted of revenge porn is subject to 1 to 3 years in prison and up to a $25,000 fine.

While changes in laws are necessary to keep pace with changes in technology and social patterns, problems can arise as lawmakers scramble to enact laws to address cybercrimes. One problem is that new laws may be misplaced because of a lack of understanding about the phenomena. By misplaced, we mean that they may not address the actual phenomenon they are intended to. As mentioned earlier, much media attention has been placed on the catfishing aspect of the story. Some have called for the possession of a false identity online to be made illegal to curtail catfishing. But being anonymous online is an important aspect of the digital environment. Consider a person who may be thinking about a change of identity—gender, religious, political. They may wish to explore aspects of this identity away from their current social networks. They may want to connect with and interact in online forums with people who share that identity. They will need the freedom to create a new persona and interact with others without obligating themselves. Or consider a whistle-blower who wants to share sensitive information about government misconduct without revealing their identity. Speaking truth to power may require creating a fake Facebook or Twitter account. Thus, uninformed laws that are misplaced, such as banning of false identities, may end up doing more harm than good.

A second problem is the appropriateness of penalties. On the one hand, a revenge porn law is meant to protect people who have been justly victimized. On the other hand, some may question the harshness of the punishment. In the example of Sauer, is prison time a just punishment for Sauer's actions? In other words, does the punishment for violating a law fit the crime? The answer to that question is always debatable. Unfortunately, the rapidity in which new questionable behaviors arise and the relative lack of understanding by the public makes it more possible that overly harsh penalties can be attached to legislation.

CHALLENGE 3: CHANGING POLICING

As we will show at various points in this text, research suggests that the perpetrators of most cybercrime come from different backgrounds and social contexts than perpetrators of the crimes that have traditionally dominated media narratives like murder and assault and battery. Cybercrime scholars are still coalescing on the profiles of cybercriminals. This is a challenge that must be addressed, but we can be confident that profiles of cybercriminals will be different than the profiles of people who commit street crime. This is especially so for the more technologically based cybercrimes such as hacking and phishing. Cybercriminals are more likely to be educated. They are more likely to be white and come from less challenging social and family circumstances.

To combat rises in cybercrimes, law enforcement will have to reorient themselves to this new criminal. Law enforcement infrastructure and cultural patterns, as of now, are oriented towards street crimes and the types of individuals who are more likely to commit them. For example, in Chapter 8, we will talk about the use of algorithms in predictive policing. These algorithms are designed to predict street crime. There is not yet an equal effort to predict cybercrime. As cybercrime increases, efforts will be needed to reorient law enforcement agencies, especially local police, towards cybercriminals.

Another change in law enforcement has been the learning and institutionalizing of investigative techniques unique to cyberspace. In this regard, law enforcement has responded in at least three ways:

1. Law enforcement has had to learn how and when to request evidence from intermediaries (through court order, subpoena, and warrant). In the Sauer case, Instagram is a third party that potentially holds inculpatory or exculpatory evidence and at the minimum a subpoena or warrant will likely be needed to obtain relevant evidence.
2. Law enforcement has developed strategies for following the breadcrumbs of a person online—their digital trail. People place a lot of information about themselves on social media or leave or on websites that harvest personal information. This public information—the posts, tweets, and images—are often enough to place a suspect at a scene or connect the suspect to the victim.
3. Specially trained professionals can identify and extract digital evidence at the binary level on a hard drive—digital forensics. With a warrant they can acquire Sauer's computing hardware and examine it for potential evidence.

Despite the new techniques developed, cybercrimes can be more difficult to investigate and solve than street crimes. This is because of the unique properties of cyberspace, one of which is the ability of computer users to form connections across time and space. This property creates new opportunities for criminals, who can target victims across jurisdictions. Kelly was in some ways fortunate that she could contact the local police in which the alleged perpetrator, Sauer, lived. In many cases, local police struggle to investigate cybercrimes because the perpetrator lives in a state or country different from the victim. For many cybercrimes such as hacking, ransomware, or denial of service attacks, this means that federal agencies conduct the investigations. However, even federal agencies can run into difficulties when a suspect is in another country. Agencies in other countries may not wish to share information or the laws in the perpetrator's country are different than the laws in the victim's country.

CHALLENGE 4: UNDERSTANDING THE CONTEXT

In 2017 Hollywood film producer Harvey Weinstein was charged with several counts of sexual misconduct. Weinstein's case was high-profile, with many well-known actresses alleging they were sexually assaulted by Weinstein. In October of that year, the hashtag #MeToo spread via social media. The "#MeToo Movement" has been instrumental in publicizing sexual misconduct. By February of 2018, one account had 71 men holding positions of power being fired or forced to resign because of sexual misconduct (Almukhtar et al., 2017). Sauer's reactions to the allegations cannot be understood without taking into account the current cultural climate towards power imbalances and sexual misconduct. Sauer's resignation is as much about informal norms of sexual behavior in the digital environment—digital deviance, as it is about formal violations of law—cybercrime. In decades past, Sauer may have been able to withstand the negative press associated with Kelly's complaint. In times past, many male authority figures have been able to mistreat women with few negative sanctions. Today, however, these allegations are difficult to dodge.

Cybercrime scholars cannot ignore the cultural context in which cybercrime occurs. Indeed, the argument can be made that because so much of cybercrime is symbolic in nature, how the crimes and the victimizations are socially constructed and interpreted matter more than for other types of crimes. In other words, a physical assault on one's person is less subject to interpretation than the effects of cyberbullying or the theft of someone's identity online. Consider a negative post on social media. It can be understood lightly as "just words," or taken with more gravity as "potentially causing psychological trauma" depending upon the context.

CHALLENGE 5: CONDUCTING AND APPLYING RESEARCH

Academic studies of cyber phenomena may not be as exciting to students who want to learn about the practical matters of cybercrime and cyberdeviance. However, good research forms the foundation for insights into cyber phenomena.

For example, Bates (2017) conducted in-depth interviews with 18 revenge porn survivors to understand their experiences. The 18 survivors who volunteered to participate in the study covered a wide range of revenge porn forms, from survivors who "experienced a widespread web release of naked photos, to photos being shared on a smaller scale (such as with a social circle), and to being threatened or blackmailed with naked photos. Some participants also experienced harassment, stalking, and other unwanted behaviors from their ex-partners in addition to the revenge porn" (p. 29). In her interviews Bates found that the victims of revenge porn suffered a variety of negative consequences including posttraumatic stress disorder (PTSD), depression, and suicidal thoughts.

The advantage of research like Bates' is that it can be applied in the real world. For example, most people are unaware of exactly what a victim of revenge porn goes through, and probably imagines that the main consequence is shame. Shame is certainly an aspect that must be considered, however Bates' work demonstrates that there are more serious consequences. Now consider how knowing these more serious consequences can impact society's response to offenders of revenge porn laws and their victims. Legislators are more likely to propose and society more likely to accept harsher punishments for violation of revenge porn laws. Meanwhile, governments will be more willing to make mental health counseling freely available to victims.

The fifth challenge of conducting and applying research is by far the most important, and really underpins the previous four challenges. Understanding and applying good research can help us more precisely define cyber phenomena (Challenge 1), better understand what laws and policies are needed to address crime and deviance (Challenge 2), help police develop more effective investigation techniques (Challenge 3), and properly unde stand social and cultural factors are important for any give cyber phenomena (Challenge 4).

The Four Categories of Cybercrime

This last section helps us organize our thinking by categorizing the myriad types of cybercrime. There are many ways of doing this. For example, one way has been to place crimes into two broad categories—crimes in which the computer is used as a tool, and crimes in which a computer is a target. This is a useful typology, but it can be too broad. The typology we use in this text is David Wall's four-category typology of cybertrespass, cyberpornography, cyberviolence, and cyberfraud. This typology is a common one and is often used in cybercrime literature. In the following paragraphs, we define each type of cybercrime and give examples. In future chapters, we will explore these categories in more detail.

CYBERTRESPASS

Cybertrespass is the "unauthorized crossing of the boundaries of computer systems into spaces where rights of ownership or title have already been established" (Wall, 2001, 3). For practical purposes, cybertrespass is synonymous with hacking (Taylor, 1999). Gaining access to a computer network at a university without permission, finding a way into a company's database, and unlocking a personal laptop by finding the password are all examples of cybertrespass.

Hacking is arguably the most talked about cybercrime in the media. A major news story about a company or organization being hacked appears every few months or so. These hacks are often called "data breaches," and usually the purpose of crossing computer boundaries without authorization is ultimately to gain access to valuable data. Some hacks are ransomware attacks, where a hacker gains unauthorized access to a hard drive, encrypts it so that the owner cannot access data, and then demands payment from the owner to regain access. Some high-profile hacks include:

- Ashley Madison—in 2015 a hack of this dating site exposed the information of 32 million users. This information included credit card numbers, names, and addresses. Because of the nature of Ashley Madison—a dating site for adulterers—many customers were concerned about their activities being exposed.
- Equifax—in 2017 the credit bureau was hacked, exposing the personal information of around 148 million customers. The Equifax data breach was especially worrisome because of the sensitivity of the information their databases housed: Social security numbers, birth dates, addresses, and in some cases credit card numbers and driver's license numbers.
- Costa Rican Government—in 2022 the Costa Rican Ministry of Finance was victim to a ransomware attack by the Russia-linked cybercrime gang Conti. The attack crippled that country's import/export businesses. The president of Costa Rica had to declare a national emergency in response to the attack.

CYBERFRAUD

Wall uses the term cyberdeception to refer to "the different types of acquisitive harm that can take place" in the digital environment (Wall, 2001, 4). This type of cybercrime covers all aspects of deception in the digital environment in which theft, usually of money or information, is the endgame. With respect to Dr. Wall's typology, we find the term cyberdeception to be inadequate for our purposes. Cyberdeception signifies one aspect of the phenomena in question—the lying or misrepresenting of oneself. This is cyberdeviance. However, most of the public focuses on what happens *after* the deception—the theft of information or money. The public is concerned with fraud. For this reason, we have decided to deviate from Wall's typology and term the different types of acquisitive harm in the digital environment as cyberfraud.

One type of cyberfraud is stealing intellectual property in the form of movies, music, and software. This property is understood as intellectual because the property is not material but based on someone's idea and creativity. Movies and music are the most common forms of intellectual property. Algorithms, computer code, and logos are other examples of products of the mind that are the property of a person or company. Intellectual property theft is one of the more common instances of cybercrime. This is often called digital piracy (Herings et al., 2018; Smallridge & Roberts, 2013).

Another type of theft is the stealing of information. Information theft is usually the end game, with the means for data theft being hacking. After gaining unauthorized access to a computer network a hacker may download information from a person's computer or a company's database. Indeed, in the previous examples of Costa Rican Government, Equifax, and Ashley Madison, the emphasis is less on the breach but instead on the consequences of data theft. It is crucial, however, to not conflate cybertrespass and cyberfraud. It is a crime to gain unauthorized access, even if nothing is stolen or altered.

While theft is readily understood as a crime, deception is more ambiguous. Some forms of deception may be frowned upon but not illegal (here we can make a distinction between deviance and crime). For example, misrepresenting oneself on dating websites does not reach the level of a punishable offense and may even be expected by people participating on those sites. It is a fact of life that individuals construct public images of themselves that are at variance with their private selves. To say to a potential romantic partner that one "loves taking walks on the beach" when one dislikes sand and sun is bad behavior, maybe mildly deviant (it could receive informal sanctions from one's date), but not a crime. People lie about their height, age, weight, use younger pictures of themselves, and so on. However, when those false pretenses are used to extract money or resources from someone, this then becomes a punishable offense. Many people are defrauded yearly through these "romance scams" (Kopp et al., 2016; Whitty, 2015).

CYBERPORNOGRAPHY

Cyberpornography, as defined by Wall, is "the publication or trading of sexually expressive materials" in the digital environment (Wall, 2001, 6). As Wall has noted, pornography has been a catalyst for the growth of the Internet. People interested in consuming pornography created an early base of Internet users. Pornography producers, looking to monetize men's interest in sexual imagery, developed online credit card transactions and streaming video early on in the history of the Internet. The pornography industry also pioneered innovations such as monthly membership fees for access to sites and the concept of "upselling" where a customer is sold related services once they have joined a site (e.g., a customer pays $10 per month for one site and is offered access to a second site for an additional $5 per month).

As we will discuss in the chapter on cyberpornography, most forms of pornography are legal. In countries with strong free speech protections like the United States, a high bar must be passed before the production, distribution, or consumption of pornography is prohibited. For this reason, a large portion of criminological analysis surrounding cyberpornography is about its deviant characteristics. The topic of pornography engenders strong debate between many groups in society, and it is usually suffused with moral overtones (Paasonen, 2015). Many feminists, parents, and conservative groups want to restrict pornography. They see pornography as exploiting women or reducing women to sexual objects. They also see pornography as lowering the moral standards of society and teaching children improper sexual behaviors. Meanwhile, civil liberties groups, citizens interested in preserving free speech, and people who openly enjoy pornography support its production and consumption.

In this textbook, we have extended Wall's definition beyond the publication and trading of materials in two ways. First, we believe that communication about sex (what can be considered the trading of symbolic content) is an important phenomenon. While many communities form online around the subject of sex and sexual expression, we will focus our attention on communities in the digital environment that support lifestyles considered by some to be sexually deviant. Second, we place erotic services facilitated in the digital environment in the category of cyberpornography. With the success of websites like OnlyFans and Chaturbate, people can buy and sell erotic services online without ever meeting or physically contacting a person. Because there is no sexual activity through physical contact these services are generally legal for adults in Western countries. Like pornography, society groups continuously debate the morality of selling erotic services online.

CYBERVIOLENCE

Cyberviolence describes "the violent impact of the cyberactivities of another upon an individual or a social or political grouping. While such activities do not have to have a direct physical manifestation, the victim nevertheless feels the violence of the act and can bear long-term psychological scars as a consequence" (Wall, 2001, 6). There is a clear link between the use of Internet technologies and the eventual harm inflicted upon an individual. For most types of cyberviolence, however, the subjective feeling of harm—either actual or threatened—determines if a behavior is thought of as cyberviolence. Because there are so many ways of producing feelings of harm online, a wide range of behaviors falls under the category of cyberviolence, from hate speech to trolling and flaming.

The type of cyberviolence that arguably garners the most media attention is cyberbullying (Hinduja & Patchin, 2015; Madlock & Westerman, 2011; Payne & Hutzell, 2015). Cyberbullying is "any behavior performed through electronic or digital media by individuals or groups that repeatedly communicates hostile or aggressive messages intended to inflict harm or discomfort on others" (Tokunaga, 2010, 278). Examples of cyberbullying include posting insults on a victim's social media page, sending hateful text messages to a victim, or sharing embarrassing or degrading images of a victim via the Internet. Over the past several decades, many young people have committed suicide entirely or in part because they have been cyberbullied. Variations of hurtful communications, including trolling, flaming, and hate speech are also instances of cyberviolence because the receiver of the communications experiences psychological harm.

Child pornography or sex trafficking may appear to be about sex, and thus fit within the category of cyberpornography. But few people debate the morality of these crimes. Globally, child pornography and sex trafficking are understood to be immoral. With respect to child pornography, much effort has been invested in combatting it, and researchers have studied the dynamics of this crime extensively (Martin & Alaggia, 2013; Merdian et al., 2013, 2016). Sex trafficking is also universally condemned, with states investing many in apprehending sex traffickers. Society has pushed to call child pornography "child sexual abuse images," or CSAIs. This change highlights that the sharing of images of children should not be confused with sex, but should be understood as an act of violence towards a minor. This argument can also be made for sex trafficking. Although the victims of sex trafficking are indeed having sex with another person, they are being coerced. As such they, too, are victims of sexual violence. The authors agree with this sentiment, and so although child pornography and Internet-facilitated sex trafficking may ostensibly fit within the category of cyberpornography, we will instead talk about this issue in the chapter on cyberviolence.

Conclusion

In this chapter, we introduced some ideas fundamental to understanding cybercrime. We started with the most fundamental idea of all, which is defining what cybercrime is. Although there are many definitions, we chose one that we think is widely shared amongst cybercrime scholars: Crimes against a computer or computer network, or (2) crimes against a person in which the primary means of committing that crime is a computer or computer network. Because so many technologies work together to produce the digital environment where crime occurs, we adopted the layering model used in computer engineering. We show how each layer houses a particular class of technologies that contribute to the operation of the digital environment, and what crimes can occur in each of these layers. We then defined what we mean by digital deviance and its relationship to cybercrime. We end the chapter by discussing the five challenges a person studying cybercrime may encounter. To illustrate these challenges, we used the case of former state representative Nick Sauer and accusations of revenge porn.

In the coming chapters, we will explore key aspects of cybercrime and digital deviance. We attempt to make the text as readable and engaging as possible. One way is by using clear, everyday language. We aim to be informative but not confusing and avoided jargon whenever possible. We are fortunate in that our topic is interesting enough to garner much media coverage worldwide. We have a plethora of news stories to choose to engage the reader, and we use them liberally throughout this text. Finally, we want to make this text as international in scope as possible. The media stories we use to illustrate the concepts in this text are drawn from Europe, Asia, Africa, and the Americas. The authors are in the United States. As such we may have some biases towards events in the United States and are and limited to stories from English-language media outlets. However, we made a concerted effort to seek out cyber events from across the globe, understand them as much as possible, and include them in this text. We believe the clear language and emphasis on real-world events from across the globe should make this an engaging text to wide range of readers.

CHAPTER 1 CURRENT EVENTS AND CRITICAL THINKING:

Can a Law Enforcement Agency do a Good Job Without Arresting Anybody?

One of the challenges faced by cybercrime scholars is understanding the impact of new police practices. Recently the United States Federal Bureau of Investigations (FBI) celebrated a law enforcement victory in which there was no arrests, no courtrooms, and no punishments. In January of 2023, Attorney General Merrick Garland announced that his justice department "…dismantled an international ransomware network responsible for extorting and attempting to extort hundreds of millions of dollars from victims in the United States and around the world" (*Office of Public Affairs | U.S. Department of Justice Disrupts Hive Ransomware Variant | United States Department of Justice*, 2023).

The network was the cybercrime syndicate called Hive. Hive used what cybersecurity professionals call a "ransomware-as-a-service (RaaS)" model. There was a core of administrators who developed a strain of ransomware and a graphical user interface (GUI) that makes it easy for someone to implement the ransomware and receive payment, in cryptocurrency, from victims. These administrators provided this service to affiliates who chose the targets and deployed the ransomware.

Attacks were in the form of double extortions. First, sensitive data was stolen from a victim's computers. Second. those computers were encrypted. Victims were told their sensitive data would not be released to the public and they would be given the keys needed to decrypt their computers if they paid a ransom. Ransom from a successful attack would be split 20/80 between administrator and affiliate. The syndicate had a site on the dark web where data from targets who did not pay was published.

Hive was an aggressive organization, initiating over 1500 attacks and collecting the equivalent of around 100 million United States dollars in ransom. The Tampa, Florida office of the FBI oversaw the case because it was closest to its first reported victim. The Tampa team, led by Agent Justin Crenshaw, interviewed many of the victims of the group to learn how they operated. Over time, Crenshaw and his team were able to gain access to the group's remote administrative panel, where the keys for decrypting data were held. Once they had access to the keys, the team could help organizations who had been attacked by hive decrypt their data. Through what can be called "mitigation efforts," the team was able to provide keys to 300 victims and save them over 130 million dollars.

Eventually, the interviews and other investigative work paid off. The FBI learned that the group staged attacks from servers rented in Los Angeles – within American borders. These servers – which housed the ransomware strain, keys, and GUI used to deploy the ransomware - were seized. The seizure led to Attorney General Garland announcing the takedown to the public. The FBI claimed victory.

But was it?

Critical Thinking Question(s)

If no criminals were apprehended, can a law enforcement agency claim they have made progress in fighting crime? Why or why not? Does your answer change if the crime is cybercrime or traditional crime? Why or why not?

REFERENCES

Almukhtar, S., Gold, M., & Buchanan, L. (2017, November 10). After Weinstein: 71 men accused of sexual misconduct and their fall from power. *The New York Times.* https://www.nytimes.com/interactive/2017/11/10/us/men-accused-sexual-misconduct-weinstein.html, https://www.nytimes.com/interactive/2017/11/10/us/men-accused-sexual-misconduct-weinstein.html

Amatulli, J. (2018, August 2). Illinois lawmaker resigns after ex says he catfished men with her nudes | HuffPost Latest News. *The Huffington Post.* https://www.huffpost.com/entry/illinois-lawmaker-resigns-catfish-nudes_n_5b631767e4b0de86f49ec7ec

Amman, M., & Meloy, J. R. (2023). Stochastic terrorism: A linguistic and psychological analysis. *Perspectives on Terrorism, 15*(5).

Bates, S. (2017). Revenge porn and mental health: A qualitative analysis of the mental health effects of revenge porn on female survivors. *Feminist Criminology, 12*(1), 22–42. https://doi.org/10.1177/1557085116654565

Belleville, M. (2019, September 24). *About the Hubble space telescope* [Text]. NASA. http://www.nasa.gov/mission_pages/hubble/about

Elias, J. (2023, February 1). *Google is asking employees to test potential ChatGPT competitors, including a chatbot called "Apprentice Bard."* CNBC. https://www.cnbc.com/2023/01/31/google-testing-chatgpt-like-chatbot-apprentice-bard-with-employees.html

Giddens, A., & Sutton, P. W. (2021). *Essential concepts in sociology* (Third Edition). Polity.

Herings, P. J.-J., Peeters, R., & Yang, M. S. (2018). Piracy on the Internet: Accommodate it or fight it? A dynamic approach. *European Journal of Operational Research, 266*(1), 328–339. https://doi.org/10.1016/j.ejor.2017.09.011

Hinduja, S., & Patchin, J. W. (2015). *Bullying beyond the schoolyard: Preventing and responding to cyberbullying* (2nd edition). Corwin.

Jones, B. (2017, April 1). We tested AOL dial-up to see whether a 56K connection is enough for today's Internet user. *Digital Trends.* https://www.digitaltrends.com/cool-tech/aol-dial-up-a-relic-of-the-past/

Kopp, C., Layton, R., Sillitoe, J., & Gondal, I. (2016). *The role of love stories in romance scams: A qualitative analysis of fraudulent profiles.* https://doi.org/10.5281/ZENODO.56227

Madlock, P. E., & Westerman, D. (2011). Hurtful cyber-teasing and violence: Who's laughing out loud? *Journal of Interpersonal Violence, 26*(17), 3542–3560.

Martin, J., & Alaggia, R. (2013). Sexual abuse images in cyberspace: Expanding the ecology of the child. *Journal of Child Sexual Abuse, 22*(4), 398–415. https://doi.org/10.1080/10538712.2013.781091

McKetta, I. (2021, September 8). *Despite all odds, global Internet speeds continue impressive increase.* Ookla – Providing network intelligence to enable modern connectivity. https://www.ookla.com/articles/world-internet-speeds-july-2021

Merdian, H. L., Curtis, C., Thakker, J., Wilson, N., & Boer, D. P. (2013). The three dimensions of online child pornography offending. *Journal of Sexual Aggression, 19*(1), 121–132. https://doi.org/10.1080/13552600.2011.611898

Merdian, H. L., Moghaddam, N., Boer, D. P., Wilson, N., Thakker, J., Curtis, C., & Dawson, D. (2016). Fantasy-driven versus contact-driven users of child sexual exploitation material: Offender classification and implications for their risk assessment. *Sexual Abuse,* 1079063216641109.

Office of Public Affairs | U.S. Department of Justice Disrupts Hive ransomware variant | United States Department of Justice. (2023, January 26). Office of Public Affairs, US Department of Justice. https://www.justice.gov/opa/pr/us-department-justice-disrupts-hive-ransomware-variant

Paasonen, S. (2015). Online pornography. In *International encyclopedia of the social & behavioral sciences* (pp. 217–222). Elsevier. https://doi.org/10.1016/B978-0-08-097086-8.64109-0

Payne, A. A., & Hutzell, K. L. (2015). Old wine, new bottle? Comparing interpersonal bullying and cyberbullying victimization. *Youth & Society,* 0044118X15617401.

Roy, I. (2023, March 8). This is the best-selling phone of all time (it's not iPhone). *Reader's Digest*. https://www.rd.com/article/nokia-all-time-best-selling-phone/

Smallridge, J. L., & Roberts, J. R. (2013). Crime specific neutralizations: An empirical examination of four types of digital piracy. *International Journal of Cyber Criminology, 7*(2), 125–140.

Taylor, P. A. (1999). *Hackers: Crime in the digital sublime*. Routledge.

Thelwall, M. (2003). Can Google's PageRank be used to find the most important academic Web pages? *Journal of Documentation, 59*(2), 205–217. https://doi.org/10.1108/00220410310463491

Tokunaga, R. S. (2010). Following you home from school: A critical review and synthesis of research on cyberbullying victimization. *Computers in Human Behavior, 26*(3), 277–287. https://doi.org/10.1016/j.chb.2009.11.014

Wall, D. (Ed.). (2001). *Crime and the Internet*. Routledge.

Whitty, M. T. (2015). Anatomy of the online dating romance scam. *Security Journal, 28*(4), 443–455. https://doi.org/10.1057/sj.2012.57

Chapter 2

Cybertrespass

Introduction

Property crimes are the class of offenses in which a victim's property is damaged or illegally acquired without the threat of physical violence. The United Kingdom conducts an annual "Crime Survey for England and Wales" that compiles data on crime rates in that country. Of the main crime types recorded, theft, burglary, vehicle offenses, and robbery are the offenses that could be classified as property crimes. In the United States, the FBI produces an annual crime report, in which property crimes are burglary, larceny (theft of personal property), motor vehicle theft, and arson. There is a class of crimes in the digital environment that mirrors property crimes in the physical environment, where a person's property is illegally entered into and goods stolen or damaged.

Cybertrespass refers to "the unauthorized crossing of the boundaries of computer systems into spaces where rights of ownership or title have been already established" (Wall, 2001, 3). Cybertrespass is grounded in the idea that areas of the digital environment are pieces of real estate that someone owns. The owner can grant or restrict access to areas in the digital environment, just as they would real estate or property in the physical environment. People who gain unauthorized access and damage property are committing cybertrespass.

Gaining unauthorized access can be illustrated with a simple example. Imagine you have a website where you are displaying your professional skills (which is not a bad idea!). On the website, you display your educational credentials, a personal biography, and maybe some of your work samples for prospective employers to see. This is public, front-end information. It can be accessed, copied, and distributed without any special credentials from a user. This front-end information is like the front yard of a home.

Your website will also have a back end. It will contain various types of data including analytics about who comes to the website, drafts of unpublished posts, and uploaded files that have not been posted to the front end. This back-end information is considered private because access is restricted to only those with the appropriate credentials. This is like the

DOI: 10.4324/9781003283256-2

inside of a house where only someone with a key may enter. These credentials (or keys) are usually a username and password. Accessing that back-end information is a criminal offense.

Cybersecurity in the Digital Environment

We can extend this understanding to other layers of the digital environment. All layers of the digital environment use procedures that restrict access to only users with the appropriate credentials. The development and implementation of these procedures encompass the profession of cybersecurity in broad strokes. Table 2.1 lists some of these practices.

EDUCATION

An obvious cybersecurity measure is educating people and organizations vulnerable to attack. Hackers will attempt to deceive the users of computers into willingly giving them access. This is easier than finding a technological way into a computer system. If we consider machines as hardware, and the operating system and applications that run on this hardware software, then the human brain can be called the "wetware." To deter hackers from "hacking the wetware," computer users are educated in hackers' tactics. Cybersecurity professionals may conduct training programs that train computer users to recognize what a phishing email may look like or how to evaluate the integrity of someone who contacts them via phone or email.

AUTOMATED DETECTION

Cybersecurity researchers use artificial intelligence, machine learning, or a combination of these to detect malicious behavior online. Artificial intelligence is a discipline

Table 2.1 Cybersecurity Measures by Layer

Type of Layer	Description	Cybersecurity Measure
Human	The connections between users	Education
Content	The information that is produced and shared on the Internet	Automated Detection
Application	Programs that allow users to perform operations on a computer	Multifactor Authentication, Install Updates
Operating System	The software that manages the operation of applications on a computer	Install Updates
Hardware	The machines that compute and manipulate data	Encryption
Infrastructure	The technologies that transmit data between machines	End-to-End Encryption, Network Segmentation

that focuses on building machines that can simulate human intelligence. An example is Amazon's Alexa technology, which can listen to human communication and respond intelligently. Machine learning is a subfield of artificial intelligence that focuses on programming computers to identify patterns in data and make decisions based on those patterns. Using machine learning in cybersecurity is possible because malicious activity tends to follow predictable patterns. Researchers can collect data about malicious activities in the past and use this data to train a computer to detect those same types of activities in the future. Using machine learning to detect suspicious behavior automatically is a part of all the layers of the digital environment (Dasgupta et al., 2022). However, of major interest to cybercriminologists is how automated detection can be used to prevent crime and deviance in the content layer.

Phishing attacks, romance scams, hate speech, and disinformation are content-based forms of cybercrime and digital deviance. In the case of phishing attacks and romance scams, an offender uses words, images, symbols, or website design to deceive a victim into divulging money or information. In the case of hate speech or disinformation, those same tools are used to spread inaccurate information or inflict psychological harm on someone.

For example, Akhtar et al. (2022) developed a disinformation detection model using artificial intelligence and machine learning. The impetus for their research was to prevent business supply chain disruptions caused by disinformation. The spread of a false news report such as "UK economy collapses" or "COVID vaccine causes sudden death" could lead to individuals acting irrationally on false information. They may choose to stockpile products or avoid buying them. Ahktar et al. (2022) used past news articles to train the detection model. Past articles were labeled as "real" or "fake," and a model was proposed to detect future instances of fake news.

MULTIFACTOR AUTHENTICATION, INSTALLING UPDATES

Simple passwords are not very secure for at least two reasons. First, they are easily guessed using automated password crackers. An automated password cracker would submit passwords until the right one is submitted and the hacker can access the user's data. For example, if a user's password was "cybercrime," it could be guessed by an automated password cracker in about six minutes.

Companies have responded by using CAPTCHAs to detect if a human is trying to enter credentials. We have all seen CAPTCHAs (Completely Automated Public Turing test to tell Computers and Humans Apart). You must match or select from these images to show that you are human. CAPTCHAs can be effective against password crackers but negatively affect the user experience. Second, a single password is not a strong defense should a password be stolen or a hacker "hacks the wetware" and tricks a user into providing a password. Consider the common scenario in which a password is written on a notepad and placed inside someone's desk. This is a weak line of defense and can easily be overcome by a hacker. Therefore, another type of cybersecurity measure is multifactor authentication. Multifactor authentication requires that a user provide two forms of authentication to access an application or a network. Forms of authentication fall into three categories: Something you know (password or pin), something you own (your phone or a card), and something you are (a fingerprint or an iris scan).

Cybersecurity professionals must always ensure that software applications and operating systems are updated to their latest versions. Updates are made available by the manufacturers of applications and operating systems to fix bugs, improve the product's operation, and patch found vulnerabilities. Frequently installing updates will deter hackers by strengthening the security of applications and operating systems.

ENCRYPTION AND NETWORK SEGMENTATION

Encryption is an essential tool for cybersecurity. Encryption uses an algorithm to scramble data; only the person with the encryption "key" can unscramble the data. The key is usually a password or passphrase. Sensitive information stored on computer hardware can be encrypted, and even if a hacker gains access to that hardware, they cannot read the data without the key. Encryption is also useful for communications. Data sent between computers can be encrypted by the sender and sent to the client. If only the users at the ends of the communication have the encryption key (end-to-end encryption), a hacker who uses a man-in-the-middle attack to intercept those communications will not be able to read them.

Within corporations with many users having different roles and responsibilities, it may be useful to segment a network. Network segmentation is the process of dividing a larger network into segments in which users have access to only certain data or websites. This can improve security because it restricts who has access to data. For example, a large corporation may only allow users with specific credentials to access servers housing the corporation's financial documents. This limits the number of user accounts that can potentially be hacked.

Demystifying Hacking

Unlike less technologically advanced cybercrimes to be discussed in later chapters, cybertrespass appears to be the domain of cybersecurity professionals and computer scientists. The protection of computer networks is indeed a highly technical and specialized field. However, this does not exempt cybercriminologists and other social scientists from addressing hacking. There are at least three ways in which their competencies and knowledge base can be applied to the understanding of cybertrespass: (1) understanding the effects of law and policy, (2) assisting law enforcement in preventing or investigating cybercrimes and (3) conducting research on cybercrimes—especially concerning cybercrime victims.

UNDERSTANDING THE EFFECTS OF LAW AND POLICY

Recall from Chapter 1 that a challenge cybercriminologists must meet for all cybercrimes is the impact of rapidly changing laws and policies. Questions can be asked about the effectiveness of a law or policy—does it address the phenomena at hand? Questions can also be asked about the appropriateness of law and policy—does the punishment for breaking the law fit the crime?

These questions are especially relevant for crimes of cybertrespass. Hacking is a complex activity, and legislation must be crafted such that problematic behavior is being addressed, and that the punishments meted out to offenders are just. Cybercriminologists can identify instances where cybertrespass laws are ineffective or unjust and inform the public.

Consider the case of Matthew Keys. Keys was a journalist who worked for a news organization in Sacramento, California. In 2010, Keys gave his username and password to the organization's content management system to a member of the hacking organization Anonymous. The member of Anonymous then defaced a *Los Angeles Times* article by altering a title and subtitle. The company was able to remove the changes within an hour. According to American federal cybertrespass laws, Keys' actions were hacking because the organization did not authorize him to give his credentials to another person. In April 2016, Keys was found guilty of hacking, and sentenced to two years in prison.

On the one hand, we could interpret the Keys' case as "if you did the crime, you must do the time." Because ultimately, Keys did break American law. And although the damage was insignificant, one can imagine a situation in which giving away one's credentials can lead to serious damage. Consider a soldier giving access to their military unit's computer system to an enemy, or a disgruntled worker in a bank giving their credentials to someone looking to steal money. But as cybercriminologists who must think critically about law and policy, we can also ask ourselves if the way we understand hacking is too broad and whether two years in prison for changing a headline is a just penalty.

ASSISTING LAW ENFORCEMENT

Law enforcement—whether it be local, state, or federal—often requests that academics provide insight into their investigations. As with other social scientists focused on crime, cybercriminologists have insights into the profile of offenders, the factors that increase the odds of victimization, what police practices lower crime rates, and more. Law enforcement can also ask cybercriminologists to consult in investigations.

Cybercriminologists indirectly assist law enforcement by teaching future and current law enforcement officers about hacking. Most individuals interested in law enforcement major in criminal justice, criminology, sociology, psychology, and other social science disciplines. The authors of this textbook work in social science departments that attract many students interested in law enforcement careers. Students in those disciplines can benefit from learning about cybertrespass from a social science perspective.

CONDUCTING RESEARCH ON CYBERTRESSPASS

The primary way in which cybercriminologists can address hacking is through their research. Asking questions about hacking and then using proper research methods to answer those questions can produce valuable insights. These insights inform law enforcement, military personnel, legal scholars, lawmakers, and everyday citizens.

For example, imagine this question: "How can we explain the hacking behavior of young people?" The answer to this question is of clear benefit to society. Parents and educators do not want the young people they are responsible for engaging in deviant or criminal behavior. Professionals in the criminal justice system would be interested in answering this question because of the established understanding that the best way to deal with criminal behavior is not through excessive punishment but by prevention. If scholars can identify why young people become hackers, they can work proactively to reduce the number of young people committing cybertresspass violations.

A team of researchers (Back et al., 2018), attempted to answer why young people hack. The team surveyed about 19,000 high school students in the United States, Venezuela, Spain, France, Germany, Poland, Hungary, and Russia. The two explanations they posited are well-known theories in criminology—Self-Control Theory and Social Bonding Theory. Criminological theory will be discussed in Chapter 10. Self-control theory posits that people with low levels of self-control will commit crimes when the opportunity arises. On the other hand, Social Bonding Theory asserts that criminal behavior occurs amongst individuals lacking social connections. The research team found more support for lacking self-control than lacking social connections. This study is one example of many types of research that help inform society's understanding of hacking.

The Culture of Hacking: From Heroes to Hooligans

One area in which criminologists and other social scientists have contributed to an understanding of cybertrespass is by exploring the culture and motivations of hackers (Jecan, 2011; Jordan, 2008, 2017; Nikitina, 2012; Nissenbaum, 2004; Taylor, 1999). The term "hacking" originated in the 1960s at the Massachusetts Institute of Technology and was generally a positive label:

> To anyone attending the Massachusetts Institute of Technology during the 1950s and 60s, a hack was simply an elegant or inspired solution to any given problem. Many of the early MIT hacks tended to be practical jokes. One of the most extravagant saw a replica of a campus police car put on top of the Institute's Great Dome. Over time, the word became associated with the burgeoning computer programming scene, at MIT and beyond. For these early pioneers, a hack was a feat of programming prowess.

During this time, the students at the Massachusetts Institute of Technology worked within a subculture in which a "hack" meant finding a better, more efficient, or cleverer way of using something or accomplishing a goal. The classic book on by journalist Steven Levy entitled *Hackers: Heroes of the computer revolution* (Levy, 1984) describes the early culture of hacking and hackers. Levy identified a series of beliefs that he describes as the "hacker ethic." These include:

- Access to technology and information should be unfettered
- Political structures should be decentralized
- Computers can improve one's life

Although Levy's work was done in the 1980's it seems as if the "hacker ethic" lasted well into the 21st century. For example, criminologist Majid Yar (2005) argued that hacker culture can be organized around four characteristics that are similar to those written about by Levy:

- The right to freely access and exchange knowledge and information
- A belief in the capacity of science and technology to enhance individuals' lives

- A distrust of political, military, and corporate authorities
- A resistance to mainstream lifestyles, attitudes, and social hierarchies

But there has been change over time in how the public views hackers. Cornell University information scientist Helen Nissenbaum (2004) argues that hackers have gone from "heroes to hooligans" in Western society. Nissenbaum describes a gradual change from seeing hackers as beneficial influences on technological innovation to dangerous agents capable of obstructing businesses and governments. As mentioned in Chapter 1, the original users of computers and then the Internet were primarily academics, people in the military or government, and some financial institutions. Thus, the percentage of the population using the Internet at this time was small, and there were few economic transactions.

The type of users and the type of activities changed in the 1990s with the growth of the modern Internet. More users went online. The average user was no longer an academic or computer scientist but a non-tech person using the Internet for entertainment and communication. People began putting more of their personal information online. Commerce became an important aspect of the online experience with people buying more things online and conducting financial transactions online.

These changes meant that "hacks" and the people who did them were dangerous. The desire to tinker with technology ran counter to the desire to control and exploit computer technology for economic gain. It also raised the fears of everyday users who believed that the archetypal "hacker in a basement" would find a way to steal their money or identity.

Scholars stress that hacker practices are not primarily unlawful and that reducing all hacker motivations to those of a criminal nature is imprecise (Holt et al., 2017; Steinmetz, 2015; Turgeman-Goldschmidt, 2005, 2008). Despite the variety of hacker practices and motivations, it is clear that the characteristics of hacker culture described above can be paths to deviant and criminal behavior. The anti-authoritarian bent of hackers means that the rules and policies of law enforcement, government, and businesses are often rejected. Rules regarding information, for example, are routinely ignored. Consistently, hackers have found ways to gain access to sensitive government documents or intellectual property and share this data publicly.

The Types of Hackers

Not all hackers are the same. Hackers differ in their motivations for cybertresspass, and the amount of technical skill they possess. Hackers can be labeled as social engineers, script kiddies, white, black, or grey hackers, and hacktivists.

SOCIAL ENGINEERS AND SCRIPT KIDDIES

Social engineers and script kiddies are low-tech hackers. Social engineers have minimal computer programming skills—or, at any rate, do not use them to hack. Their strategies for cyber trespassing revolve around getting others to provide access to their networks by directly manipulating a victim or finding indirect ways into a system. One tactic is to send emails that purport to be from legitimate companies or authorities, asking for personal information. This tactic, called phishing, has proven to be very effective. Phishing can be very low-tech, as when social engineers use it. However, as we will discuss in a later section, it can also be very sophisticated. Two other ways include shoulder surfing, looking over the shoulder of someone as they key in their personal information, and dumpster diving, looking through the discarded documents of a target. Dumpster diving is often a preparatory technique for high-tech hackers, as they can gain information about how to infiltrate the computer networks of a business. However, social engineers can also use dumpster diving to find discarded passwords or personal information that will allow them to guess passwords.

Script kiddies are unskilled hackers who find code, tools, and technologies already produced by more skilled hackers and use them to gain unauthorized access to computer networks. The label is meant to be insulting, as it implies that someone does not have the actual ability to produce their own hacking technologies. Numerous hacker forums and websites exist where individuals with criminal intent can find worms, viruses, or other malware. Script kiddies can also buy hardware on these online forums, such as keyloggers and credit card scammers.

In 2020, cybersecurity researchers observed that the source code for the Dharma ransomware strain was being sold on hacking forums. According to ZDNet:

> *Several ransomware experts…said the sale of the Dharma ransomware code would most likely result in its eventual leak on the public Internet, and to a wider audience. This, in turn, would result in the broader proliferation among multiple cybercrime groups, and an eventual surge in attacks.*
>
> (Source code of Dharma ransomware pops
> up for sale on hacking forums, n.d.)

The experts' predictions were correct. Later that same year, news agencies reported that "unsophisticated Iranian hackers" were targeting companies in Russia, Japan, China, and India with ransomware (*Unsophisticated Iranian hackers armed with ransomware are targeting companies worldwide | Fox News*, n.d.)

WHITE, BLACK, AND GRAY HAT HACKERS

Hackers with a high degree of technical skill can be divided into three types: Black, white, and gray (Holt, 2010). The labels are inspired by the tropes of old Hollywood Western movies, where the good guys wore white clothes, and the bad guys wore black clothes.

Black hat hackers find vulnerabilities in software and networks and exploit them for malicious purposes. Money is a major motivation. However, many black hat hackers hack for political or ideological reasons. For example, they may hack into databases or emails and release sensitive information to the public to further a political goal. Recall the hacker values described previously, such as "information should be free" and a "mistrust of authorities." These values lead to hackers often breaking into the systems of large corporations or businesses, stealing data, and making that data available to the public.

White hat hackers attempt to break into computer networks to identify and patch vulnerabilities. The term often attached to this practice is "ethical hacking or "pen(etration) testing." When working for security firms or law enforcement, white hat hackers may attempt to identify black hat hackers or anticipate their movements.

Gray hat hackers occupy a middle position. They are often freelancers looking to identify exploits and vulnerabilities. Once they find these exploits, they sell their information to law-abiding corporations, governments, or criminals on the black market. Gray hat hackers may even sell their software or hardware to script kiddies.

HACKTIVISTS

Hacktivists are distinguished from the hackers described above in that their motivations are political. In this way, hacktivists are like cyberterrorists (discussed in Chapter 7), but do not attempt to harm civilians. Hacktivists commit acts of cybertrespass as a form of protest against a worldview or political group. Hacktivists can be analogized to civil rights groups, anti-war groups, animal rights groups, and environmental groups performing acts of civil disobedience to publicize their causes. Whereas the latter groups have traditionally used sit-ins and public marches, hacktivist groups may hack into a computer system to deface a website or perform a distributed denial of service attack to prevent a website from operating properly.

Arguably the most well-known hacktivist group is Anonymous. Anonymous rose to prominence in the early 2000s and 2010s with a series of attacks that shut down or defaced several highly trafficked websites owned by governments and corporations. For example, Anonymous was linked to attacks on Sony's PlayStation network in 2011 and the Donald Trump-owned Trump Towers website in 2015.

One study explored an Anonymous cell involved in the 2012 university student protests in Québec, Canada. The protests were in response to a proposed tuition hike. The proposed hike would raise tuition by 75%. "This caused students to protest on the streets, blocking entrances to university buildings, and clash with police over the course of several months" (Fortin et al., p. 36). The Québec government then proposed a bill prohibiting rallies with more than 50 people unless pre-approved by the police. This bill drew the attention of the cell in Québec, which then hacked several police and government servers and websites. The demonstrations, marches, and other forms of protest lasted over several months and were called the "Maple Spring." Eventually, the Québec government dropped its proposed tuition hike.

The study examined the communications in two chatrooms frequented by Anonymous members during the Maple Spring. The goal of the study was to identify the main topics discussed. The researchers identified five:

- Collective identity—The scholars observed several attempts by Anonymous members to describe what the group is and what it stands for, with no real consensus or disagreement. The multiple definitions create inclusivity, they argue, because each member's understanding of the collective is honored.
- Freedom of expression—Anonymous members' concerns, as expressed on the forums, were not about the socioeconomic issue of tuition hikes. Instead, their concern was over freedom of expression and the free flow of information. The Québec government's attempt to stifle demonstrations was an attack on expression.
- Immunity of the media—One of the few articulated rules on the forums was not attacking the media. The media is seen as a disseminator of information and as such needs to be protected.

- Target selection—The members discussed at length what websites to target. There was not always a consensus, but targets that were generally selected went against the values of freedom of expression and the free flow of information.
- Reception and perception of the attacks—members were proud of the websites and servers they hacked into and shared their successes in the chat rooms. "A collective sense of joy and pride was visible in the chatroom after a success was reported through the use of emoticons" (48).

The Process of Cybertrespass

This section gives an overview of the hacking process from beginning to end.

In his book *Hacking the hacker: Learn from the experts who take down hackers* (2017), cybersecurity professional Grimes outlines the basic steps in the hacking process. Grimes describes it as the hacking methodology. We list the steps in Grimes' hacking methodology below and add further elaboration and vocabulary.

1. INFORMATION GATHERING

Hackers begin by conducting reconnaissance, and learning as much about the target as possible. There are at least two ways to gather information—spycraft and collecting open-source information.

Spycraft in this text will refer to techniques used to collect information from a target in the physical world without being detected. One technique is shoulder surfing. Shoulder surfing refers to the act of looking over a target's shoulder as they key in personal information. Shoulder surfing has also been called visual hacking and can be done at close range by looking over someone's shoulder or at a distance using binoculars. Shoulder surfing is such a common technique that in response to the practice hardware manufacturers have developed countermeasures to protect users from shoulder surfing attacks. Some newer laptops have a privacy mode that makes viewing the screen at an angle difficult, thereby discouraging shoulder surfing, and cell phone users can buy screen protectors that approximate the same effect.

Dumpster diving, another form of spycraft, refers to the act of searching for discarded information about a potential target. The term dumpster is both literal—in that hackers may indeed search in dumpsters, and metaphorical—signifying the fact that the search is for discarded information that has been thrown away or neglected. As such, a hacker will look for discarded information in any number of areas—both physical and digital. Information can be found, for example, in trash bins as well as old hard drives. Dumpster diving is a precursor to more sophisticated social engineering or hacking forms. An organizational chart or phone list found through dumpster diving could be the information needed to make a phishing email look more legitimate.

Open-Source Intelligence (OSINT) can be defined as "the collection, processing and correlation of public information from open data sources such as the mass media, social networks, forums and blogs, public government data, publications, or commercial data" (Pastor-Galindo et al., 2020). Hackers can learn a lot about a target from mass media. According to Grimes (2017):

> *[the hackers] use the news media and public financial reports to find out who the senior executives are or to find other employee names for social engineering. The hacker looks up news stories to see what big software the target has bought recently, what mergers or divestitures are happening (these are always messy affairs often accompanied by relaxed or missed security), and even what partners they interact with.*

(11)

OSINT also includes less obvious, more technical information such as IP addresses and domain names. Hackers can also create a digital profile of their target, a process called fingerprinting. A target's fingerprint will include information about the type of hardware, software, and services the target uses, (for example, the target could be using Dell Optiplex 7040 machines, with Windows 11 installed, using Zoom version 5.13.7 for videoconferencing, and a Logitech C920 webcam operated by Logitech webcam software version 2.4).

2. PENETRATION

This stage is when the hacker initially "hacks" into a system. Grimes argues that if they have collected enough information, hackers *will* find a vulnerability in the system, exploit it, and gain access. The tools used for penetration will be discussed in a later section. However, at this time it is worth noting Grimes' assertion that if a hacker or hacking team is diligent enough, they will eventually gain access to a system. This claim has been supported by research. Cybersecurity company Positive Technologies did research on a global sample of organizations (*Business in the Crosshairs*, n.d.). The company used its cybersecurity experts to attempt to breach the computer networks of the company sampled. *They were able to do so 93% of the time.*

On the one hand, this high percentage of successful hacks is surprising. One can imagine that there is a great incentive for these companies to protect themselves from cyberattacks. A successful attack will damage their reputation with customers and cost them millions. As such, millions of dollars and thousands of hours of employee work time are invested in protecting their networks. On the other hand, consider the number of technologies that allow a networked computer system to function (think of the layers discussed in Chapter 1), and then think of the number of users in a company—all of whom are using computers on the network and are susceptible to being manipulated in some way. With these factors in mind, the 93% seems more plausible.

3. GUARANTEEING FUTURE EASIER ACCESS

Hackers may want to ensure they can remain inside of a compromised system by finding additional exploits. Companies routinely change passwords, update software, or modify security protocols. One tactic Grimes mentions is installing a backdoor into the computer system. A backdoor refers to a way of getting around the cybersecurity measures on a computer system. One common backdoor type is installing undetectable spyware on a machine in the target's network. The hackers can then spy on the activities of that particular machine even if the initial vulnerability they used to enter the system is patched.

4. INTERNAL RECONNAISSANCE

Internal reconnaissance is information gathering within a network. Hackers do internal reconnaissance by "looking in memory, on the hard drive, for network connectivity, and enumerating users, shares, services, and programs" (Grimes, 2017, p. 18). A major goal of internal reconnaissance is to understand the target better. Imagine if the target is a large multinational company, and the hackers have hacked into one machine from a low-level user. This machine or user of that machine may not have access to the information the hacker wants. Internal reconnaissance can help the hackers zero in on where that information is and how to get to it.

5. MOVEMENT

Hackers now may want to move through the computer network—compromising more user accounts or machines. This may be necessary in order to get to the most valuable information in the system. Grimes argues that moving to additional targets within the same system is easier once an initial foothold is gained in a system.

Consider a sample organizational table below (Table 2.2). Imagine a company has implemented the sound cybersecurity practice of limiting who has access to data, and a hacker has managed to gain access to a computer in the company's customer service division. The hacker's goal is to steal some of the company's intellectual property. The hacker gained access to this computer because they found that the client management software used by employees to communicate with customers did not adequately check for viruses when customer documents were uploaded. Customer service employees do not have access to the company's intellectual property, and so the hacker will need to find a way to access top management's computers.

6. INTENDED ACTION EXECUTION

In a later section of this chapter, we will talk about the different types of hackers and what their motivations are. But whatever their motivations, most hackers have an end goal in mind. In this stage, hackers will conduct the activity they planned before entering the network.

Table 2.2   Company Organization Chart by Data Access

Unit	Data Access
Management	All data below and the company's intellectual property
Sales and Accounting	Company's financial information, customer's financial information
Customer Service	Past and Present Customer PII (name, address, contact info, purchase history)
Human Resources	Past and Present Employee PII (names, address, contact info, health information, social security numbers)
Support (Custodians and Physical Security)	Their own personal log-in credentials

7. COVERING TRACKS

The hackers may wish to make sure that their presence in a system once they've left cannot be detected. But Grimes (2017) argues that this stage is less necessary today:

> *This used to be what almost all hackers did years ago, but these days computer systems are so complex and in such great numbers that most asset owners don't check for hacker tracks. They don't check the logs, they don't check the firewall, and they don't look for any signs of illegal hacking unless it hits them in the face.*

(19)

How do Hackers Penetrate a Network?

There are three broad ways in which hackers gain access to a network: Impersonation, interception, and using malware. These ways are often used in conjunction with each other—for example, a phishing email (impersonation) is used to install ransomware (malware) on a computer. They are separated here for teaching purposes.

IMPERSONATION

A common way of hacking into a computer is through impersonating a legitimate entity. That entity could be a person, a communication from a person in the form of an email, text, or phone call, a website, or a computer.

One of the more common techniques is to impersonate a government official. This tactic works because people are socialized into listening to and trusting authority figures. The United States' Internet Crime Complaint Center reported government impersonation as being the 15th most reported crime in 2015, with 11,832 complaints. This is most certainly an undercount, as many people are unaware that they have been duped, are too embarrassed to admit they have been scammed, or do not know that the crime complaint center is available.

Phishing is another instance of impersonation. Phishing is an email, webpage, or other communication that purports to be legitimate but is designed to infect a computer with malware (Hutchings & Hayes, 2009; Konradt et al., 2016), or to deceive the user into providing sensitive information. Phishing has evolved over the years to incorporate other technologies in the digital environment. Vishing is phishing via telephone, where a hacker attempts to fool a target into providing sensitive information. Meanwhile, smishing is phishing via text messages, with links or phone numbers sent to cell phones.

Spoofing is also a type of technological social engineering. Spoofing refers to falsifying the origin of communication, thereby misleading or deceiving the receiver of the communication. In the case of social engineering, the receiver of the false communication is a computer user; however, spoofing can also be done by deceiving computers.

One common type of spoofing is email spoofing. Email spoofing occurs when the identifying attributes of a sent email are falsified. These attributes include from what email address the message is sent, to whom the message is sent, the path along which the email traveled from sender to recipient, and the IP address of the computer from which the email was sent. Scammers may use software often called "ratware" to change some of these identifying attributes.

Another type of spoofing is web spoofing. In web spoofing, a website is created that approximates the look of a more well-known website. The URL for the fake website may also be quite similar. For example, a spoofed website may use a logo like that of the iconic half-eaten apple used for the Apple Corporation and a URL of www.apple.com. Such websites usually trick someone to input personal information that can be harvested, or have them download malware onto their computers.

INTERCEPTION

Hackers can find ways to insert themselves between two machines communicating and intercept the data or messages they share. For example, consider a student sitting in a coffee shop doing their term paper, using the coffee shop's Wi-Fi connection. The communication is between the student's laptop and the coffee shop's router. A hacker could intercept the signal from the student's laptop, read the information, and then send that signal on to the coffee shop's router, where it then goes to its destination. The student does not know that their information is being intercepted. There are many names for this type of attack, but a common one is the man-in-the-middle attack. The purpose of these attacks can be to steal information, spy on someone, or sabotage communications.

In 2018, Dutch security services foiled a man-in-the-middle attack by Russian agents. The agents were members of Russia's military cyber unit GRU (Glavnoye Razvedyvatelnoye Upravlenie) 26165. In April of that year, four members of the unit came to the Dutch city of The Hague with diplomatic passports. The team loaded a car with technical equipment, including Wi-Fi spoofing equipment, that would allow them to conduct their attack.

Their target was the Organization for the Prohibition of Chemical Weapons (OCPW). The OCPW is the world's foremost chemical weapons watchdog. The organization was investigating the poisoning of a Russian ex-spy and his daughter in the UK. According to a BBC report:

> They [the agents] planned to carry out a closed access hack operation targeting the OPCW's Wi-Fi network, officials say. In the rear of the car they had set up specialist equipment for doing this, and parked the vehicle in the car park of a nearby Marriot hotel. The equipment included an antenna which was hidden under a waterproof jacket and aimed at the OPCW office. This was being used to intercept login details...The goal was to compromise and disrupt computers in the building, officials say.
>
> ("How the Dutch foiled Russian 'cyber-attack' on OPCW," 2018)

MALWARE

Malware simply means malicious software. Historically, the three classes of malware have been viruses, worms, and trojans. Ransomware is neither a virus, worm, nor trojan but a class of software with its own characteristics. These four types are discussed below.

Viruses

Viruses are malware that infect a computer and change the functionality of the computer or programs running on that computer. Viruses are embedded in other files and need interaction from a human user to drop their "payload" (executable action) and replicate. Viruses can be direct-action viruses and immediately perform the desired action once installed. They may also be memory-resident viruses and remain inactive until the user performs a desired action. Memory-resident viruses are often called "time-bomb" viruses.

Worms

Worms can be understood as self-replicating malware that performs its actions without the intervention of a user. Once a worm has gained entry into a computer network—through an email or hyperlink—it will spread or replicate without additional user interaction. Worms are self-contained programs and do not need to attach themselves to programs or files and operate surreptitiously within the computer system.

Unlike viruses, worms usually do not have a "payload." However, they are very damaging because they recruit computer memory to replicate and spread, slowing down computing speed. One indicator of an infected machine is that it is running slower than usual or crashes repeatedly. Worms are also damaging because they can clog the connections between networks, simulating the same difficulties observed in a denial-of-service attack. The common ways worms spread are through vulnerabilities in the protocols in a computer network, emails, and the sharing of infected portable media.

Trojans

Trojans are named after the mythological Trojan Horse used to smuggle Greek soldiers during the Trojan War. Subterfuge is the defining characteristic of computer Trojans. Trojans appear to the user to be legitimate software. Once the user clicks on the software, the Trojan's payload is installed onto the computer. Trojans are not characteristically designed to replicate across computer or systems or to interfere with the computer's normal operations. These behaviors would alert a user or cybersecurity professional to the presence of the Trojan, which would defeat its purpose. By being undetected, Trojans allow a hacker to perform unwanted functions unbeknown to computer users. Trojans can be used to:

- Create backdoors so that hackers can gain future access to a computer. An example of this is the "Linux.BackDoor.Fgt" backdoor. This backdoor targeted Linux servers running a specific Internet Relay Chat (IRC) server. Hackers compromised the official download site for the IRC software and replaced the legitimate software package with a version containing the backdoor. Users who downloaded and installed this tampered version unknowingly introduced the backdoor into their systems. The backdoor allowed them to execute arbitrary commands, read and write files, and execute commands remotely.

- Control computers for a for a denial-of-service attack (DoS). The goal of a DoS attack is to overwhelm the target with an excessive amount of traffic, data, or requests. A common type of DoS attack is the distributed denial-of-service (DDoS) attack. In a DDoS attack, multiple compromised computers or devices (known as a botnet) are used to flood the target with requests simultaneously. This can cause the target to shut down.
- Install a keylogger (or keystroke logger) onto a computer to record a user's keystrokes. Once installed, keyloggers run in the background, recording what a user types of their machine. Some keyloggers can also capture screenshots or record mouse movements.

Ransomware

Ransomware is a type of malware that encrypts a computer's files or locks the authorized user out of the device. To gain access to the files or device, the victim must pay the hacker money (ransom), usually in cryptocurrency.

There have been several high-profile ransomware attacks over the past several years. In January of 2023, the British multinational postal service Royal Mail was hit with a ransomware attack from the Russia based "Lockbit cartel" ("Royal Mail hit by Russia-linked ransomware attack," 2023). The gang encrypted files on the company's servers causing disruption to its overseas deliveries. They also threatened to leak sensitive data if an 80-million-dollar ransom was not paid. Royal Mail refused to pay the ransom and restarted their international mail services six weeks later.

Some victims of ransomware attacks are not able to survive the attack. Lincoln College, a college in the United States, closed after 157 years in 2022. The college had already been struggling financially because of the COVID-19 pandemic. In December of 2021, they were hit with a ransomware attack believed to have originated in Iran. The attack "walled off the school's access to its data and halted its recruitment, retention and fund-raising campaigns" (Chung, 2022). The school eventually paid $100,000 to gain access to their data. Once they gained access to their data, administrators at the college saw significant enrollment shortfalls. The attack, along with COVID-19, meant the school did not have enough funds to remain in operation.

The Crimes of Cybertresspass

This chapter has so far discussed ways of protecting from cybertresspass, a general process by which hackers commit cybertresspass, and the various types of hackers who participate in this activity. The final section discusses the three activities that can be done once a "hack" has been successful.

DATA THEFT

The hacks that have gotten the most media coverage have been those in which hackers have stolen credit card or financial information. The Target hack of 2013 resulted in an estimated 40 million credit and debit card information stolen, as well as the names, addresses, phone numbers, and email addresses of around 70 million customers. In 2017, the credit rating company Equifax was hacked, resulting in the theft of social security numbers, addresses, and other identifying information from over 140 million customers.

The theft of data is not always motivated by economic gain. Data theft can also be politically motivated. Nations are perpetually spying on each other. In 2015, the United States government computer systems were hacked with over 21 million people's records stolen, including 19.7 million people who had been subject to a government background check. The theft was the largest cyberattack on government systems to that date, and industry professionals believe that China was the perpetrator.

DATA MANIPULATION

An action committed after unauthorized access is the manipulation of data. For example, a hacker can gain access to a sensitive document or software application and modify records or values. Data manipulation could be more difficult to detect than theft. Cybersecurity professionals often detect intrusions when they are alerted to massive amounts of data are detected leaving the network. Data being extracted from a network is called exfiltration. Data manipulation does not require the exfiltration of data.

One form of data manipulation is encrypting someone's data without their authorization. A particular type of malware, called ransomware, encrypts a victim's files and demands payment for them to be decrypted. A ransomware attack can be especially difficult for the victim and for law enforcement. Once a computer is infected, it is practically impossible to reverse the infection as decrypting files without a decryption key can be extremely difficult. Other types of attacks, by contrast, can be combatted with software that can clean a system of the malware. Furthermore, payment is demanded in the form of cryptocurrency. Cryptocurrency is difficult to trace making it hard for law enforcement to identify the perpetrators.

Data manipulation can be rather simple. Consider, for example, a student who has managed to obtain their professor's college account password. They can then go into the grading system using the professor's credentials and change their grades. In essence, they have manipulated the data that is associated with their account.

ALTERING COMPUTER OPERATIONS

Hackers can alter the way in which a computer or network operates. Distributed denial-of-service (DDoS) attacks are examples in which a hacker alters a computer's functionality. DDoS attacks are carried out by a hacker who first spreads a malware across a number of computers or devices, taking control of them. These infected computers are called "bots." A collection of bots called a botnet are used to send numerous requests to a website or server. The victim's machines shut down or are severely slowed because of the traffic, and legitimate users are blocked.

As computers become more integrated into everyday machines and appliances, altering computer functions will become a greater issue. Individuals and families are beginning to use computer networks to turn on home power and lights, operate ovens and stoves, and drive cars. These machines and appliances—or more specifically, the Internet enabled computers that animate them—can be hacked and manipulated. This creates a potentially dangerous situation that will need to be addressed in the future.

Conclusion

In this chapter, the topic of cybertrespass was explored. Cybertrespass, commonly called hacking, refers to "the unauthorized crossing of the boundaries of computer systems into spaces where rights of ownership or title have been already established" (Wall, 2001, p. 3). Hacking is the most technologically sophisticated cybercrime, often requiring in-depth computer programming and networking knowledge. In each layer of the digital environment, cybersecurity professionals must develop strategies to protect computers and their users from hackers. Hackers' success rates are still high even as cybersecurity professionals implement these strategies. This is because of the sheer number of ways a system can be breached, from the infrastructure layer to the human layer, and using tactics from dumpster diving to social engineering.

The technical nature of hacking does not mean that cybercriminologists and law enforcement personnel are not important to understanding cybertrespass. Criminologists can apply social science theory and methods to understanding cybertrespass. Both criminologists and law enforcement personnel can understand the impacts of laws and policies, help develop effective criminal investigation practices, and they can conduct research on aspects of hacking.

Hacking is an ever-changing, complex activity. Hacking was initially seen positively—a person finding a clever way to accomplish a goal. Scholars studying hacking have demonstrated that many hackers were powered by a "hacker ethic" that was not of itself criminal. Moreover, some hackers are explicitly criminal (black hat), work in cybersecurity (white hat), and still others who will offer their services to either commit or combat crime (grey hat). Still other hackers are hacktivists who hack as a form of protest. This complexity speaks to the need for social scientists to continue exploring cybertrespass in the future.

CHAPTER 2 CURRENT EVENTS AND CRITICAL THINKING:

Should Some Things Never be Online?

Electric vehicles use little or no fossil fuel, leaving a smaller carbon footprint. Many people see electric vehicles as a way of combatting climate change. Some nations have passed laws either mandating electric vehicles or mandating that cars lower their carbon dioxide emissions. As such, the number of people buying electric vehicles is steadily rising. Because these electric vehicles and the technologies they rely upon are connected to computer networks, they can be hacked.

Consider an excerpt from a 2023 story published in the technology magazine *Wired*:

At the beginning of the war in Ukraine, hackers tweaked charging stations along the Moscow–Saint Petersburg motorway in Russia to greet users with anti-Putin messages. Around the same time, cyber-vandals in England programmed public chargers to broadcast pornography. (Root, 2023)

The consequences of these breaches were relatively minor. But what if more nefarious hackers had breached the charging systems? A cybersecurity expert, quoted in the *Wired* story remarked:

If a hacker were to switch thousands, or millions, of chargers on or off simultaneously, it could destabilize and even bring down entire electricity networks…We've inadvertently created a weapon that nation-states can use against our power grid.

This danger highlights an enduring problem. Having an Internet enabled device increases its usability and efficiency, but it also means that the device is now at risk of being hacked. Think about automobile operating systems (Apple's CarPlay or Google's Android Auto are two examples). If they are connected to the Internet, then it is theoretically possible for hackers to breach the security of those systems. A hacked system can be fatal to a driver whose car malfunctions while on the highway. Or consider that some pacemakers now wirelessly transmit information to a doctor. This allows a doctor to monitor the performance of the pacemaker. But it also means that a hacker can possibly hack into that pacemaker. Like a hacked operating system in an automobile, malfunctions caused by hacks can be fatal.

There are many devices or systems that are Internet enabled and thus vulnerable to hacks. Should some things never be online, given the catastrophic damage that could be caused should they be hacked? Why or why not?

REFERENCES

Akhtar, P., Ghouri, A. M., Khan, H. U. R., Amin ul Haq, M., Awan, U., Zahoor, N., Khan, Z., & Ashraf, A. (2022). Detecting fake news and disinformation using artificial intelligence and machine learning to avoid supply chain disruptions. *Annals of Operations Research*. https://doi.org/10.1007/s10479-022-05015-5

Back, S., Soor, S., & LaPrade, J. (2018). Juvenile hackers: An empirical test of self-control theory and social bonding theory. *The International Journal of Cybersecurity Intelligence and Cybercrime*, 1(1), 40–55. https://doi.org/10.52306/01010518VMDC9371

Business in the crosshairs: Analyzing attack scenarios. (n.d.). Ptsecurity.Com. Retrieved July 21, 2023, from https://www.ptsecurity.com/ww-en/analytics/pentests-2021-attack-scenarios/

Chung, C. (2022, May 9). Lincoln College to close, hurt by pandemic and ransomware attack. *The New York Times*. https://www.nytimes.com/2022/05/09/us/lincoln-college-illinois-closure.html

Dasgupta, D., Akhtar, Z., & Sen, S. (2022). Machine learning in cybersecurity: A comprehensive survey. *The Journal of Defense Modeling and Simulation: Applications, Methodology, Technology*, 19(1), 57–106. https://doi.org/10.1177/1548512920951275

Fortin, F., Campisi, F., & Neron, M.-E. (2022). Hacktivists from the Inside: Collective Identity, Target Selection and Tactical Use of Media during the Quebec Maple Spring Protests. *Rivista di Criminologia, Vittimologia e Sicurezza*, XVI, 1–3, 2022. https://doi.org/10.14664/rcvs/242

Grimes, R. A. (2017). *Hacking the hacker: Learn from the experts who take down hackers* (1st edition). Wiley.

Holt, T. J. (2010). Examining the role of technology in the formation of deviant subcultures. *Social Science Computer Review*, 28(4), 466–481. https://doi.org/10.1177/0894439309351344

Holt, T. J., Freilich, J. D., & Chermak, S. M. (2017). Exploring the subculture of ideologically motivated cyber-attackers. *Journal of Contemporary Criminal Justice*, 1043986217699100.

How the Dutch foiled Russian "cyber-attack" on OPCW. (2018, October 4). *BBC News*. https://www.bbc.com/news/world-europe-45747472

Hutchings, A., & Hayes, H. (2009). Routine activity theory and phishing victimisation: Who gets caught in the "Net"? *Current Issues in Criminal Justice, 20*(3), 433–451.

Jecan, V. (2011). Hacking Hollywood: Discussing hackers' reactions to three popular films. *Journal of Media Research, 4*(2).

Jordan, T. (2008). *Hacking: Digital media and technological determinism.* Polity Press.

Jordan, T. (2017). A genealogy of hacking. *Convergence: The International Journal of Research into New Media Technologies, 23*(5), 528–544. https://doi.org/10.1177/1354856516640710

Konradt, C., Schilling, A., & Werners, B. (2016). Phishing: An economic analysis of cybercrime perpetrators. *Computers & Security, 58*, 39–46. https://doi.org/10.1016/j.cose.2015.12.001

Levy, S. (1984). *Hackers: Heroes of the computer revolution* (1st edition). Anchor Press/Doubleday.

Nikitina, S. (2012). Hackers as tricksters of the digital age: Creativity in hacker culture. *The Journal of Popular Culture, 45*(1), 133–152.

Nissenbaum, H. (2004). Hackers and the contested ontology of cyberspace. *New Media & Society, 6*(2), 195–217. https://doi.org/10.1177/1461444804041445

Pastor-Galindo, J., Nespoli, P., Gómez Mármol, F., & Martínez Pérez, G. (2020). The not yet exploited goldmine of OSINT: Opportunities, open challenges and future trends. *IEEE Access, 8*, 10282–10304. https://doi.org/10.1109/ACCESS.2020.2965257

Root, T. (2023, July 5). EV charger hacking poses a 'catastrophic' risk. *Wired.* https://www.wired.com/story/electric-vehicle-charging-station-hacks/

Royal Mail hit by Russia-linked ransomware attack. (2023, January 12). *BBC News.* https://www.bbc.com/news/business-64244121

Source code of Dharma ransomware pops up for sale on hacking forums. (n.d.). ZDNET. Retrieved April 17, 2023, from https://www.zdnet.com/article/source-code-of-dharma-ransomware-pops-up-for-sale-on-hacking-forums/

Steinmetz, K. F. (2015). Craft(y)ness: An ethnographic study of hacking. *British Journal of Criminology, 55*(1), 125–145. https://doi.org/10.1093/bjc/azu061

Taylor, P. A. (1999). *Hackers: Crime in the digital sublime.* Routledge.

Turgeman-Goldschmidt, O. (2005). Hackers' accounts: Hacking as a social entertainment. *Social Science Computer Review, 23*(1), 8–23. https://doi.org/10.1177/0894439304271529

Turgeman-Goldschmidt, O. (2008). Meanings that hackers assign to their being a hacker. *International Journal of Cyber Criminology, 2*(2), 382.

Unsophisticated Iranian hackers armed with ransomware are targeting companies worldwide | Fox News. (n.d.). Retrieved July 21, 2023, from https://www.foxnews.com/tech/unsophisticated-iranian-hackers-armed-with-ransomware-are-targeting-companies-worldwide

Wall, D. (Ed.). (2001). *Crime and the Internet.* Routledge.

Yar, M. (2005). Computer hacking: Just another case of juvenile delinquency? *The Howard Journal of Crime and Justice, 44*(4), 387–399.

Chapter 3

Cyberpornography

Introduction

Cyberpornography, as defined by Wall, is "the publication or trading of sexually expressive (explicit) materials in the digital environment" (Wall, 2001, p. 6). We will extend Wall's definition in two ways.

First, we extend cyberpornography to include communication about sexual behaviors and lifestyles. In particular, we are interested in online communities that may be considered sexually deviant by large segments of Western society. Second, we place forms of sex work that occur or are facilitated in the digital environment in the category of cyberpornography. Phenomena such as providing virtual sexual services through camming or through websites like OnlyFans are considered in this chapter, as well as the use of the digital environment to facilitate sexual services that are ultimately delivered in person.

A unique aspect of this chapter is that we are primarily writing about a series of *behaviors* that may be considered deviant or immoral as opposed to a series of *crimes*. Communicating about and ultimately acting upon sexual fetishes is not usually illegal in most countries. However, they are by definition, non-normative behaviors and would be perceived as deviant by many. Similarly, the consumption of "normal" pornography—depictions of vaginal or anal sex between two cisgender adults—is not illegal, but considered deviant by many. Indeed, despite the evidence that *most* young to middle-aged males and many females consume legal pornography, few are willing to admit it (One of the authors of this text used to walk into class on the day of the cyberporn lecture and ask for a show of hands of who watches pornography. Few students raised their hands).

Of course, some behaviors are criminalized. Sexting is, in most cases, a deviant but not illegal behavior. But when sexting occurs between an adult and a minor, it is considered an instance of trafficking in child pornography. Similarly, the production of pornography, while regulated in some contexts, is generally seen as free expression and permitted in society. However, some pornography is seen as so morally egregious it is prohibited.

DOI: 10.4324/9781003283256-3

We will use the American "Miller Test" to illustrate this. Whether the phenomena in this chapter are seen as deviant or criminal, morality is usually a primary factor involved. If we can think of cybertrespass as "crimes against property" and cyberviolence (to be covered in Chapter 4) as "crimes against persons," then the crimes in this chapter are "crimes against morality."

Sexual Deviance in Online Spaces

Recall from Chapter 1 that deviance is defined as normative violations that will elicit social control sanctions if detected. Sexual deviance occurs when norms about sexuality—norms of sexual identity and sexual expression—are violated. Sociologist Meredith G. F. Worthen (2016) writes:

> *Almost any sexual behavior can, and may, in some societies or cultures, be considered a forbidden act or one that deserves criminal sanction. For example, pornography, premarital sex, and prostitution have all been defined as deviant and criminal, and by contrast, they have also been viewed as normative. Sexual deviance, then, is a social construct...*

> (p. 119)

The constructed nature of most deviance, including sexual deviance, is axiomatic in social science. We *make* something deviant. A majority of people may simply choose to adopt one way of living over another and then perceive the minority of people who choose a different way as deviant. Yet another way is when powerful or influential people or groups pass laws labeling a behavior deviant. We will not explore the process of making deviance in this book. However, it is important to realize that the online communities forming around sexual "deviance" are not inherently deviant and may not be so at a different space or time. As an example, trans persons are becoming more visible in Western societies. While being trans is still considered by many in society to be deviant, there are many spaces where identifying as trans is celebrated as an example of self-expression and being true to one's identity. Moreover, we can expect that over time, society will become more tolerant of people adopting a sexual identity that differs from the one recorded on their birth certificate.

The temporal and spatial variations in what is considered deviant mean that people with deviant identities or behaviors can seek out spaces where they are not negatively sanctioned. Many of these spaces are online (Campbell et al., 2019; Cavalcante, 2016; Jenzen, 2017). Sundén (2023) conducted an ethnographic study of the Swedish digital BDSM, fetish and kink platform Darkside. The participants in her study were in the kink "closet"—an analogy to the gay and lesbian "closet" of withholding sexual identity from the public. Sundén (2023) identified tactics that allow sexually marginalized groups to "exist, resist, and transgress without becoming fully visible or graspable" (p. 2). To prevent nonconsensual image sharing, community members blurred their faces on the uploaded images – a form of concealed exhibitionism. Members also embrace what Sundén calls an "opacity" (not being clear or transparent) in how they understand themselves. To many outsiders their sexual identity and behaviors are hard to categorize and define. This is embodied in the phrase, "your kink is not my kink, but your kink is ok."

There are other examples of people exhibiting deviant behaviors and/or possessing deviant identities finding connections online. In the United States many Americans who identify as politically conservative have been historically hostile towards LGTBQ communities. However, many conservatives are LGTBQ and must navigate conservative spaces—offline and online. Brody et al.'s (2022) research explores conservative LGBTQ—whom they call "gayservatives" on the conservative social media website Gab. The researchers explored 11 public groups catering to gayservatives and identified several communication patterns. One pattern was communicating about finding one's place. For example, the scholars quote one user as saying: "I'm an old, Christian, gay, gun-toting Republican, so it's taken me a while to find my tribe" (Brody et al., 2022, p. 5). Another pattern was the establishing of a gayservative community. Website users were open in relating their need to find people with a similar sexual identity and then using the community to crowdsource advice to questions such as dating as a gayservative. Yet another pattern is reinforcing traditional norms of masculinity by embracing a masculine form of homosexuality. For example, one meme circulating on the website during their research states: "Yeah, I'm gay. But you won't catch me acting like a f—g."

Pornography Consumption

With pornography referring to materials showing sexual organs or activity intended to produce arousal, research on rates of pornography tend have at least two conclusions. First, most people report consuming pornography sometime in their recent past. Second, men consume pornography far more than women, with most studies showing rates above 90%. For example, Solano et al. (2020) report that 91.5% of men and 60.2% of women report having consumed pornography in the past month of their research. More recently, Ballester-Arnal et al. (2023) provided one of the more comprehensive studies on pornography. They divided respondents into five age groups (less than 18 years old, between 18–25, 26–40, 41–60, over 60 years old) and found that pornography usage rates for *all* male groups were over 85%. This finding supports the claim that most people report consuming pornography.

For men, 97% of respondents in the age groups less than 18 years old, between 18–25, and 26–40 report consuming pornography. For women, the rates are somewhat lower, but still clear majorities. The age groups less than 18 years old, between 18–25, and 26–40 report consuming pornography at 78%, 75%, and 83%, respectively.

We can also get a sense of the popularity of pornography by comparing the most visited sites worldwide. Figure 3.1 (p. 47) lists the 15 most popular sites measured by the number of visits. The search engine Google, the video sharing site YouTube, and the social media site Facebook are the top of the list. This was not unexpected. *But the next two most visited sites worldwide were sites specializing in pornographic content—Pornhub and Xvideos.* They receive more visits than Twitter (now X), Wikipedia, Reddit, and Instagram. This could be surprising for those who may be unaware of the popularity of porn in the digital environment. Other pornographic sites were also listed: XNXX, Spankbang, and Xhamster.

The point being made here is that pornography consumption is not a niche activity conducted by a few unusual computer users. The survey research and the user statistics suggest it is a major aspect of the digital environment. A secondary point can be made about how deviance is a socially constructed phenomenon. As mentioned in the

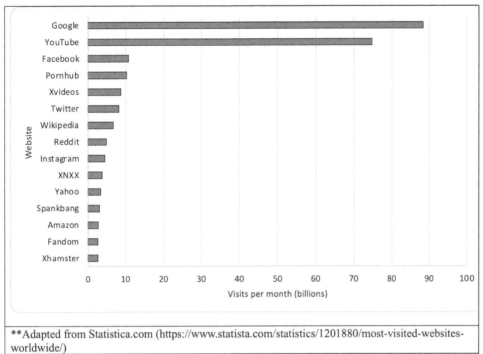

Figure 3.1 A bar chart reflecting traffic statistics of popular websites worldwide as of November 2022.

introduction, one of the authors has often asked his students for a show of hands of who has watched pornography, knowing that few (usually no) hands will be raised. In a class of 30 students, it is highly unlikely that those students are being totally truthful. But consuming pornography, or at least publicly admitting it, has been *constructed* as a less than admirable activity and there is fear of receiving mild negative social sanctions for owning up to it.

Legislating Pornography in the Digital Environment

Different countries have different laws legislating what and how pornographic content can be displayed to the public. A common tension in Western countries is between restricting expressions that may violate the moral sensibilities of some citizens, and the freedom of expression necessary for a healthy democracy. Below, we highlight the Miller test to illustrate how the American legal system attempts to navigate this tension.

THE MILLER TEST AND CRIMINALIZING PORNOGRAPHY

One can think of pornography through a lens of deviance—violating social norms, and a lens of criminality—violating formal laws. But, criminal cases against the production and consumption of pornography are somewhat rare. When they do occur, they usually involve extreme sexual acts or exploitation of children. Most pornography is legal in the United States because of the strong free-speech protections afforded by the United States Constitution. Indecent materials, of which most pornography is understood to be, are protected as free speech. The state can regulate when and where these materials can be shown, but they cannot be outright banned. For example, when pornographic magazines are sold in bookstores or on newsstands, they have covers on them to protect the sensibilities of the public and prevent children from viewing these materials. Similarly, television shows on national television being broadcast during certain "family viewing" times, cannot show nudity or use certain vulgar words. Obscene materials, however, can be regulated and prohibited by the government. Packard (2013) gives a distinction between indecency and obscenity: "In general indecency encompasses profanity, references to excretory organs, nudity, and implied sexual behavior. Obscenity refers to explicit depictions of actual sexual conduct, masturbation, violent sexual abuse, and child pornography."

While courts vary greatly by state in defining obscenity, most rely upon some variation of a three-pronged test originating from *Miller v. California* (1973):

1. An average person, applying contemporary community standards, must find that the material, as a whole, appeals to the prurient interest. In other words, is the material considered sexually explicit by the standards of the community?
2. The material must depict or describe, in a patently offensive way, sexual conduct specifically defined by applicable law. Does the material show an explicit act of sex?
3. The material, taken as a whole, must lack serious literary, artistic, political, or scientific value. Does the material have any societal value other than for sexual consumption?

This test, called the "Miller Test," places a high bar for the prohibition of pornography. A "yes" is required for all three prongs in order for the state to declare it as obscene and ban the material. Few materials can be clearly categorized as obscene.

A primary reason is because of the third prong of Miller's test: Pornography can be understood as having artistic value. Pornographic material can be understood as a recorded artistic performance, placing it into the same category as other recorded performances such as movies, television shows, and public lectures. For example, in 2022 acclaimed actress Cate Blanchett won the British Academy Film Award for Best Actress (BAFTA) in a Leading Role. Blanchett won the award over several other acclaimed actresses, including the American Viola Davis and the Malaysian star Michelle Yeoh. Meanwhile, in 2022 the Female of the Year at the American AVN (Adult Video News) awards was popular pornographic actress Gianna Dior. The American Dior won over other popular actresses including Lulu Chu from China and the Australian Angela White. In both cases, awards were given based upon their respective industry standards of acting—playing someone you are not and attempting to evoke a response in the viewer. The point here is not to draw an equivalency between the two industries, but instead to show that pornography producers and consumers can make a claim that pornography is artistic expression that needs to be protected.

Also problematic is the first prong, the "community standards" question. The Miller Test has traditionally placed the burden on deciding what is obscene on local communities. In one sense, this is a reasonable orientation to take (especially in an analog world). The purpose of regulating pornography is to protect the sensibilities and respect the tastes of the people who may be exposed to it in a given community. Who better to know what is obscene in said community than the people within it?

This logic, however, breaks down in a digital environment. Consider a company that makes pornographic content with their production facilities in Los Angeles, California. The company decides to use a cloud company to store its content, and the cloud company's servers are in the state of Virginia. Meanwhile, someone in the city of Burlington, Vermont, decides to sue the company for producing obscene content, and wants the content banned. Whose community standards should be taken into account to judge obscenity? Los Angeles, Virginia, or Burlington? The vast reach of the worldwide web blurs the lines between these respective communities such that addressing this question of jurisdiction of standards becomes quite a bit more complicated. United States courts have not settled on a definitive understanding of what community standards means in the digital environment. Thus, judgments on these grounds continue to be erratic.

Although it is difficult to determine what is obscene there are some general guidelines. Animal porn is considered obscene, and the production and distribution of it is prohibited. Porn in which scenes of violence, rape, or coercion are depicted is considered obscene and is prohibited. Because BDSM and hypnosis porn are popular genres, production companies making this type of content make it clear to the viewer that the scenes they depict do not hurt the actors involved (usually with a disclaimer). Finally, the production, distribution, and consumption of images of a sexual nature involving children are also prohibited.

Impacts of Pornography Consumption

Scholars and community leaders have raised several concerns about the impact of online pornography consumption. The narrative has focused primarily on its negative impacts. These impacts include:

- Addiction
- Perceptions of women
- Normalizing risky sexual behaviors

ADDICTION

In his book, *The medicalization of society*, sociologist Peter Conrad (2007) argued that alcoholism, ADHD, menopause, and erectile dysfunction as life problems have been redefined as requiring medical treatment. Conrad does not address pornography directly; however, one could apply the same logic. As such, the scholars Burke and MillerMacPhee (2020) apply the "medicalization of addiction" to pornography use. The phrase "medicalization of addiction" refers to the process by which society views and treats addiction as a medical issue rather than a moral failing or a criminal matter. Instead of stigmatization and punishment through incarceration or fines, society begins to treat addiction through the framework of medical science, emphasizing its physiological, psychological, and neurological aspects. Groups looking to curtail the use of pornography in society may describe their concerns through a medical framework grounded in science, claiming pornography use is addictive.

In their research, Burke and MillerMacPhee (2020) document a sharp rise in scientific and news articles describing pornography as a medical concern. For example, before 2010,

Table 3.1   Most Common Harms Cited by Proponents of the Addiction Narrative*

Type of Harm	Examples
The consumer is harmed psychologically or physically	Low self-esteem; depression and anxiety; damaged brain development; sexually transmitted infections
Men's ability to develop intimate relationships with women are impaired	Thwarted friendships or romances; marital conflict; delayed marriage; extramarital affairs; objectification or mistreatment of women
Increase in criminal behavior	Violence and aggression; robbery; sex trafficking; sex work
Increase in sexual deviance	Shocking, extreme, or deviant sexual interests including group, same-sex, hardcore, or kinky sex; misinformation about real-life sex

*Adapted from Burke and MillerMacPhee (2020)

366 newspaper articles and 27 scientific articles were published referencing pornography addiction. Since then, the numbers are 1,010 and 101, respectively. The articles could be critical of an addiction framework (e.g., there is little evidence that pornography is addictive), or choose an alternative explanation for pornography usage. However, most of these articles adopted an addiction framework—91% of newspaper articles and 72% of scientific articles. At the same time, state legislators began proposing pornography restriction resolutions—from the first in 2016 followed by 17 in 2017. All these resolutions supported an addiction framework to justify regulating pornography consumption.

It is instructive to illustrate the types of harms posited by supporters of this framework. Burke and MillerMacPhee (2020) identify four main categories, listed in Table 3.1. Some of these harms are explored in more depth below. Given these harms, one can see the logic behind state resolutions. If pornography is addictive, on the rise, and addiction leads to the harms listed in Table 3.1, then society needs to find ways to reduce pornography addiction through law and policy.

But *can* people even become addicted to pornography? As noted above, 72% of the scientific articles explored by Burke and MillerMacPhee (2020) support an addiction framework. But there is still no consensus on the issue, and it is not categorized as an addictive behavior in the psychologists' Diagnostic and Statistical Manual. There is evidence both for and against.

Some scholars suggest that the notion of pornography addiction is overhyped (Ley, 2012). In their review of pornography addiction studies, Ley, Prause, and Finn (2014) concluded that the studies asserting clinical addiction were inadequately designed and therefore misleading. Some scholars (Grubbs et al., 2018; Voros, 2009) argue that calling pornography consumption an addiction is ultimately a moral judgment powered by a person's adherence to religious strictures. In other words, individuals *perceive* they are addicted because they continue to violate the morals of their faith. Williams (2017) questioned the research done on pornography consumption and argued that the use of the addiction label is premature:

> *[In] the growing popularity among clinicians and the public in applying an addiction framework to sexuality issues, such application is not yet warranted and seems to reflect entrenched sociocultural biases. Competent social workers do not need to use the term addiction in order to help their clients resolve a range of potential problems*

associated with sexuality. Simply referring to 'problematic sexual behavior' will do, at least for now.

(p. 621)

Conversely, other scholars suggest that pornography addiction is a medical disorder that can require treatment (Wilson, 2015). In fact, a few studies estimating online gaming and pornography addiction side-by-side have proposed some parallels between the two phenomena. Both have negative outcomes like higher depression, reported anxiety, and diminished social interactions (Sallie et al., 2021). Scholars arguing that pornography consumption can reach the level of addiction note that repeated consumption of pornography alters brain functioning to the point in which the behavior negatively impacts how a person functions in life (Love et al., 2015).

PERCEPTIONS OF WOMEN

There are significant gender differences in pornography consumption, with men seeking out (Maddox et al., 2011) and consuming much more than women (Cox et al., 2022). Thus, there is a concern that excessive pornography consumption can negatively impact men's perception of women. Indeed, a 2022 study across four countries—Germany, Korea, Taiwan, and the United States—showed that people who more frequently watch pornography were more likely to exhibit sexually objectifying behaviors (Willis et al., 2022). Scholars have identified at least three ways pornography consumption can influence perceptions of women:

1. Men are more likely to accept rape myths. Rape myths are "attitudes and beliefs that are generally false, but are widely and persistently held, and that serve to deny and justify male sexual aggression against women" (Lonsway & Fitzgerald, 1994, p. 134). One common myth is that women lie about rape. Sexual activity was initially consensual, the myth goes, but because of remorse or fear of recrimination, a woman will assert that the activity was not consensual. Another common rape myth is that only certain kinds of women—presumably women who are socially marginal—are raped. A variant of the rape myth is that women feign disinterest in sexual activity until being "conquered by men."
2. Men are more likely to be sexually callous towards women. Men may presume that the purpose of the sexual act is for women to please them. They may ignore or downplay the sexual desires and needs of their female partners.
3. Men are more likely to reduce women to sexual objects. Men who watch large amounts of pornography may begin to see women only as potential sexual partners. This objectification lowers the status of women in men's eyes to things to be used.

Many of the assertions about the impacts of pornography are based upon work that was done on pornographic materials produced with older media and consumed offline (i.e., DVDs, VHS videotapes). Newer research exploring pornographic materials in the digital environment has produced a more nuanced view. Research from Gorman et al. (2010) found that the majority of videos in their sample could be classified as degrading to women, which supports the idea that viewing pornography produces attitudes in men about sex that are unfavorable to women. They, along with Vannier, Currie, and O'Sullivan (2014), found that male actors were more often depicted as dominant. However, Vannier and colleagues also found that women and men were portrayed equally in terms of sexual experience, occupational status, and the initiation of sexual activity. They further observed that male actors were more likely to appear nude than female actors. In one of the more extensive studies, Klaassen and Peter (2015) found a great deal of complexity in what is shown in pornographic videos. Their research showed that both men and women were objectified in pornography, only in different ways. Like Vannier and colleagues they found equality in terms of professional status, but men were depicted more often as dominant.

NORMALIZING RISKY SEXUAL BEHAVIOR

Some scholars have argued that one impact of excessive pornography use is an increase in risky sexual behaviors. Risky sexual behaviors are sexual behaviors that pose an unintended negative health outcome. These behaviors are of interest to scholars and professionals working with youth because engaging in these behaviors can lead to sexually transmitted infections, early pregnancies, and poor educational outcomes. Examples of risky sexual behaviors are shown in the work of Fino et al (2021), who developed and validated a Sexual Risk Behavior Scale from a survey of college students in the United Kingdom (see Table 3.2).

One way of understanding the link between pornography use and risky sexual behaviors is the sociological concept of "scripts" (Collins, 2005; Goffman, 1990). Scripts are analogous to a script an actor has in a play, and refer to sequences of actions, behaviors, and expectations that guide individuals in specific social situations. People learn scripts through social interaction with significant others and the media (e.g., they are socially

Table 3.2   Sexual Risk Behavior Scale*

	Never	Rarely	Sometimes	Often	Very Often
How often have you had anal sex without a condom?					
How often have you performed oral sex without protection (condom or dental dam)?					
How often have you had sex while under the influence of alcohol (i.e. drunk)?					
How often have you had sex while under the influence of drugs or substances?					
How often have you had sex without a condom with someone you have just met?					

Total scores can be computed by averaging individual items' scores (where 0 = "Never"; 1 = "Rarely"; 2 = "Sometimes"; 3 = "Often"; 4 = "Very often"). Higher total scores indicating higher risk to engage in sexual risk behaviors.

*Adapted from Fino et al. (2021)

constructed). Scripts are like mental templates that help people understand how to behave, what to say, and what to expect when interacting with others in specific contexts. People rely on scripts especially when they have no real-world experience.

Young people who are still learning how to interact with a potential sexual partner, may uncritically accept the behavior they see in pornography as a realistic description of sexual activity. Watching pornography can suggest what should and should not happen in a sexual encounter, how individuals should respond to the events in a sexual encounter, and the expected outcome of adopting a particular action during a sexual encounter (Huesmann, 1986). Pornography is known to depict several types of risky sexual behaviors, including scenes of multiple sex partners, sexual activity between strangers, and sexual activity without protection from sexually transmitted diseases. Watching these scenes can give a person sexual scripts that they then use in everyday encounters (Sun et al., 2016).

The link between pornography, the scripts they suggest, and actual behaviors is not entirely theoretical. Wright and Randall's (2012) study of a national sample of Americans showed that pornography consumption was positively associated with having sex with multiple partners, engaging in paid sex, and having had extramarital sex. Braithwaite et al. (2015) explored the link between pornography usage and what happens during hookups. The researchers surveyed over 1,200 American students who had hookups in the past 12 months before the survey was conducted. They found that higher frequencies of pornography consumption among male students was associated with a higher likelihood of being intoxicated and when intoxicated at higher levels. For women, this is reversed with a less likelihood of being intoxicated and when intoxicated at lower levels. The researchers theorize that "...women who view pornography are more sexually savvy than women who do not...so it is possible that those who do so are more sexually educated and thus less likely to do risky things during hookups, such as be intoxicated" (Braithwaite et al., 2015, p. 1167). However, with respect to penetration without a condom during hookups, *both* males and females show higher likelihoods with higher frequencies of pornography consumption.

Revenge Porn

Revenge porn refers to the nonconsensual sharing of images that are sexual in nature. The sharing of the images are often done by an ex-partner to humiliate the victim, thus the colloquial label revenge porn. Revenge porn can be seen as a form of cyberviolence. Indeed, many female revenge porn victims experience trust issues, lowered self-esteem, PTSD, anxiety, depression, and loss of control (Bates, 2017). For this reason, the logical place for revenge porn is in the cyberviolence chapter (Chapter 4). However, the authors have been reading and writing about revenge porn for about a decade and our prior understandings have carried over even into this second edition.

The phenomena were often linked to celebrities in the early national discussions around revenge porn. During 2014, Apple's cloud services were hacked, and the nude selfies taken by celebrities on their IPhones were pasted onto image boards. There was also a spate of private sex tape releases that many speculated were intentionally released to raise the profile of those involved. These considerations led us to think of revenge porn in pornographic, not violent terms. Moreover, our understanding of cyberviolence has developed markedly in the last several years to be more attuned to how violence—especially against women—occurs online. Society as a whole was also slow to catch up, with state and federal legislatures not passing specific laws prohibiting the practice until the 2010s (McGlynn et al., 2017).

Should there be future editions of this text, revenge porn will be discussed as a form of cyberviolence. We put our thought process here to illustrate to the reader two of the challenges of cybercriminology mentioned in Chapter 1—defining cybercrimes and rapid changes in law and policy.

Reliable data on revenge porn victimization rates is difficult to obtain. A compilation of prior studies done in 2020 shows that about 9% of people have had their image or video-based sexts shared without consent (Patel & Roesch, 2022). Most research shows that women (especially younger women) are disproportionately the targets of image-based sexual abuse (Foody et al., 2021). For example, the United Kingdom's Revenge Porn Hotline's (https://revengepornhelpline.org.uk/) annual report shows that in 2019 73% of call-ins were from women. A 2017 report from the American organization the Cyber Civil Rights Initiative (https://cybercivilrights.org/) found that 62% of respondents who said photos had been shared of them online were women.

One aspect of revenge porn is that it is easy to victim blame: "[W]hy did [the victim] send it in the first place?" or "[the victim] has to take responsibility for allowing someone to take a nude photo of them." Research from Mckinlay and Lavis (2020) help us to understand this phenomenon more. The researchers presented respondents with one of two scenarios in an experiment. In one scenario, the respondents were read a scenario where a female uploaded their own intimate images to Facebook (the control condition). In the other, the respondents were read a scenario where an ex-partner uploaded an image without consent (the revenge porn condition). Each scenario included one of two levels of nudity—a low nudity scenario where the female is wearing lingerie, and a high nudity scenario where the female has her breasts exposed. Respondents were then asked questions for both scenarios to measure how promiscuous and "blameworthy" the female was. For both conditions high nudity led to respondents viewing the female as more promiscuous and blameworthy. What does this mean? Similar to rape myths, in which women are deemed to be "asking for it" when they dress provocatively, more nudity in a revenge porn case may lead the public to believe the woman is more to blame.

Sexting

Sexting in the broadest sense is the consensual sharing of sexually explicit material. The archetypal example of sexting is two people in a current or future sexual relationship sharing sexual images of each other via text messages on their mobile phone (i.e. "sext"). Though mobile phones and other handheld communication devices are what we normally think of here, there are numerous variations on what is considered sexting and how it can occur. The material can also be shared via email or direct messaging through social media; it is the sharing dynamic that matters. Moreover, sexting is not exclusively the sharing of images. The consensual sharing of words, video, and audio of a sexual nature are also considered forms of sexting.

When exploring the phenomenon of sexting, a question can be asked: Who is the actual sexter? Consider an exchange where one person asks another to send them a sexually explicit image. The image is then sent and opened. In this exchange, who then is the sexter? Is it the originator of the image, the receiver, or both? This matters in an academic sense because how sexting is defined determines its prevalence rate. In a review of sexting literature, Barrense-Dias, Berchtold, Surís, and Akre (2017) reported that sexting prevalence ranged from 7.1% to 60% for passive sexting—those who ask for and receive sexts, and 2.5% to 27.6% for active sexting—those who send sexts. In addition, it may determine how a sexter is profiled. Active sexters may be different demographically and psychologically than passive sexters. Young people, as one would expect, are more likely to both send and receive text messages of a sexual nature. Klettke, Hallford, and Mellor (2014) found that girls send more sexually explicit texts than boys. They suggest that this may be because females perceive pressure to send texts of a sexual nature.

In a study of Canadian and American cell phone users, Galovan, Drouin, and McDaniel (2018) showed that sexters can be divided into four groups distinguished by who sends, who receives, and whether it is words, pictures, or both. Non-sexters comprised 71.5% of those surveyed. This group did not send words or pictures. About 14.5% were word-only sexters. This group sent word only sexts a few times a week, but rarely sent pictures. A third group, labeled frequent sexters (8.5%), sent and received both texts and images a few times a week. A fourth group was labeled "hyper sexters." Hyper sexters were 5.5% of the sample and reported that they sent and received sexually explicit text messages and pictures every day.

The above categorization of sexters relies primarily on the frequency of the individual sexter. However, another approach could include the motivations of the sexter and the dynamics they have with their partner. To this end, Dodaj and Sesar (2020) review prior literature on sexting and posit four categories:

1. Relational sexting—Sexting between two people who are building or have healthy intimacy between each other.
2. Reactive sexting—The researchers describe this as a playful and "opportunistic form of sexting" where sexters "send, receive, post, or forward to others sexts with intent, as a form of self expression, or to explore their identity by experimenting with their sexuality. It can also be a way of gaining popularity amongst one's peer group." Dodaj and Sesar (2020, p. 18).
3. Forced sexting—Sexting done because of pressure from a potential or current partner. The partner may require a sext be sent in order to move forward with the relationship or maintain the relationship. The sexter may also feel obligated to send a sext if their partner sends sexts to them.
4. Violent sexting—This form of sexting include "additional criminal or abusive elements beyond the creation, sending or possession of sexual images produced by young people. These elements are related to adults soliciting sexts from minors or minors sexting with adults, and abusive behaviour such as sexual abuse, extortion, deception or even exchanging images without the knowledge or against the will of minors who were photographed" (2020, pp. 19–20).

On the one hand, sexting can be seen as a harmless activity between two people who wish to share intimate details of themselves. It can be a way to bond with one's partner. On the other hand, scholars have identified some negative consequences to sexting. Klettke and colleagues (2014):

A clear finding that emerged was that sexting is associated with a higher likelihood of being sexually active, as well as engagement in a range of sexual risk behaviors, such as having unprotected sex and consuming alcohol and drugs prior to sexual activity.

(p. 52)

In other words, sexting may be an indicator of other deviant behaviors. There may also be mental health problems associated with sexting, as research has linked sexting to depression (Van Ouytsel et al., 2017) and contemplating suicide (Dake et al., 2012). Therefore, although some may see sexting as a relatively harmless activity, its presence may be a sign of more serious issues.

A second challenge with addressing sexting is that it can be an avenue for the distribution of child pornography (discussed in Chapter 4).

Sex Work

In the physical environment, distinctions are often made between different types of sex work and the spaces in which this work happens. Sex work in the physical environment is stratified by how much freedom the sex worker has and how much money they make from their labor. Street prostitutes occupy the bottom stratum. They tend to work in areas frequented by low-income clientele and exhibit less control over their time of work and the amount of money gained from their services. They are also more likely to be physically abused. Workers in massage parlors have some discretion over the clients they service, work in safer environments, and garner a larger percentage of the money from their services. Escorts are the most privileged sex workers and occupy the top stratum. They exercise the greatest amount of freedom and control in when and where they perform their services, and usually receive more compensation for their services.

Scholars of sex work in the digital environment also appreciate the complex ways in which sexual services are bought and sold. The digital environment is used to facilitate connections between clients and workers, after which sex happens in offline environments. It is also used to sell digitized sexual services in the form of videos and live shows. Another way in which sex work is facilitated in the digital environment is through advertising services and reviewing services rendered by clients. Cunningham and colleagues (2018) have produced a typology of the varied ways in which sex work occurs in the digital environment (Table 3.3; p. 57).

These spaces taken as a whole expand our understandings of sex work—where it is, how it is facilitated, and what forms it takes. Consider camming and camming platforms. Is this sex work? Given the commercial exchange, where a camming model produces content of a sexual nature that a customer then buys, it would appear so. On the other hand, there is no physical contact or actual sex between people and camming is legal in most countries – even in countries that criminalize prostitution. As of this writing only a small number of countries, South Korea being an example (Lee, 2021) have banned it. Additionally, according to Stegeman (2021), camming platforms like Chaturbate and LiveJasmin write their terms of service (ToS) to "reject conceptions of camming as sexually expressive, or as work" (p. 13). How do we make sense of this? Or consider sex worker forums—spaces where sex workers can network, get information and advice, and peer support. These spaces also allow sex workers to organize politically and advocate for policies that benefit them. These forums upend stereotypical notions

Table 3.3 Typology of Sex Work Spaces in the Digital Environment

Escort directories	Websites that allow sex workers who offer in-person direct sex work to create profiles to advertise their services
Camming platforms	Sites dedicated to the facilitation of webcam shows
Multi-service adult entertainment platforms	Websites that offer a range of different services within the one site including providing advertising for escorts, webcam shows, and instant message
Dating and hook-up platforms with commercial advertising	Websites/applications that facilitate connection between people for personal relationships and unpaid sexual encounters, but some have commercial advertising space where sex workers can advertise their services
Dating and hook-up platforms without commercial advertising	Websites/applications that facilitate connection between people for personal relationships and unpaid sexual encounters but prohibiting advertising for paid sex
Customer review forums	Spaces where customers post messages about their experiences of buying sexual services including reviews of individual sex workers. They are also a marketing space for sex workers
Agency websites	Websites run by third party agencies who act as intermediaries between sex workers who provide direct in-person services and their clients. The agencies are responsible for the running of the websites, which are used to advertise different sex workers working for the agency
Individual sex worker websites	Websites used to market individual sex workers who work independently, created and managed by sex workers or by web designers/IT specialists on their behalf
Classified websites	Advertising spaces/forums that allow individuals to post user-generated advertisements for a range of goods and services. Some classified sites permit sex work advertising and have dedicated and separate space for these while others prohibit it altogether
Social media platforms	Sex workers engage with social media (for marketing, networking, and peer support) in a range of ways and to varying degrees
Sex worker forums	Sex worker-led spaces where sex workers can network, get information and advice, and peer support
Content delivery platforms	Dedicated platforms that host and sell user-generated adult content online

*(Modified from Cunningham et al., 2017.)

of prostitutes being controlled by handlers or pimps, in favor of an empowered class of service workers.

The digital environment has also changed *who* participates in sex work. As Jones (2015) argues, the digital environment has "helped to create new opportunities for sex workers and to craft a labor environment that is more appealing to workers across social classes" (pp. 560–561). Jones discusses the particular affordances provided by the digital environment:

- It is safer. A filtering process occurs through information sharing online, and sex workers are exposed to less risk. Moreover, there is a self-selection process, where customers who use the Internet to find prostitutes/escorts are likely less prone to violence and wealthier than customers who prefer street prostitutes.
- The wages are better. Sex workers can more easily recruit and select high-end clientele online.

- It is easier to advertise, screen, and recruit. This not only increases wages, but also lowers the barriers to entry.
- There is less contact with police. Sex workers have historically had a conflictual relationship with police, with police often compelled to arrest them, which can lead to exploitation. Moving their activities out of public view reduces this contact.
- There may be benefits for political organization. Sex worker forums allow sex workers to connect with each other and discuss organizing and mobilizing.

The stereotype of the sex worker who *must* choose sex work to pay for life's necessities, while it was never completely accurate, is less so in the Internet age. People may choose to do sex work for additional funds (e.g., a "side hustle"). They may choose sex work because it is more interesting, exciting, or provides more freedom than their current employment. Or they may perform sex work while they complete their studies and then leave the profession once their education is completed.

Trans sex workers have also taken advantage of the liberties of the digital environment. Vartabedian (2019) explored websites where Portuguese and UK trans women prostitutes advertise their services. The research was conducted because most scholarship focused on street or female workers. She argues that prostitution presents an empowering opportunity for trans women:

> *For many trans women prostitution is the main (and only) place where they can be admired and desired in a social environment that otherwise enables great discrimination and structural violence against them. They present themselves as good lovers who are able to perform virile sexual practices, but, at the same time, their 'beautiful' and feminine bodies are of great importance.*

(p. 225)

In closing, we should note that although this section presents the benefits of the digital environment for sex trafficking, it is not an unqualified good and certainly not all groups in society agree with its benefits. Just as sex work has expanded sex work opportunities, it has also expanded sex trafficking opportunities, a topic we will explore in Chapter 4. Even when the sale of sexual services are voluntary, some groups still wish to seriously curtail or even prohibit it. These objections are beyond the purview of this chapter. However, in brief religious groups may object to sex work on moral grounds and some feminist groups argue that the sale of sex, voluntary or involuntary, is inherently exploitative of women.

Conclusion

Cyberpornography, is "the publication or trading of sexually expressive (explicit) materials in the digital environment" (Wall, 2001, 6). We extended this definition to communication about sexual behaviors and lifestyles and to forms of sex work occurring or facilitated by the digital environment. With this broadened understanding, we discussed several topics: Sexual deviance in online spaces, pornography consumption, revenge porn, sexting, and sex work.

When criminalized, most of the topics in this chapter represent what can be called "victimless crimes." The exception to this is revenge porn, which has a clear victim. The production and consumption of pornography, people discussing sexual fetishes, and the buying and selling of sex work are behaviors that do not have clear victims. Instead, these behaviors are understood by many to be affronts to the moral order and are regulated as such. However, we should be careful not to take the "victimless crimes" or "violations of the moral order" descriptions as a complete summary of these behaviors. For example, to the extent that pornography consumption can lead to the perpetuation of rape myths or the objectification of women, we can say that others in society can be harmed indirectly by these behaviors.

CHAPTER 3 CURRENT EVENTS AND CRITICAL THINKING:

OnlyFans…To Be or Not To Be?

OnlyFans is a subscription-based social media platform that allows creators to share content, often adult-oriented, with their subscribers in exchange for a monthly fee. The site began in 2016, and by 2019, about 120,000 content creators were registered. During the global pandemic, the site's popularity grew exponentially when people were on lockdown and staring at their screens all day. By the end of 2021, it had over a million creators and 90 million users (Shane, 2021).

One major reason for the growth in OnlyFans was that sex workers began using the site—so much so that the site gained a (somewhat unwarranted) reputation of being a site just for porn. The popularity of OnlyFans, and its reputation as a space where sexual services are sold, attracted the attention of organizations combatting sex trafficking and child exploitation. Organizations like The National Center for Missing and Exploited Children and Exodus Cry assert that many of the sex workers using online spaces are not doing so voluntarily but are coerced. These organizations have targeted platforms like OnlyFans, urging them to crack down on the sale of sexual services on their sites. The outcry from these organizations eventually led to banks and other payment processors refusing to provide their services to OnlyFans because of reputational damage.

In 2021, OnlyFans temporarily banned sexually explicit material from their servers in response to the public outcry and the threats from financial institutions. The decision was an unpopular one with its users. Sex workers felt betrayed—OnlyFans was biting the hand that fed it. The company was skewered on social media for their decision. Eventually, the company reversed its decision—allowing sex workers to continue to sell content on the site. As of this writing, the company still allows sexual content on their platform, even as it goes through an "upcycling [of] its image from an adult content subscription platform to a Patreon-like home for all kinds of creators" (Lunden, 2022).

Many websites have been presented with the same problem as OnlyFans – should they allow popular sexual content—the content that helped build their platform, or should they restrict that content to appease third parties who are concerned with sexual exploitation or reputational damage? Tumblr chose to remove all nudity from its website. The decision came after Apple decided to drop the company's software from its Apple Store because child pornography was found on its website. After accusations that it hosted illegal content were published in the *New York Times* (Kristof, 2020) and credit card companies threatening to cut ties, Pornhub made changes to its platform—only verified accounts could upload material and downloads were banned. In 2017, Patreon banned sex workers and adult content of a sexual nature.

Critical Thinking Question(s)

Businesses have to make decisions that allow them to stay solvent. As such, decisions to appease financial institutions may be unavoidable. Moreover, few would disagree with a decision to ban illegal content such as child pornography.

However, we can ask questions about individual free expression on the one hand, and standards of public decency on the other. Should the public support the platforming of sexual content on sites like OnlyFans? Why or why not? Should societies have standards of decency that are enforced in the digital environment? Why or why not?

REFERENCES

Ballester-Arnal, R., García-Barba, M., Castro-Calvo, J., Giménez-García, C., & Gil-Llario, M. D. (2023). Pornography consumption in people of different age groups: An analysis based on gender, contents, and consequences. *Sexuality Research and Social Policy*, 20(2), 766–779. https://doi.org/10.1007/s13178-022-00720-z

Barrense-Dias, Y., Berchtold, A., Surís, J.-C., & Akre, C. (2017). Sexting and the definition issue. *Journal of Adolescent Health*, 61(5), 544–554. https://doi.org/10.1016/j.jadohealth.2017.05.009

Bates, S. (2017). Revenge porn and mental health: A qualitative analysis of the mental health effects of revenge porn on female survivors. *Feminist Criminology*, 12(1), 22–42. https://doi.org/10.1177/1557085116654565

Braithwaite, S. R., Givens, A., Brown, J., & Fincham, F. (2015). Is pornography consumption associated with condom use and intoxication during hookups? *Culture, Health & Sexuality*, 17(10), 1155–1173. https://doi.org/10.1080/13691058.2015.1042920

Brody, E., Greenhalgh, S. P., & Sajjad, M. (2022). Gayservatives on Gab: LGBTQ+ communities and far right social media. *Social Media + Society*, 8(4), 205630512211370. https://doi.org/10.1177/20563051221137088

Burke, K., & MillerMacPhee, A. (2020). Constructing pornography addiction's harms in science, news media, and politics. *Social Forces*, soaa035. https://doi.org/10.1093/sf/soaa035

Campbell, R., Sanders, T., Scoular, J., Pitcher, J., & Cunningham, S. (2019). Risking safety and rights: Online sex work, crimes and 'blended safety repertoires.' *The British Journal of Sociology*, 70(4), 1539–1560. https://doi.org/10.1111/1468-4446.12493

Cavalcante, A. (2016). "I Did It All Online:" Transgender identity and the management of everyday life. *Critical Studies in Media Communication*, 33(1), 109–122. https://doi.org/10.1080/15295036.2015.1129065

Collins, R. (2005). *Interaction ritual chains* (2nd print., and first paperback print). Princeton University Press.

Conrad, P. (2007). *The medicalization of society: On the transformation of human conditions into treatable disorders*. Johns Hopkins University Press.

Cox, D., Lee, B., & Popky, D. (2022, May 3). *How prevalent is pornography?* Institute for Family Studies. https://ifstudies.org/blog/how-prevalent-is-pornography

Cunningham, S., Sanders, T., Scoular, J., Campbell, R., Pitcher, J., Hill, K., Valentine-Chase, M., Melissa, C., Aydin, Y., & Hamer, R. (2018). Behind the screen: Commercial sex, digital spaces and working online. *Technology in Society*, 53, 47–54. https://doi.org/10.1016/j.techsoc.2017.11.004

Dake, J. A., Price, J. H., Maziarz, L., & Ward, B. (2012). Prevalence and correlates of sexting behavior in adolescents. *American Journal of Sexuality Education*, 7(1), 1–15. https://doi.org/10.1080/15546128.2012.650959

Dodaj, A., & Sesar, K. (2020). Sexting categories. *Mediterranean Journal of Clinical Psychology*, 8(2). https://doi.org/10.6092/2282-1619/MJCP-2432

Fino, E., Jaspal, R., Lopes, B., Wignall, L., & Bloxsom, C. (2021). The Sexual Risk Behaviors Scale (SRBS): Development & validation in a university student sample in the UK. *Evaluation & the Health Professions, 44*(2), 152–160. https://doi.org/10.1177/01632787211003950

Foody, M., Mazzone, A., Laffan, D. A., Loftsson, M., & O'Higgins Norman, J. (2021). "It's not just sexy pics": An investigation into sexting behaviour and behavioural problems in adolescents. *Computers in Human Behavior, 117*, 106662. https://doi.org/10.1016/j.chb.2020.106662

Galovan, A. M., Drouin, M., & McDaniel, B. T. (2018). Sexting profiles in the United States and Canada: Implications for individual and relationship well-being. *Computers in Human Behavior, 79*, 19–29. https://doi.org/10.1016/j.chb.2017.10.017

Goffman, E. (1990). *The presentation of self in everyday life* (Nachdr.). Doubleday.

Gorman, S., Monk-Turner, E., & Fish, J. N. (2010). Free adult Internet web sites: How prevalent are degrading acts? *Gender Issues, 27*(3–4), 131–145. https://doi.org/10.1007/s12147-010-9095-7

Grubbs, J. B., Wilt, J. A., Exline, J. J., Pargament, K. I., & Kraus, S. W. (2018). Moral disapproval and perceived addiction to Internet pornography: A longitudinal examination: Moral disapproval and perceived addiction. *Addiction, 113*(3), 496–506. https://doi.org/10.1111/add.14007

Huesmann, L. R. (1986). Psychological processes promoting the relation between exposure to media violence and aggressive behavior by the viewer. *Journal of Social Issues, 42*(3), 125–139. https://doi.org/10.1111/j.1540-4560.1986.tb00246.x

Jenzen, O. (2017). Trans youth and social media: Moving between counterpublics and the wider web. *Gender, Place & Culture, 24*(11), 1626–1641. https://doi.org/10.1080/0966369X.2017.1396204

Jones, A. (2015). Sex Work in a Digital Era. *Sociology Compass, 9*(7), 558–570. https://doi.org/10.1111/soc4.12282

Klaassen, M. J. E., & Peter, J. (2015). Gender (in)equality in Internet pornography: A content analysis of popular pornographic Internet videos. *The Journal of Sex Research, 52*(7), 721–735. https://doi.org/10.1080/00224499.2014.976781

Klettke, B., Hallford, D. J., & Mellor, D. J. (2014). Sexting prevalence and correlates: A systematic literature review. *Clinical Psychology Review, 34*(1), 44–53. https://doi.org/10.1016/j.cpr.2013.10.007

Kristof, N. (2020, December 4). Opinion | The children of Pornhub. *The New York Times.* https://www.nytimes.com/2020/12/04/opinion/sunday/pornhub-rape-trafficking.html

Lee, M. J. (2021). Webcam modelling in Korea: Censorship, pornography, and eroticism. *Porn Studies, 8*(4), 485–498. https://doi.org/10.1080/23268743.2021.1901602

Ley, D. J. (2012). *The myth of sex addiction.* Rowman & Littlefield Publishers, Inc.

Ley, D., Prause, N., & Finn, P. (2014). The Emperor has no clothes: A review of the 'pornography addiction' model. *Current Sexual Health Reports, 6*(2), 94–105. https://doi.org/10.1007/s11930-014-0016-8

Lonsway, K. A., & Fitzgerald, L. F. (1994). Rape myths. In review. *Psychology of Women Quarterly, 18*(2), 133–164.

Love, T., Laier, C., Brand, M., Hatch, L., & Hajela, R. (2015). Neuroscience of Internet pornography addiction: A review and update. *Behavioral Sciences, 5*(4), 388–433. https://doi.org/10.3390/bs5030388

Lunden, I. (2022, October 19). OnlyFans CEO says adult content will still have a home on the site in 5 years. *TechCrunch.* https://techcrunch.com/2022/10/19/onlyfans-ceo-says-adult-content-will-still-have-a-home-on-the-site-in-5-years/

Maddox, A. M., Rhoades, G. K., & Markman, H. J. (2011). Viewing sexually-explicit materials alone or together: Associations with relationship quality. *Archives of Sexual Behavior, 40*(2), 441–448. https://doi.org/10.1007/s10508-009-9585-4

McGlynn, C., Rackley, E., & Houghton, R. (2017). Beyond 'revenge porn': The continuum of image-based sexual abuse. *Feminist Legal Studies, 25*(1), 25–46. https://doi.org/10.1007/s10691-017-9343-2

Mckinlay, T., & Lavis, T. (2020). Why did she send it in the first place? Victim blame in the context of 'revenge porn.' *Psychiatry, Psychology and Law, 27*(3), 386–396. https://doi.org/10.1080/13218719.2020.1734977

Packard, A. (2013). *Digital media law* (2nd edition). Wiley-Blackwell.

Patel, U., & Roesch, R. (2022). The prevalence of technology-facilitated sexual violence: A meta-analysis and systematic review. *Trauma, Violence, & Abuse, 23*(2), 428–443. https://doi.org/10.1177/1524838020958057

Sallie, S. N., Ritou, V. J. E., Bowden-Jones, H., & Voon, V. (2021). Assessing online gaming and pornography consumption patterns during COVID-19 isolation using an online survey: Highlighting distinct avenues of problematic Internet behavior. *Addictive Behaviors, 123*, 107044. https://doi.org/10.1016/j.addbeh.2021.107044

Shane, C. (2021, May 18). OnlyFans isn't just porn ;). *The New York Times.* https://www.nytimes.com/2021/05/18/magazine/onlyfans-porn.html

Solano, I., Eaton, N. R., & O'Leary, K. D. (2020). Pornography consumption, modality and function in a large Internet sample. *The Journal of Sex Research, 57*(1), 92–103. https://doi.org/10.1080/00224499.2018.1532488

Stegeman, H. M. (2021). Regulating and representing camming: Strict limits on acceptable content on webcam sex platforms. *New Media & Society,* 146144482110591. https://doi.org/10.1177/14614448211059117

Sun, C., Bridges, A., Johnson, J. A., & Ezzell, M. B. (2016). Pornography and the male sexual script: An analysis of consumption and sexual relations. *Archives of Sexual Behavior, 45*(4), 983–994. https://doi.org/10.1007/s10508-014-0391-2

Sundén, J. (2023). Digital kink obscurity: A sexual politics beyond visibility and comprehension. *Sexualities,* 136346072211244. https://doi.org/10.1177/13634607221124401

Van Ouytsel, J., Torres, E., Choi, H. J., Ponnet, K., Walrave, M., & Temple, J. R. (2017). The associations between substance use, sexual behaviors, bullying, deviant behaviors, health, and cyber dating abuse perpetration. *The Journal of School Nursing, 33*(2), 116–122. https://doi.org/10.1177/1059840516683229

Vannier, S. A., Currie, A. B., & O'Sullivan, L. F. (2014). Schoolgirls and soccer moms: A content analysis of free "teen" and "MILF" online pornography. *The Journal of Sex Research, 51*(3), 253–264. https://doi.org/10.1080/00224499.2013.829795

Vartabedian, J. (2019). Bodies and desires on the Internet: An approach to trans women sex workers' websites. *Sexualities, 22*(1–2), 224–243. https://doi.org/10.1177/1363460717713381

Voros, F. (2009). L'invention de l'addiction à la pornographie. *Sexologies, 18*(4), 270–276. https://doi.org/10.1016/j.sexol.2009.09.008

Wall, D. (Ed.). (2001). *Crime and the Internet* (1st edition). Routledge. https://doi.org.proxy.lib.odu.edu/10.4324/9780203299180

Williams, D. J. (2017). The framing of frequent sexual behavior and/or pornography viewing as addiction: Some concerns for social work. *Journal of Social Work, 17*(5), 616–623. https://doi.org/10.1177/1468017316644701

Willis, M., Bridges, A. J., & Sun, C. (2022). Pornography use, gender, and sexual objectification: A multinational study. *Sexuality & Culture, 26*(4), 1298–1313. https://doi.org/10.1007/s12119-022-09943-z

Wilson, G. (2015). *Your brain on porn: Internet pornography and the emerging science of addiction.* Commonwealth Publishing.

Worthen, M. G. F. (2016). *Sexual deviance and society* (1st edition). Routledge. https://doi.org/10.4324/9781315744858

Wright, P. J., & Randall, A. K. (2012). Internet pornography exposure and risky sexual behavior among adult males in the United States. *Computers in Human Behavior, 28*(4), 1410–1416. https://doi.org/10.1016/j.chb.2012.03.003

Chapter 4

Cyberviolence

Introduction

Violence has historically been understood as a behavior using physical force to harm someone. As such, violent crimes are those crimes in which a perpetrator uses or threatens to use violence against a victim. Murder, rape, robbery, assault, kidnapping, and torture are all types of violent crimes. This chapter will explore the phenomena of cyberviolence. Wall (2001) defines cyberviolence as:

> ...the violent impact of the cyberactivities of another upon an individual or social grouping. Whilst such activities do not have to have a direct physical manifestation, the victim nevertheless feels the violence of the act and can bear long-term psychological scars as a consequence.
>
> (1998)

Wall's notion of cyberviolence is contingent upon a different framing of how we understand violence. Violence is not indicated by whether the perpetrator uses physical force, but instead by the harm that is visited upon the victim. If the core of violence is harm, then that harm can be produced in a variety of ways. One way is symbolically. Using this logic, Wall labels activities that produce "long-term psychological scars" as cyberviolence. Cyberbullying, cyberstalking, and hate speech are all forms of cyberviolence.

The authors of this text extend the notion of cyberviolence to instances of sexual violence, including pornographic images of children produced and shared online and internet-facilitated sex trafficking. Scholars have begun replacing the more well-known term child pornography with the terms child sexual abuse images (CSAI) for pictures or child sexual abuse material (CSAM) for other sexual representations and content associated with children (Guerra & Westlake, 2021). This change aims to signify that sexual content involving children is not about sex between consenting parties but about abuse.

DOI: 10.4324/9781003283256-4

This line of reasoning can also be applied to sex trafficking. Internet-facilitated sex trafficking, is ultimately one of consent. Being coerced by another person or group into providing sexual services is about violence for the victim, even if the person receiving the services sees it primarily as a sexual act. This is the case even if the coerced person is providing sexual services in the same space as a sex worker willingly providing services.

These extensions to Wall's original idea of cyberviolence make the category the most varied of the four categories of cybercrime and digital deviance discussed. Cyberviolence ranges from issues of identity to sexuality to trauma, and from relatively minor deviant acts to horrific crimes.

Thinking Critically About the Differences Between Physical Violence and Cyberviolence

There are several similarities between physical violence and cyberviolence. First, and most importantly, someone is hurt. Because the hurt in the digital environment is not physical does not necessarily mean the damage is less. Indeed, the argument can be made that because some acts of cyberviolence lead to lifelong psychological problems and even suicide, symbolic violence can be equally or *more* damaging than some forms of physical violence.

Consider the events surrounding the suicide of Brandy Vela. Vela was an 18-year-old high school student living in the American state of Texas. On the morning of November 29, 2016, Vela sent an email to her family saying she would kill herself. Family members rushed home and saw her leaning against the wall with a gun to her chest. They could not convince her to put the gun down, and Vela committed suicide. She had been receiving text messages from an untraceable cell phone saying hurtful things. Using her photo, fake Facebook pages were set up, saying she would "offer sex for free." In 2017, a former boyfriend and his current girlfriend were arrested and charged in association with Vela's death.

A second similarity is that emotions often power violence in both environments. Domestic violence—someone battering their spouse—is often a spontaneous reaction of anger. Although movies and television dramas depict sexual assaults as premeditated acts coming from strangers, most sexual assaults are committed by an angered acquaintance of the victim attempting to assert dominance. The perpetrator believes they are entitled to sexual activity and react with violence when permission is not granted. Emotion also underpins acts of cyberviolence. As we will discuss below, flaming, trolling, hate speech, and cyberbullying are primary ways for an individual or group to lash out against another individual or group.

Although there are similarities between physical violence and cyberviolence, there are also differences. One difference is the means by which the harm is caused. The means by which violence is committed in the physical environment is primarily through one's own body or by some weapon that acts as an extension of the body. When someone physically attacks another person, they use their body to inflict harm. Even when there is no actual assault, but instead the fear of assault, the logic is that there is a credible threat from the perpetrator. The tools used in committing the assault—weapons like handguns and knives—are extensions of the body. By contrast, cyberviolence is committed through the mind, and the tools are the affordances (or design features) of technologies in the digital environment. These technologies are primarily found in the application layer, as these are the technologies used to produce content. The tools used in committing the assault—words, phrases, emojis, and means—are extensions of the mind.

All individuals can commit physical harm to another person. However, not everyone has an equal ability or predisposition to do so. An infant with a water pistol does not pose a credible threat to an adult. They do not have the physical presence (they are a small child) or a weapon (a water pistol) to commit harm. Also, while children can be aggressive in their actions, their motivations are presumably playful in intent. However, as that child grows into a young man, his physical presence alone will likely make him appear threatening to smaller and weaker others. He may have in his possession or capable of acquiring a handgun instead of a water pistol. Additionally, he may have higher testosterone levels than older males and females, making him more impulsive and willing to use physical force. These reasons—along with social conditions such as poverty and challenging home circumstances that are motivations to commit armed robbery or lash out physically—make young men the primary candidates for committing physical violence.

Similarly, all individuals can commit cyberviolence to some degree. However, everyone is not equally likely to have the means or predisposition to do so. Many forms of cyberviolence require a facility with symbolic communication. Constructing a particularly biting post or reply on Facebook, a clever tweet, or finding an appropriate meme requires some level of social awareness and communicative ability. Moreover, understanding the nuances of a software platform to the degree that your attacks can be more effective requires a level of familiarity with a platform and the dynamics of social media that others do not possess.

Therefore, a second difference between physical violence and cyberviolence is likely the type of perpetrator. Another way of saying this is that the profile of the perpetrator of cyberviolence may be different than the profile of the perpetrator of physical violence. One area of focus from scholars has been gender differences. For example, there is some evidence that girls are more likely to be both the perpetrators and victims of cyberbullying—one form of cyberviolence (Peterson & Densley, 2017). Similarly, research has shown that women are more likely to commit intimate partner cyberstalking than men (Smoker & March, 2017). We would also expect that individuals more technologically proficient will be more likely to commit cyberviolence (Wang & Ngai, 2022).

Research is still in its infancy, and scholars continue to conduct studies on the causes of cyberviolence and profiles of those persons more likely to use the digital environment to harm others.

Types of Cyberviolence

Violent crimes can be organized by type of perpetrator and type of victim. The violent crime of rape, for example, can be understood as an individual perpetrator committing an act of sexual violence towards an individual victim. Meanwhile, acts of terrorism are often individuals committing indiscriminate acts of violence against people within a group (nation, religious group, racial group, etc.). The violence associated with gang warfare can be understood as groups committing acts of physical violence against other groups. We use this way of thinking to organize types of cyberviolence. In Table 4.1 (p. 66) we compare physical violence to cyberviolence, organizing type of crime by perpetrator and victim.

Table 4.1   Classification Scheme for Types of Violent Crimes

Perpetrator	Victim	Cyberviolence
Individual	Individual	Cyberbullying
		Cyberstalking
		Flaming
		Trolling
		CSAI/CSAM
		Internet-facilitated sex trafficking
Group	Individual	Online shaming
Individual	Group	Trolling
		Hate speech
		Cyberterrorism*
Group	Group	Cyberwar*

*Cyberterrorism and cyberwar will be discussed in Chapter 7

CYBERBULLYING

One of the myths of cyberbullying is that everyone knows what it is. However, one of the challenges of cybercriminology is properly defining cybercrime and digital deviances, and cyberbullying is emblematic of this challenge. Consider a poll done in 2022 by The Pew Research Center, which reported that "nearly half of teens have ever experienced cyberbullying, with offensive name-calling being the most commonly reported" (Atske, 2022). This may seem quite high—*half of all teens are getting cyberbullied?*

But the question asked teens if they ever experienced any of these things online or on their cell phone (the percentage saying yes is in parentheses):

- Offensive name-calling (32%)
- Spreading of false rumors about them (22%)
- Receiving explicit images they didn't ask for (17%)
- Constantly being asked where they are, what they are doing, etc. (15%)
- Physical threats (10%)
- Having explicit images of them shared without their consent (7%)

At least 46% of all teens said they had experienced as least one of these things. And this indicated cyberbullying. But does it? If someone calls you an offensive name, are you necessarily being bullied? Insulted, yes. Bullied, maybe not. Or consider receiving explicit images they didn't ask for or having explicit images of them shared. This sounds more like revenge porn than cyberbullying. Even being physically threatened does not always mean someone is being bullied. What if two angry teens are physically threatening each other because of a disagreement? PEW is not unique in measuring cyberbullying in this way. Consider a report on bullying published by the Australian Institute of Health and Welfare, stating that of young people aged 12–17, "4 in 10 (44%) had at least 1 negative online experience" (2021).

There needs to be a clearer understanding of cyberbullying. One possible approach is identifying the behaviors and conditions likely to cause serious emotional harm to a victim. These harms include decreased self-esteem, social isolation, poorer educational outcomes, juvenile delinquency, and suicidal ideation. As such, Tokunaga (2010) defines cyberbullying as "any behavior performed through electronic or digital media by individuals or groups that repeatedly communicates hostile or aggressive messages intended to inflict harm or discomfort on others" (278). Here, the particular behaviour is less important than where it happens (in the digital environment), the function of the behavior (to communicate hostile or aggressive messages), and the intent (to inflict harm or discomfort).

Tokunaga's definition of cyberbullying is standard in the social science literature. We want to add another component to this definition: Power imbalance. Power imbalance is a basic component of how social scientists understand traditional bullying (Olweus, 1993) and is implied in social science research. However, we want to make it explicit. Individuals without some form of power over their victim—physical strength, strength in numbers, social status, age, intelligence, money, connections—cannot bully others. Power can be indicated in a number of ways. For example, a study done on Chinese youth showed that teens who are more technologically proficient (an indicator of power) were more likely to cyberbully their peers (Wang & Ngai, 2022).

Arguably the most reliable cyberbullying estimates are produced by the Cyberbullying Research Center,[1] which uses a variation of Tokunaga's definition of cyberbullying. According to that center's survey done in 2021 on American youth, about: 23% of young people, 24% of females, 22% of males, 35% of transgender youth, and 29% of multiracial youth were cyberbullied. If we look at racial identity, 26% white, 18% Hispanic, and 16% African American youth reported being cyberbullied.

Myths of Cyberbullying

The Cyberbullying Research Center provides evidence-based tips and strategies on cyberbullying. However, there are several myths people have about cyberbullying. We list some of these myths (from Sabella et al., 2013) and describe them below:

1. *Everyone knows what cyberbullying is.* This myth opened this section on cyberbullying. There is wide variation in what is considered cyberbullying. Indeed, cyberbullying is often conflated with cyberstalking or revenge porn.
2. *Cyberbullying causes suicide.* This myth is media-driven. There are certainly cases, including those we highlighted previously. However, Sabella and colleagues (2013) note the vast majority of cyberbullying victims do not kill themselves, and those who do typically have experienced a constellation of stressors and other issues operating in their lives, making it difficult to isolate the influence of one specific personal or social problem as compared to others. Cyberbullying is an issue that needs to be addressed, but when suicides occur it may be because the victim has experienced other harmful experiences.
3. *Like traditional bullying, cyberbullying is a rite of passage all teens experience.* Many adults believe that navigating these experiences is a way to teach young people the adult skill of dealing with adversity. Bullying will "toughen them up." However, the notion that bullying teaches someone how to live in the world is a myth. In fact, bullying can cause long term psychological damage.
4. *Cyberbullies are outcasts or just mean kids.* There is a sense, again coming from the media, that cyberbullies are always mean kids hell-bent on destroying the lives of others. However, this does not seem to be the truth in most cases. Many who participate in cyberbullying are only trying to have some fun and are not

attempting to inflict lasting harm. In this sense, cyberbullying for many kids is "a joke" where the perpetrator has no sense that his or her actions can permanently damage the victim.

5. *To stop cyberbullying, just turn off your computer or cell phone.* Parents may determine that the most effective way of shielding their children from cyberbullying is by taking them out of the digital environment. This, however, is not realistic for two reasons. First, the young person loses out on important life experiences. Modern society requires that a person enter and navigate the digital environment. Young people must learn how to seek, interpret, and produce symbolic communication on the Internet. In the long run, restricting computer access only makes it harder for the young person to anticipate and defend against cyberbullying in the future. Second, this is practically impossible. The digital environment is made up of interconnected networks that are not under the control of individuals. Young people cannot avoid cyberbullying by turning off their cell phone or computer. Even if they turn off their phone, they will eventually have to check their email, be required to go online for school, or connect with family and friends through social media.

Can Someone Cyberbully...Themself?

Hannah Smith, a 14-year-old from the United Kingdom, was found hanged in her bedroom by her older sister. It was ruled a suicide, and her family believed she had been cyberbullied. Indeed, there had been vile messages posted about Hannah online. However, in an examination of Smith's laptop, it was determined that Smith had posted the messages herself.

The case of Hannah Smith is an example self-cyberbullying, or digital self-harm. Digital self-harm occurs in two ways. One way is the "anonymous online posting, sending, or otherwise sharing of hurtful content about oneself" (Patchin & Hinduja, 2017, p. 762). This is the type of digital self-harm done by Smith. Digital self-harm is not a rare occurrence. The Cyberbullying Research Center reports that about 9% of young people posted something online about themselves that was mean at some point in their lifetime in 2019. This had increased from around 6% in 2016. A second way someone can commit digital self-harm is by seeking out conflicts that will lead to one's humiliation or goading others into posting demeaning or hateful things about oneself.

Some scholars have posited that digital self-harm may be a form of self-regulation (Soengkoeng & Moustafa, 2022). Young people may be alienated from peers or feel unsafe in their environments. Like physical forms of self-harm (e.g., cutting, pulling hair) they use digital self-harm to manage those negative feelings and gain self-control. By hurting themselves, they take control of when and where they are hurt.

TROLLING AND FLAMING

Trolling is the act of generating conflict online, often for a prank or to cause controversy. Flaming, on the other hand, can be defined as the uninhibited expression of hostility, insults, and ridicule (Kayany, 1998). A major difference between trolling and flaming is that a troll has no vested interest in the conflict-generating content they produce or have no relation to the victims they target. It is primarily a game or prank, encompassed in the catchphrase "doing it for the lulz," or doing it for the humor.

Milner (2013) describes trolling through what he calls the logic of lulz. The logic of lulz, Milner argues, is to generate a "hyper-humorous, hyper-ironic, hyper-distanced mode of discourse" (2013, p. 89). He argues that trolls seek out normative discussions, ideas, and images and intentionally try to mock or subvert them. An example of this would be joining an online forum for people struggling with alcoholism, and repeatedly posting comments about the joys and health benefits of drinking beer.

Milner's view of trolling is a common one, but there are other behaviors that can be considered as trolling:

- Deceiving people in online forums simply to sow discord
- Cultivating needless arguments
- Using abusive or offensive words and harassing others
- Using sexist, racist, or queerphobic words

Many of these behaviors can also appear to be other forms of cybercrime or cyberdeviance. Harassing others can be seen as cyberbullying and participating in acts of sexism or racism can be seen as hate speech. However, a key difference is the motivation. Trolls may not necessarily want to cause harm like cyberbullies or demean like bigots. Instead, they are more interested in provoking reactions for the sheer entertainment of it.

Graham (2019), exploring trolling through a sociological perspective, argues that trolling began as a form of boundary maintenance for people navigating spaces in the digital environment. For sociologists, boundary maintenance refers to the processes insiders use to identify and maintain distinctions between outsiders. An example of this provided by Graham is the "gendertrolling" observed in online spaces during the 1990s, when the Internet was understood to be a masculine space. Women were trolled, in an effort to exclude them from online spaces.

In some countries, trolling can rise to a punishable offense. Trolling is covered in the UK under its "Malicious Communications Act."[2] In 2011 Sean Duffy was sent to prison in the United Kingdom for Internet trolling. Many families set up Facebook tribute pages for their loved ones who have died. Duffy had posted derogatory messages on several of these pages. He also posted videos on YouTube mocking the deceased. On one tribute site to a young girl who died in a car crash, Duffy defaced a picture of her by adding stitches to her head and placing a caption under one picture reading "Used car for sale, one useless owner."[3] For these acts he was given an 18-week jail sentence. Duffy did not know the victims, and his actions appeared to be just for "the lulz."

Flaming, in contrast to trolling, often occurs in online spaces where controversial issues are discussed. Like face-to-face discussions that lead to raised voices and strong emotions, Internet users may express disagreement rudely and use profanity. Thus, a key difference between flaming and trolling is that a genuine interest underlies flaming motivations. A person who flames may themselves feel aggrieved because a sentiment was expressed that they strongly disagree with. A second difference between flaming and trolling is that flaming is an "in the moment" act that does not carry over to another context or a subsequent post.

While flaming is not discussed as much in society or in research as much as trolling, the practice may have more wide-ranging societal implications. Inflamed passions often result from perceived cultural, ideological, or political differences that manifest in online forums or social media. We are more likely to communicate harshly towards a person we believe to be of a different race, creed, or political affiliation—and thus not deserving of civility.

HATE SPEECH

The United Nations defines hate speech as:

> *any kind of communication in speech, writing or behaviour, that attacks or uses pejorative or discriminatory language with reference to a person or a group on the basis of who they are, in other words, based on their religion, ethnicity, nationality, race, colour, descent, gender or other identity factor.*
>
> (United Nations, n.d.)

This is likely the way most people think about and understand hate speech.

Although this is the definition adopted by the United Nations and is likely acceptable to most people, they note that "*there is no universal definition of hate speech under international human rights law. The concept is still under discussion, especially in relation to freedom of opinion and expression, non-discrimination and equality.*" Different nations may evaluate the same communication differently. Or even if there is agreement that something is hate speech, they may respond to hate speech differently. These differences are often based upon the history and social context of the nation. For example, several nations—Austria, Germany, and Poland are examples—have criminalized Holocaust denial. Given the histories of those countries, where Jews were persecuted and killed in concentration camps, the prohibition is understandable. Meanwhile, in the United States, expressing a belief that the Holocaust never happened is protected under free speech laws. People may levy informal social sanctions on a Holocaust denier for their deviance, but the state cannot formally punish the person with fines or prison time.

The variations in hate speech laws across the globe can present unique challenges for companies operating in the digital environment. Content deemed lawful in one jurisdiction, may be illegal in another. For example, Facebook in 2021 and Twitter in 2022 have had complaints lodged against them in Australia by the Australian Muslim Advocacy Network (AMAN). The organization used Australia's Racial Discrimination Act. A section in that act makes it unlawful to offend, insult, humiliate or intimidate someone because of their race. The organization's complaint was that the social media companies had not removed content vilifying Middle Eastern, African, South Asian, and Asian people.

A Sociological Understanding of Hate Speech

The definition of hate speech from the United Nations discussed above is satisfactory in most contexts. However, sociologists and other social scientists are also interested in the impact of hate speech on individuals and groups. In this light, a different approach to hate speech is needed, one that identifies the conditions that can lead to hate speech becoming a form of violence.

The approach used in this text will adopt a three-pronged criteria (adapted from Matsuda, 1989): (1) the speech implies or states that the target group is inferior or undeserving, (2) the speech is aimed at a group that has been historically oppressed or disadvantaged, and (3) the speech is intended to be harmful. This understanding adds power differences and intent. We deviate somewhat from Matsuda's stipulation that the group needs to be *historically* oppressed. Newly identified minority groups—people with different lifestyles, religions, or sexual identities—may not have a history of oppression but face contemporary challenges.

Before moving forward, we must point out that all individuals can be victims of hateful words, and states apply hate speech laws accordingly. However, like our approach to cyberbullying, we are interested in the conditions in which hate speech produces serious psychological harm, which has historically meant harm to oppressed minority groups.

As such, examples of harmful hate speech include:

- A website arguing that people of European ancestry are more intelligent than people of African ancestry
- A troll in an online forum replying to a person they think is Hispanic, saying that all Hispanics should go back to Mexico because they are all gang members
- Twitter comments aimed at a tweet celebrating the marriage of a gay couple, with the tweets calling the marriage "disgusting" or "sinful"

Using this sociological understanding, hate speech can be harmful in at least two ways. First, hate speech can lower the status of the group in the eyes of others. In this sense, hate speech is sociologically harmful. Hate speech can be used to paint a group as violent, unintelligent, or unpatriotic. This type of labeling can prepare members of dominant groups psychologically for more egregious types of behavior towards the minority group. Hate speech can be a "gateway act" to discrimination, the support of harmful social policies, or physical violence. Numerous historical episodes show this pattern. The Third Reich in 1930s Germany, white supremacists in Jim Crow Era United States, and the Hutu majority in early 1990s Rwanda all used hate speech against a minority group. This speech produced a sense in the dominant group that Jews, African Americans, and the Tutsi minority were "others." Once a minority group has been "otherized," dominant groups can more easily generate the justification for discriminatory laws or for committing acts of violence towards these groups.

Second, hate speech is psychologically harmful to the individuals within the groups it is directed at. In this sense, hate speech is functionally equivalent to the taunts and insults used by bullies. There are negative consequences to consuming content asserting one's person or group is inferior. Like cyberbullying, this can include psychological distress and a lowering of self-esteem. For example, Gelber and McNamara (2016) explored the consequences of hate speech directed towards members of indigenous communities and minority groups in Australia. In their interviews, respondents reported the pain caused by hate speech (333):

- *To me the saddest thing is [there] not a recognition of the special status of what we add to this country. We don't take away from; we add ... but it's always put up*

> *there as a negative, that Aboriginals don't add to the fabric of this country, that we don't—and … I think that it is painful … Yes, it does hurt and it strikes at your very being.*

- *You can never, you can never repair damage in that content once it's been put out there. It lingers, it stays, it smells, it hangs around. You can't get rid of it and racism is racism, it builds and feeds on that.*
- *Our kids also feel hopeless and ask why their parents as Muslims are doing something wrong.*

The difference between hate speech and other forms of cyberviolence we have discussed is that hate speech is generally understood to be aimed at a group. Flaming, trolling, and cyberbullying are generally aimed at individuals, and it is easier to identify a clear victim. Nevertheless, hate speech is potentially more damaging for society because it can be a factor supporting discrimination and injustice towards large swaths of a population.

CYBERSTALKING

Stalking is generally defined as an "ongoing course of conduct in which a person behaviorally intrudes upon another's life in a manner perceived to be threatening" (Nicastro et al., 2000, 69). When this intrusion occurs in the digital environment, we can consider this cyberstalking. Reyns and colleagues (2011) define cyberstalking as "the repeated pursuit of an individual using electronic or Internet-capable devices" (1).

Cyberstalking is prevalent within romantic relationships (Marcum et al., 2017), and especially amongst young people who spend a lot of their time in the digital environment. Indeed, the connection between intimate relationships and stalking is strong enough that cyberstalking and "cyber dating abuse" are often used interchangeably (Marcum et al., 2017).

The potential for cyberstalking has increased over the years. This is because there are more ways of entering and communicating in the digital environment. For example, in the early 2000s, people entered the digital environment primarily through their home computers and used mainly emails for communication. Consequently, cyberstalking was somewhat limited to those devices, locations, and means of communication. Today, consider the number of ways in which a person can enter the digital environment—phones, computers, laptops, appliances, automobiles, and wearable devices. Also, consider the number of ways in which a person can communicate in the digital environment—email, text, and hundreds of social media applications. These ways of entering and communicating in the digital environment present more opportunities for a victim to be pursued and more ways in which a victim's life can be intruded upon. Examples of cyberstalking include:

- Seeking online communication in the form of emails, texting, social media correspondence, constantly from a victim
- Collecting social media or other online information about a victim. This information could be photographs, replies, and comments by the victim, or other digital footprints such as likes, upvotes, and retweets
- Logging into a victim's social networking accounts without their permission
- Installing or activating GPS tracking devices on mobile devices without their permission

Table 4.2 Types of Intimate Partner Cyberstalking

Passive	*Invasive*	*Duplicitous*
Check their online accounts to see what they've been up to	Check their messages (e.g., email, Facebook) without them knowing	Pose as someone else over social media or email
Monitor their behaviors (e.g., friendships, movements, activities) through social media	Log into their accounts (e.g., email, Facebook) without them knowing	Use a fake account (e.g., Facebook, Instagram) to check up on them
Check their last "online" status	Check their phone/computer history	Use location settings on their phone/computer to see where they've been or are going

(Adapted from March et al., 2022)

Many perpetrators of cyberstalking know their victim intimately—meaning that their victim is a current or former romantic partner. March et al. (2022) explored the behavioral patterns of intimate partner cyberstalking. The researchers asked participants on a survey to indicate which behaviors they would do if they were trying to retain or attain a partner. Their research showed that cyberstalking behaviors were clustered into passive, invasive, and duplicitous (see Table 4.2). For both men and women, the most common type of cyberstalking was passive.

ONLINE SHAMING

Online shaming refers to a group subjecting an individual to harassment, bullying, and condemnation because of some real or perceived transgression. The fundamental aspect of shaming, as described by Braithwaite (1989), is the "societal processes of expressing social disapproval" (100). The perpetrators of online shaming are collections of individual users acting as a group. Research has shown that when individuals perceive themselves as being a part of the group, they lose their inhibitions and become more vitriolic and combative (Suler, 2004). Thus, the target of online shaming may be the recipient of particularly malicious comments that are out of proportion to the transgression. There are at least two motivations for online shaming—social control and vigilantism.

Online Shaming for Social Control

One motivation for online shaming is to identify what behaviors are unacceptable publicly. In this way, shaming is a form of social control. For example, the author J.K. Rowling experienced an online backlash for her comments on transgender persons. The backlash has been particularly severe, with calls for boycotting her famous Harry Potter books and the movies derived from them.

From a sociological perspective, this response is an attempt to negatively sanction Rowling for comments perceived as harmful, and in the process, signal to others what behaviors are unacceptable. Online shaming for social control has become pervasive in societies worldwide, as social media users can easily register their anger or disgust with a person or their actions. Several commentators have lamented this trend, calling it "cancel culture."

A famous example of online shaming for the purposes of social control is the case of Justine Sacco (Ronson, 2015). Sacco was a public relations executive for a company called IAC. As she waited for her flight at London's Heathrow Airport, she began tweeting jokes:

- Weird German Dude: You're in First Class. It's 2014. Get some deodorant.—Inner monologue as I inhale BO. Thank God for pharmaceuticals
- Chilly—cucumber sandwiches—bad teeth. Back in London!
- Going to Africa. Hope I don't get AIDS. Just kidding. I'm white!

After this last tweet, Sacco boarded her 11-hour flight, and went to sleep. Sacco had only 170 followers at the time, and her jokes could have easily melted into the Twittersphere. Unfortunately for Sacco, when she awoke, she realized that her third joke—about AIDS, Africa, and whiteness—was the number one trending tweet on Twitter. Sacco had crossed a boundary of social acceptance, and she was unfortunate in that other Twitter users—possibly those with a high number of followers—read and retweeted her joke.

Sacco experienced severe online shaming in the hours and days that followed. An article on Sacco (Ronson, 2015) lists some of the responses to Sacco's tweet:

- "In light of @Justine-Sacco disgusting racist tweet, I'm donating to @care today" and "How did @JustineSacco get a PR job?! Her level of racist ignorance belongs on Fox News. #AIDS can affect anyone!"
- "I'm an IAC employee and I don't want @JustineSacco doing any communications on our behalf ever again. Ever."
- "This is an outrageous, offensive comment. Employee in question currently unreachable on an intl flight." [This tweet is from her employer, IAC.]
- "We are about to watch this @JustineSacco bitch get fired. In REAL time. Before she even KNOWS she's getting fired."

A popular hashtag was used to comment on Sacco—#HasJustineLandedYet, as people expressed pleasure in watching her lose her career. Sacco was eventually fired from IAC. Whatever one thinks about Sacco's poor taste in humor, or even if one imagines that her jokes reveal unhealthy racial views, it is clear that Sacco experienced a high degree of stress because of online social shaming.

Online Shaming as Vigilantism

Another motivation for online shaming is to punish a person for an actual or perceived transgression that has not been adequately addressed through institutional or legal means. Collections of individuals may decide to "right the wrong" using the tools they have available in the digital environment, what can be called digital vigilantism (Trottier, 2017). There are many reasons why groups decide to seek justice on their own:

- There may be no formal laws against the behavior in question
- Law enforcement may have historically ignored the transgression or place a low priority on it

- Law enforcement may be ineffective in bringing criminals to justice
- A person may have been convicted of a crime and punished, but the punishment does not meet the expectations of the group

As an example, in 2011, riots broke out in Vancouver, Canada, after the home team lost a hockey game. The riots caused major damage to the city and injured many people. Nathan Kotlyak was photographed attempting to light a police car on fire, and the photo was shared across numerous social media platforms. Arvanitidis (2016) writes about the experience:

> *Shortly after, the backlash he suffered from the public was immediate, merciless, and overwhelmingly public. As the photograph continued to make its way across the Internet, Kotlyak found himself subjected to a torrent of verbal abuse, demands for punishment, and threats, until eventually he and his family were forced to flee their home following the publication of their home address online.*
>
> (19)

Kotlyak released a written statement, taking full responsibility for his actions, apologizing, and expressing remorse. The response to Kotlyak was so severe, and it can be categorized as vigilantism, because the Vancouver citizens wanted him and other rioters to be punished for their crimes.

A more recent example of online vigilantism is the death threats received by the American physician Dr. Anthony Fauci. As the chief medical advisor to the United States President, and a member of Presidents Donald Trump and Joe Biden's White House Coronavirus Task Force, Fauci was the public face of the American government's response to the COVID-19 pandemic. Fauci's recommendations for addressing the pandemic were unpopular among some groups in American society. Additionally, Fauci was the victim of much misinformation, and citizens attributed statements or motives to Fauci that turned out to be false.

The unpopular recommendations and misinformation created a climate in which Dr. Fauci became the target of many disgruntled people. In March 2020, law enforcement began protective operations around Dr. Fauci, which included vetting threats received by mail, voicemail, and emails. Figure 4.1 (p. 76) shows evidence from an email collected during an investigation into threats against Fauci. This email and similar threats can be understood as digital vigilantism. The purpose was not to shame Fauci for inappropriate actions; instead, the motivation is to punish him for what is perceived as criminal actions during the pandemic.

Comparing Motives

The motives of social control and vigilantism are related, as both are about levying sanctions for bad behaviors. However, shaming for social control is primarily a cultural transgression, and vigilantism is linked to transgressions that are either criminal or that the group imagines should be criminalized. Another difference is the severity of sanctions. Online shaming as social control may never rise above the level of vitriolic comment—or a public outcry. This outcry may lead to punishment from other authorities;

From:	naturtheateralhena
To:	Fauci, Anthony (NIH/NIAID) [E]
Cc:	
Subject:	Hope you get a bullet in your compromised satanic elf skull today
Date:	Monday, December 28, 2020 10:32:35 PM

Dear Anthony Fauci,

Every time I see your sickening elf visage I literally get sick. You are a lying sack of shit, all the way back to your bullshit HIV scam. You are a sickening, compromised, satanic freemason criminal, and I hope you get a rope around your vile elf neck, and a bullet in your disgusting elf face tonight. Hope someone takes a baseball bat to your dirty lying elf skull and puts your out of your misery, you sickening vile piece of criminal DOG SHIT.

Why were you afraid to debate Kary Mullis about the PCR test, you dirty little fucking elf? HOPE SOMEONE TAKES A BASEBALL BAT AND SMASHES YOUR EYEBALLS OUT, SICKENIONG VILE LITTLE FUCKING ELF

Sent with ProtonMail Secure Email.

Figure 4.1   An image of the e-mail to Anthony Fauci from Thomas Patrick Connally, Jr.

however, this punishment does not come from the shamers themselves. Vigilantes tend to undertake more severe forms of punishment that in and of themselves are crimes. For example, they may hack personal accounts to doxx targets or make threats of physical violence.

THE DISTRIBUTION AND CONSUMPTION OF ONLINE CHILD PORNOGRAPHY

The distribution and consumption of online child pornography causes severe harm to children. It is an act of violence. The United States Department of Justice highlights this important point on their website:

> *Experts and victims agree that victims depicted in child pornography often suffer a lifetime of re-victimization by knowing the images of their sexual abuse are on the Internet forever. The children exploited in these images must live with the permanency, longevity, and circulation of such a record of their sexual victimization. This often creates lasting psychological damage to the child, including disruptions in sexual development, self-image, and developing trusting relationships with others in the future.*
>
> (The United States Department of Justice, 2015).

The authors of this text also see the presence of child pornography as an act of violence and support the transition to using terms such as child sexual abuse material (CSAM) and child sexual abuse images (CSAIs) to signify that fact. However, this textbook continues to use child pornography because it is still the term used most often by policy makers and laymen in English speaking countries.

THE AMOUNT OF CHILD PORNOGRAPHY IN THE DIGITAL ENVIRONMENT

It is difficult to know how much child pornography is present in the digital environment. Most of the images of children are encrypted or shared on darknets like Tor and Freenet. Despite these difficulties, researchers who have explored darknets have found a high prevalence of child pornography (Jardine, 2016; Owen & Savage, 2015). In one study exploring a year's worth of child pornography sharing on a peer-to-peer network, researchers found that on an average day, 122,687 known child pornography files were shared (Wolak et al., 2014).

PROFILING CHILD PORNOGRAPHY OFFENDERS

As with most types of cybercrimes, it is difficult to profile child pornography offenders (CPOs). However, according to Houtepen et al., (2014), some broad characteristics can be drawn. They are primarily white, between the ages of 25 and 50 years, and compared to child sexual abusers, more likely to be employed. They have above average intelligence, and 30% of known CPOs have completed some form of higher education. They often have jobs that either require little to no social interaction or where they have daily contact with children. CPOs are less likely to be employed in jobs requiring consistent interaction with adults, such as college professor, police officer, or bank manager.

One assumption about CPOs is that their consumption of images is either a temporary substitute or a gateway to child contact. One study done in 2007 showed that at least 80% of CPOs are active child molesters (Schell et al., 2007). However, some recent research has questioned this tight link between the consumption of images and actual child contact. Henshaw et al (Henshaw et al., 2017) write that a large percentage of CPOs do not move to actual child contact, are not deviant or criminal in other ways, and as a result have a rather normal life.

The CPO population is complex. Merdian et al. (2013) argue that there are three dimensions to online child pornography offending:

- *Fantasy driven versus contact driven.* CPOs that were fantasy-driven had a wide array of motivations for consuming child pornography. Contact-driven CPOs were those who had an encounter with a child in the past.
- *Different motivations for fantasy-driven CPOs.* There are several motivations for CPOs who were driven by fantasy:
  - Paedophilic motivation—These CPOs have a sexual interest in children
  - General deviant sexual interest—These CPOs are sexually deviant in general, and are not specifically interested in children (e.g. they may also be interested in bestiality, sadomasochism, etc.)
  - Financial motivation—These CPOs are interested in profiting from the sale of child pornography and are not necessarily interested in children sexually
  - Other—CPOs can have a wide range of motivations that are not easily categorized. Some are simply collectors of pornography, and others simply wish to defy the legal codes against consuming child pornography

- *Low or high networking.* Some CPOs consume child pornography in isolation, while others consume child pornography in a social context that reinforces their behavior. Low networking CPOs tend to consume a smaller amount of child pornography and are not linked to other forms of deviance or child contact. However, high networking CPOs are more serious offenders. They are involved in online victim grooming or will eventually pursue contact with children.

Research providing evidence of several types of CPOs allows society to move away from the common stereotypes seen in the media. CPOs on fictionalized crime shows such as *Law and Order* or *Luther* are often depicted as maladjusted, awkward, or otherwise "creepy" individuals who have uncontrollable desires for child sexual contact. Research shows that this is only a small percentage of the population. As a result, law enforcement and policy makers will need to adjust their investigations and their policies to this reality. For example, because the link between the consumption of images and actual child contact is not as clear as once imagined, it may be necessary to treat individuals who have consumed images differently than those who have had actual contact. Preventative or therapeutic measures may be available for offenders of the first type that may prevent them from graduating to more serious contact-related offenses.

INTERNET-FACILITATED SEX TRAFFICKING

Sex trafficking is the buying, selling, and sexual exploitation of people. This requires varying levels of coercion and threats of physical violence. According to the International Labor Organization, there were 4.8 million victims of sex trafficking worldwide in 2016. At least a million of those victims were children.[4] Sex trafficking is a global phenomenon, with almost every country in the world being affected. Countries may be the point of origin for a trafficking victim, countries could be in the victim's transit path, or a country can be the victim's destination.

Although the digital environment is not the primary space of exploitation, traffickers use the digital environment to facilitate crime. The phenomenon of human trafficking – which includes trafficking for sex—can be organized into three elements: The act, the means, and the purpose (see Figure 4.2; p. 79):

- The first element is the act: Recruiting, transporting, transferring (moving from one mode of transport to another), harboring, or receiving a victim of human trafficking. These are acts that are necessary for global sex trafficking and can be performed by different actors in a trafficking organization
- To commit these criminal acts, traffickers use threats of force, deception, and money—the second element of human trafficking
- The third element is the ultimate purpose of the trafficking enterprise. This chapter is focused on prostitution or other forms of sexual exploitation. However, trafficking can also be for other purposes such as slavery or removal of organs

The United Nations Office on Drugs and Crime (*Global Report on Trafficking in Persons 2023*, 2023) produces an annual report on global human trafficking. The latest report

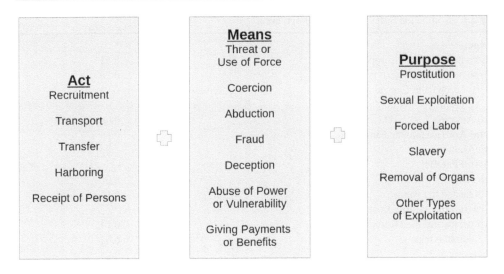

Figure 4.2   An illustration of the three dimensions of human trafficking.

published during the writing of this textbook was for the year 2022. According to the report, the majority of sex trafficking victims were female—64% women and 27% girls. Around 10% were males—5% men and 4% boys. Not all United Nations member countries provided data on trans persons. However, in the nine countries that reported data on transpersons, about 2% of their victims identified as trans.

The report stated that the number of sex trafficking victims detected declined globally by 24% from pre-pandemic 2019 numbers. This can be a positive or negative data point depending upon the explanation. On the one hand, sexual exploitation often begins with a potential trafficking victim being contacted in public spaces—night clubs, bars, shopping areas. With the closing of public spaces, fewer potential victims can be contacted and exploited. On the other hand, the pandemic may have driven sex trafficking further underground into less visible and less safe locations. Suppose the explanation for the decline in victims is that sex trafficking has been driven underground. In that case, lower detection rates do not mean lower victimization rates, and those victimized may be in even more danger.

Another finding speaks to the global nature of sex trafficking. Countries in sub-Saharan Africa and South Asia are convicting fewer traffickers (see Table 4.3; p. 80). For example, countries in South Asia (e.g., Afghanistan, Bangladesh, India) have a conviction rate per 100,000 people of 0.01. Meanwhile, Central and Southeastern Europe (e.g., Albania, Poland, Russia, Ukraine) have conviction rates of 0.28 per 100,000.

The lower conviction rates in South Asia and sub-Saharan Africa are not because there are fewer victims in those regions. Indeed, in analysing the origin and destination of victims—the trafficking flow, the UN's report suggests that these countries are the origin of many victims, and these victims are being detected in a wider range of destination countries. This suggests that traffickers in these regions are operating more freely within Sub-Saharan Africa and South Asia and are trafficking victims to people in other regions.

Table 4.3 Conviction Rates Per 100,000 Population*

Europe	
Western and Southern Europe	0.12
Central and South-Eastern Europe	0.28
Eastern Europe and Central Asia	0.12
The Americas	
North America	0.08
Central America and the Caribbean	0.11
South America	0.06
Asia and Pacific	
South Asia	0.01
East Asia and the Pacific	0.12
Africa and the Middle East	
North Africa and the Middle East	0.10
Sub-Saharan Africa	0.02
Global	0.04

*(*Global Report on Trafficking in Persons 2023*, 2023)

SEX TRAFFICKING AND TECHNOLOGY

A major focus for the cybercriminologist is how the digital environment facilitates the act and provides the means for that purpose. For the act of trafficking, the digital environment makes it easier to recruit victims. Victims can be found online and groomed. Traffickers can coordinate their activities amongst themselves across wide distances using mobile phones, making it easier to transfer, transport, and harbor victims. For the means of trafficking, the digital environment makes it easier to communicate with a victim through space and time. A trafficker can more easily and more often make threats, coerce, and deceive. With the growing use of cryptocurrencies such as bitcoin, it may be easier for traffickers to send and receive payments without the risk of being detected by law enforcement.

Another way in which the digital environment facilitates sex trafficking is by hiding it from mainstream society. As Leary (2014) argues, "The migration of sex trafficking to a digital space can both make the crime more public, but also remove it from places where it has been traditionally recognized and identified" (291). Traffickers can recruit victims and coordinate their activities within relatively secure spaces. Prior to the growth of the Internet, traffickers would have needed to venture into spaces where children or young women frequented, such as schools, parks, shopping malls, etc. Now, traffickers can enter online spaces anonymously and entice victims with promises of money and travel.

In a study of sex trafficking court cases from 2001 to 2011 by Mary Graw Leary (2014), technology played a role in approximately 78% of all cases. Leary argues that technology is most prevalent in recruiting and connecting purchasers and victims. Leary's research also highlights the response of law enforcement. Local and federal police units have moved their operations into the digital environment. Law enforcement set up investigations online to identify offenders. They surveil digital spaces where traffickers meet victims. They, like the traffickers, take advantage of online anonymity. They impersonate a potential victim in an attempt to learn the identity of the traffickers and impersonate traffickers to learn the identity of purchasers. Law enforcement also undertake undercover sting operations conducted entirely online. Leary argues that these operations have met with success:

it would seem that an aggressive and successful approach to intervention in child sex trafficking cases necessarily includes utilizing technologies such as false online advertisements, false child sex tourism companies, or posing as fictitious offenders in certain online communities.

(2014, 289)

Conclusion

Cybertrespass, and to a lesser degree cyberdeception/theft, receives a lot of attention from the public because of the financial loss involved. Cyberpornography can also receive a lot of attention the public always has a fascination with activities associated with sex and sexuality. However, the phenomena associated with cyberviolence also causes immense harm to individuals. A significant amount of young people are cyberbullied and cyberstalked.

Trolling and flaming are prevalent features of the digital environment, with almost every computer user having experienced aggressive or hostile communications aimed at themselves or others. Hate speech has been historically associated with subsequent discrimination, unfair social policies, and in extreme cases genocide. Children and adults are being victims of sexual violence in the digital environment through child sexual abuse images/materials and through sex trafficking. The challenge for scholars and law enforcement professionals moving forward is to develop ways of mitigating the effects of preventing altogether these cybercrimes and digital deviances.

CHAPTER 4 CURRENT EVENTS AND CRITICAL THINKING:

Meta and Sex Trafficking

Several reports, from *The Guardian* have concluded that the applications owned by the social media company Meta—Facebook, Instagram, and WhatsApp—are used by traffickers to target victims.

In a 2023 study commissioned by the US state of Florida, 90 law enforcement agencies were asked to review instances of Internet-facilitated human trafficking. In a meeting discussing the results, Ashley Moody, Attorney General of the United States state of Florida, reported that "the findings of our statewide survey and other reports make it clear that Meta platforms are the preferred social media applications for human traffickers looking to prey on vulnerable people." (https://www.myfloridalegal.com/newsrelease/attorney-general-moody-calls-meta-ceo-zuckerberg-florida-testify-about-use-meta)

A separate investigation from *The Guardian*, also in 2023, linked Meta applications to trafficking. "Our two-year investigation suggests that the tech giant Meta is struggling to prevent criminals from using its platforms to buy and sell children for sex," said *The Guardian*, in a write-up of the investigation (https://www.theguardian.com/news/2023/apr/27/how-facebook-and-instagram-became-marketplaces-for-child-sex-trafficking)

Facebook, Instagram, and WhatsApp are applications that allow people to make connections with people. They are often the primary ways in which we build platonic and intimate connections, share special moments with family, or just pass the time at our office desk or while waiting on the subway. In other words, these applications provide value to the people who use them. But the same affordances that provide this value for law abiding citizens can also be used for criminals.

If a technology is being used to facilitate sex trafficking, do the owners have an ethical responsibility to combat such trafficking? Should they be held criminally liable for sex trafficking because their technology was used in the commission of the crime?

NOTES

1 https://cyberbullying.org/
2 www.legislation.gov.uk/ukpga/1988/27/contents
3 www.theguardian.com/uk/2011/sep/13/internet-troll-jailed-mocking-teenagers
4 https://www.ilo.org/wcmsp5/groups/public/@dgreports/@dcomm/documents/publication/wcms _575479.pdf

REFERENCES

Arvanitidis, T. (2016). Publication bans in a Facebook age: How Internet vigilantes have challenged the Youth Criminal Justice Act's "Secrecy Laws" following the 2011 Vancouver Stanley Cup Riot. *Canadian Graduate Journal of Sociology and Criminology, 5*(1), 18. https://doi.org/10.15353/cgjsc-rcessc.v5i1.142

Atske, S. (2022, December 15). Teens and cyberbullying 2022. *Pew Research Center: Internet, Science & Tech.* https://www.pewresearch.org/internet/2022/12/15/teens-and-cyberbullying-2022/

Australian Institute of Health and Welfare. (2021, June 25). *Australia's youth: Bullying and negative online experiences.* Australian Institute of Health and Welfare. https://www.aihw.gov.au/reports/children -youth/negative-online-experiences

Braithwaite, J. (1989). *Crime, shame, and reintegration.* Cambridge University Press.

Gelber, K., & McNamara, L. (2016). Evidencing the harms of hate speech. *Social Identities, 22*(3), 324–341. https://doi.org/10.1080/13504630.2015.1128810

Global Report on Trafficking in Persons 2023 (Global Report on Trafficking in Persons, p. 166).(2023). United Nations Office on Drugs and Crime. https://www.unodc.org/documents/data-and-analysis/glotip /2022/GLOTiP_2022_web.pdf

Graham, E. (2019). Boundary maintenance and the origins of trolling. *New Media & Society, 21*(9), 2029–2047. https://doi.org/10.1177/1461444819837561

Guerra, E., & Westlake, B. G. (2021). Detecting child sexual abuse images: Traits of child sexual exploitation hosting and displaying websites. *Child Abuse & Neglect, 122,* 105336. https://doi.org/10.1016/j.chiabu .2021.105336

Henshaw, M., Ogloff, J. R., & Clough, J. A. (2017). Looking beyond the screen: A critical review of the literature on the online child pornography offender. *Sexual Abuse, 29*(5), 416–445.

Houtepen, J. A. B. M., Sijtsema, J. J., & Bogaerts, S. (2014). From child pornography offending to child sexual abuse: A review of child pornography offender characteristics and risks for cross-over. *Aggression and Violent Behavior, 19*(5), 466–473. https://doi.org/10.1016/j.avb.2014.07.011

Jardine, E. (2016). Tor, what is it good for? Political repression and the use of online anonymity-granting technologies. *New Media & Society,* https://doi.org/10.1177/1461444816639976

Kayany, J. M. (1998). Contexts of uninhibited online behavior: Flaming in social newsgroups on Usenet. *Journal of the American Society for Information Science, 49*(12), 1135–1141. https://doi.org/10.1002/(SICI)1097-4571(1998)49:12<1135::AID-ASI8>3.0.CO;2-W

Leary, M. G. (2014). Fighting fire with fire: Technology in child sex trafficking. *Duke Journal of Gender Law & Policy, 21*(2), 289–323.

March, E., Szymczak, P., Di Rago, M., & Jonason, P. K. (2022). Passive, invasive, and duplicitous: Three forms of intimate partner cyberstalking. *Personality and Individual Differences, 189*, 111502. https://doi.org/10.1016/j.paid.2022.111502

Marcum, C. D., Higgins, G. E., & Nicholson, J. (2017). I'm watching you: Cyberstalking behaviors of university students in romantic relationships. *American Journal of Criminal Justice, 42*(2), 373–388. https://doi.org/10.1007/s12103-016-9358-2

Matsuda, M. J. (1989). Public response to racist speech: Considering the victim's story. *Michigan Law Review, 87*(8), 2320. https://doi.org/10.2307/1289306

Merdian, H. L., Curtis, C., Thakker, J., Wilson, N., & Boer, D. P. (2013). The three dimensions of online child pornography offending. *Journal of Sexual Aggression, 19*(1), 121–132. https://doi.org/10.1080/13552600.2011.611898

Milner, R. M. (2013). FCJ-156 Hacking the social: Internet memes, identity antagonism, and the logic of lulz. *The Fibreculture Journal, 31*.

Nicastro, A. M., Cousins, A. V., & Spitzberg, B. H. (2000). The tactical face of stalking. *Journal of Criminal Justice, 28*(1), 69–82. https://doi.org/10.1016/S0047-2352(99)00038-0

Olweus, D. (1993). *Bullying at school: What we know and what we can do.* Blackwell.

Owen, G., & Savage, N. (2015). *The Tor Dark Net* (20; Global Commission on Internet Governance Paper Series). https://www.cigionline.org/sites/default/files/no20_0.pdf

Patchin, J. W., & Hinduja, S. (2017). Digital self-harm among adolescents. *Journal of Adolescent Health, 61*(6), 761–766. https://doi.org/10.1016/j.jadohealth.2017.06.012

Peterson, J., & Densley, J. (2017). Cyber violence: What do we know and where do we go from here? *Aggression and Violent Behavior, 34*, 193–200. https://doi.org/10.1016/j.avb.2017.01.012

Reyns, B. W., Henson, B., & Fisher, B. S. (2011). Being pursued online: Applying cyberlifestyle–routine activities theory to cyberstalking victimization. *Criminal Justice and Behavior, 38*(11), 1149–1169. https://doi.org/10.1177/0093854811421448

Ronson, J. (2015, February 12). How one stupid tweet blew up Justine Sacco's life. *The New York Times.* https://www.nytimes.com/2015/02/15/magazine/how-one-stupid-tweet-ruined-justine-saccos-life.html

Sabella, R. A., Patchin, J. W., & Hinduja, S. (2013). Cyberbullying myths and realities. *Computers in Human Behavior, 29*(6), 2703–2711. https://doi.org/10.1016/j.chb.2013.06.040

Schell, B. H., Martin, M. V., Hung, P. C. K., & Rueda, L. (2007). Cyber child pornography: A review paper of the social and legal issues and remedies—and a proposed technological solution. *Aggression and Violent Behavior, 12*(1), 45–63. https://doi.org/10.1016/j.avb.2006.03.003

Smoker, M., & March, E. (2017). Predicting perpetration of intimate partner cyberstalking: Gender and the Dark Tetrad. *Computers in Human Behavior, 72*, 390–396. https://doi.org/10.1016/j.chb.2017.03.012

Soengkoeng, R., & Moustafa, A. A. (2022). Digital self-harm: An examination of the current literature with recommendations for future research. *Discover Psychology, 2*(1), 19. https://doi.org/10.1007/s44202-022-00032-8

Suler, J. (2004). The online disinhibition effect. *CyberPsychology & Behavior, 7*(3), 321–326. https://doi.org/10.1089/1094931041291295

The United States Department of Justice. (2015, May 26). *Child pornography.* https://www.justice.gov/criminal-ceos/child-pornography

Tokunaga, R. S. (2010). Following you home from school: A critical review and synthesis of research on cyberbullying victimization. *Computers in Human Behavior, 26*(3), 277–287. https://doi.org/10.1016/j.chb.2009.11.014

Trottier, D. (2017). Digital vigilantism as weaponisation of visibility. *Philosophy & Technology, 30*(1), 55–72. https://doi.org/10.1007/s13347-016-0216-4

United Nations. (n.d.). *What is hate speech?* United Nations; United Nations. Retrieved July 22, 2023, from https://www.un.org/en/hate-speech/understanding-hate-speech/what-is-hate-speech

Wall, D. (Ed.). (2001). *Crime and the Internet*. Routledge.

Wang, L., & Ngai, S. S. (2022). Cyberbullying perpetration among Chinese adolescents: The role of power imbalance, fun-seeking tendency, and attitude toward cyberbullying. *Journal of Interpersonal Violence, 37*(23–24), NP21646–NP21671. https://doi.org/10.1177/08862605211062988

Wolak, J., Liberatore, M., & Levine, B. N. (2014). Measuring a year of child pornography trafficking by U.S. computers on a peer-to-peer network. *Child Abuse & Neglect, 38*(2), 347–356. https://doi.org/10.1016/j.chiabu.2013.10.018

Cyberfraud

Author's Note: Throughout this chapter, consider the connection between the content here and the cybertrespass/hacking material in Chapter 2. Often, a well-executed hack is a prerequisite to a successful theft of digital content, and we often find an attempted hack involves a great deal of deception. Thus, intertwined within much of the cyberfraud material in this chapter are the opportunities to invade a digital environment discussed in the preceding chapter on cybertrespass. It would be prudent to reference that material as you proceed through this chapter.

Introduction

Cyberfraud encompasses the concepts *cyberdeception* and *cybertheft*, for which Wall defined as "the different types of acquisitive harm that can take place" in the digital environment (2001, 4). *Acquisitive*, in this case, refers to the harms resulting from crimes in which the offender gains materially from the crime. In a simpler sense, cyberfraud refers to the act of lying (deception) and stealing (theft) in the digital environment; thus, cyberdeception and cybertheft. In theory, the two phenomena are distinct. Lying is commonplace in human relationships and is usually not a criminal offense, while theft is universally seen as a behavior that needs to be prohibited. However, the two phenomena are often linked. Criminals lie, construct elaborate fantasies, and engage in all types of subterfuge to steal money or information from a victim. Thus, for practical purposes, we can combine cyberdeception and theft and discuss them under the unifying concept of cyberfraud.

Cyberfraud is distinct from the other categories of cybercrime due in part to the comparatively wider array of offenders and victims impacted. Consider, for instance, that we generally find young people tend to be the perpetrators and victims of cyberviolence, the economically disadvantaged are considerably more likely the victims of online child trafficking schemes, and the wealthy are favored targets of cybertrespass offenders. Cyberfraud, on the other hand, is a crime experienced by young and old, rich and poor alike.

DOI: 10.4324/9781003283256-5

There are at least two reasons for this. First, given the volume of commercial transactions occurring today through Internet-enabled technologies, digital forms of payment like credit cards draw much attention from prospective thieves and heighten the risk of being targeted via digital means (e.g., credit card fraud or credit card skimming). Anyone inputting PII during the course of a digital transaction risks becoming a potential victim of identity theft, yet the usage of PII as a means of verifying identity and securing transactions is unavoidable. Thus, the simple act of buying goods online puts you in a position to potentially become a victim of many digitally-based crimes.

Second, there are numerous ways of deceiving someone in the digital environment, and these span from highly technical to more psychological in nature. This expands the range and options of perpetrators. Prospective offenders lacking in technical skill to commit such crime can turn to social engineering and other non-technical skills, and vice versa for offenders inept and/or unwilling to deal directly with targets in a social sense. It also expands the range of victims. A person may be aware of phishing or website spoofing, for example, but still fall victim to a romance scam because they are emotionally vulnerable to such attacks.

Types of Cyberfraud

The ways in which someone can be defrauded online are numerous and seems to grow exponentially every year. Thus, any list of fraud types is a tentative one as offenders continuously devise new schemes and add to the range of known frauds committed online. However, categorizing such theft by *money* motivation and *information* motivation is an integral way of organizing current and new schemes. Button and colleagues (2015) demonstrate as much in their organization of online frauds (see Tables 5.1a and 5.1b; p. 87).

Neither MS nor PIS frauds are mutually exclusive; prospective fraudsters often find it beneficial to employ techniques from multiple categories by first baiting their targets with a seemingly legitimate website created to harvest credentials (the PIS attack) for later use in executing an MS attack (i.e., accessing, and ultimately stealing from targeted financial accounts online). Accordingly, we will narrow our focus in this chapter to several well-known types of cyberfraud techniques where deception and/or theft are the primary goals. These are:

- *Identity Theft*—Obtaining and using another person's personal data in some way that involves fraud or deception
- *Phishing (also Vishing, Smishing, and Pharming)*—Sending fraudulent communications to obtain personal information
- *Advance Fee Frauds*—Scams in which a fraudster leads a victim to believe that they will receive a large payment in the future for some present action—usually an "advance fee"
- *Romance Scams*—A fraudster develops a deceitful relationship with a victim to extract favors from the victim, usually in the form of monetary payments
- *Selling of Counterfeit Goods*—The selling of merchandise that purports to be a product of a recognized brand company but is instead a copy of lesser value

Table 5.1a Money Seeking (MS) Frauds

419 scams: The victim is contacted by someone claiming to be an official with a large sum of money. They are looking for someone to help them obtain the money, in return for which they offer to pay a substantial fee. To start the venture, however, they require a payment in advance from the victim.

Bogus inheritance scams: Victims are contacted and told they have inherited a large sum of money from a long-lost relative but need to pay fees in advance to release the money.

Bogus lottery: Victims are contacted and told they have won a lottery but need to pay a fee in advance to release the funds.

Bogus products: Goods and services advertised on online markets that are either defective or non-existent.

Career opportunity scams: Jobs and training are offered online, usually for lucrative jobs, but the reality is there is no chance of work.

Clairvoyant and psychic scams: Victims are sent communications saying that something bad will happen to them unless they pay money.

Loan scams: Victims are sent demands for debt repayment with threats if they do not pay; alternatively, scammers offer to renegotiate debts or amend adverse credit ratings associated with the non-existent loans.

Person in distress fraud: In some cases, people are targeted with a tragic story of a stranger and asked to send money. Another variation entails a person's email account being hacked and all their contacts are addressed stating they are in distress in a foreign country and require money to be wired urgently. This is often targeted at older computer users, and the fraudster purports to be a young relative in distress.

Romance scams: There are a wide variety of different romance scams, with the most common involving the victim falling in love with (usually) a fake person and being tricked into sending gifts or money for emergencies or their costs of travel to meet with them.

Share sale scams: Victims are convinced to buy worthless or overvalued shares using high pressure sales tactics. The buying of these shares increases the values of the shares, at which time the fraudsters then sell their shares. This is also called a "pump and dump" scheme.

Table 5.1b Personal Information Seeking (PIS) Frauds

Fake websites and emails: The sending of fake emails (phishing) or the creation of fake websites (spoofing). Often executed in tandem for the purpose of harvesting credentials (personal information) in order to steal the identity of the computer users (identity theft) and/or execute systemic infiltration of targets systems or accounts.

Social networking: Entails fraudsters using fake identities to befriend individuals online and then harvest any online personal data displayed or trick them into parting with the information.

Malware: Entails more technically proficient fraudsters using programs, viruses, and hacking to secure the personal information of a victim.

- *Pump and Dump Schemes*—A fraudster or group of fraudsters urges a victim to buy stocks to artificially inflate their value. They then sell the shares they own at the inflated price. The victim is left holding shares that are decreasing in value
- *Digital Piracy*—The illegal acquisition of digital, copyrighted goods
- *Cryptocurrency Fraud*—The fraudulent buying or selling of cryptocurrencies
- *NFT Fraud*—The fraudulent buying or selling of non-fungible tokens (NFTs) either on a blockchain server or "off-market" via an independent NFT platform (e.g. OpenSea)

Identity Theft

Identify theft (also called *identity fraud*) is understood as all types of crime in which someone wrongfully obtains and uses another person's personal data in some way that involves fraud or deception. Most states have identity theft laws that prohibit the misuse of another person's identifying information. Although the term identity theft is of the 21st century, the process dates back much further:

> *…identity theft is as old as the concept of identity itself. As soon as identity acquired any sort of value, someone was going to want to steal it for nefarious purposes. Someone else's identity in ancient Egypt could gain you access to the presence, and influence, of a Pharaoh. If you were transported to the colonies in the 18th century, one way of getting back to England was to steal the identity of a sailor and blag [persuade/lie] your way onto a returning ship.*

(Kirk, 2014, 449)

In 2021, roughly 51,629 people in the U.S. reported being victims of identity theft, with losses totaling approximately 279 million dollars[1]—an average loss of just over $5,400 per victim. The same year, 226,000 cases of identity fraud were reported to the U.K.'s Credit Insurance Fraud Avoidance System (CIFAS),[2] with average losses approaching nearly four billion pounds per year since 2013.[3] Estimates from Australian authorities reflect similar outcomes: 159,600 reported victims of identity theft,[4] with approximately 1.5 million total Australian dollars lost in 2020–2021 (McAlister & Franks, 2021).

While offering some understanding of how much money is lost per incident reported, each of these estimates are likely underreported given each is restricted to those who voluntarily report or have others report on their behalf. Arguably, more accurate estimates come from victim-focused data sources like the Bureau of Justice Statistics' National Crime Victimization Survey. The 2014 iteration of the survey estimated 17.6 million people were victims of identity theft.[5] This is considerably larger in comparison to variants of theft offline; within that same year, the total number of people who were victims of burglary, motor vehicle theft, and personal theft totaled 10.4 million *combined*.[6]

According to survey responses maintained by the Identity Theft Resource Center, victims suffer losses in both time and money.[7] Table 5.2 shows the most frequent actions taken by a victim of identity theft. Note the commonality of responses pertaining to loss

Table 5.2   Most Frequent Responses to the Question: Did You Do Any of the Following as a Result of Your Identity Theft Case?*

Closed existing financial accounts	33%
Use online accounts less frequently or not at all	33%
Spent time away from other life experiences, like hobbies or a vacation	33%
Closed existing online accounts	27%
Borrowed money from family/friends	26%
Took time off from work	22%
Spend time away from family	22%

*Modified from the Identity Theft Resource Center's "Identity Theft and Its Aftermath" 2017 report (www.ftc.gov/system/files/documents/public_comments/2017/10/00004-141444.pdf)

Table 5.3 Most Frequent Physical Reactions Because of Identity Theft Victimization**

Sleep Problems	92%
Stress	88%
Persistent headaches	42%
Changes in eating/drinking	36%
New unhealthy/addictive behaviors	17%
Relapse of Unhealthy/addictive behaviors	16%

**Modified from the Identity Theft Resource Center's "2022 Consumer Impact" report (www.ftc.gov/system/files/documents/public_comments/2017/10/00004-141444.pdf)*

of time. Victims also experienced damages that extended beyond financial loss. Table 5.3 shows that victims of identity theft reported stress, lack of sleep, headaches, and more.

In sum, the data presented in this section suggests that identity theft is a common type of cyberfraud with wide-ranging impacts on those who are victimized. In the next section, we discuss exactly what is "identity" in the digital environment.

Personally Identifiable Information

Humans use observation to identify a person—usually using their eyes to see physical features or mannerisms. They also use their ears to hear a person's voice, their noses to smell, and so forth. Individuals without sight may also rely on touch to identify a person. Once someone is identified, we then know how to interact with that person: To approach, to be guarded, to be friendly, etc. This happens at a subconscious level, and we are not necessarily cognizant of this process. We are only aware of the process when our senses cannot help us. For example, someone hears noises on the bottom floor of their home and call out to ask who it is. The response, or lack of one, will then determine how one should proceed.

Just as we use our senses to convey information about objects of the physical environment, computers use information—numbers, letters, dates, biometric information—to identify a person/user and then decide how to interact with that user. Generally speaking, this information is something unique to each user and consists of at least one of three types: Something you know, something you are, or something you own (see Table 5.4). In a common scenario, a person goes to a banking website and is confronted with a screen asking for identifying information—a username and a password. The response, or lack of one, will then determine for the computer (the server owned by the bank) how to proceed.

Table 5.4 Types and Examples of Personally Identifiable Information

Type of Personally Identifiable Information	Examples
Something you know	Passwords, answer questions (e.g. your mother's maiden name, the name of your favorite dog), birthdate
Something you are (biometric data)	Fingerprints, facial composition (through facial recognition software), voice (through voice recognition software), DNA
Something you own	Key, credit card, mobile phone

This identifying information is called *personally identifiable information*, or PII. The act of stealing one's identity in the digital environment is ultimately the act of stealing a victim's PII. Thus, digital identity theft victimization is commensurate with PII vulnerability; the more exposed one's PII is, the greater the risk they'll fall victim to digital identity theft and infractions resulting from such stolen data (i.e., acts of fraud).

Some examples of PII include:

- Social security number
- Alien registration number
- Numbers issued by government organizations such as a school or the military
- Birthdate
- Address
- DNA
- Eye signature (retina display)
- Fingerprints

The requirement for PII is that it can distinguish one person from another. Some PII are by design meant to be unique, such as a social security number or military identification number. Other types of PII are not as effective at distinguishing individuals. Someone's name is technically a type of PII, but two people can have the same name. Thus, it is not an effective identifier.

The more information a computer network requires for access privileges, and the more sophisticated that information is, the less likely a legitimate user have their PII stolen. Their PII is less vulnerable and prone to exploitation. Thus, some computer networks use two or more forms of identification. This is usually something you know like a password, and something you own, like your mobile phone. This *two-factor authentication* standard is the norm at ATM machines, where a person must provide something they know (a username and password) and something they own (a credit card) to gain access.

As computer processing power and algorithms become more complex, computers are beginning to use other types of PII to distinguish people. For example, the ability of computers to distinguish handwriting samples has improved to the point that handwriting is becoming an effective type of PII. Similarly, facial recognition software has become better at accurately identifying faces, and as such facial images are another developing type of PII. At the time of this writing, all new iPhones are equipped with Apple's version of facial recognition technology—Face ID—and all major known competitors to the iPhone have adopted some version of the technology.

Phishing, Vishing, Smishing, and Pharming in Cyberfraud

One of the main ways PII is stolen is through a range of fraudulent and unsolicited communication efforts known as *phishing* (e-mail-based), *vishing* (voice- or phone-based), or *smishing* (SMS or text-based). As discussed previously in Chapter 2, these techniques are a form of subterfuge typically designed to route targeted users to online content engineered to pull PII data. False websites and other web-based content engineered for the purpose of capturing PII are features of a process called *pharming*, and thus it is included under the cyberfraud category.[8] Estimates from FBI reporting in 2021 revealed an increase of 34% in complaints for these types of offenses, with a financial impact of roughly 6.9 billion in annual losses. Phishing attacks (notably, advance fee frauds) in the UK have increased nearly tenfold since 2020 (60,000 attacks in March 2020; 599,000 attacks in March 2022).[9] Reports from several other countries around the same timeframe reflect similar problems.

Japan reported approximately 49,000 pharming websites and nearly 108,000 cases of phishing attacks in just one month during 2021; 526,000 phishing cases for the full year.[10] Vishing attacks in South Korea have plagued the country in recent years, with a reported 170,000 recorded attacks between 2016 and 2020 and losses totaling over 788 trillion South Korean won (600 million in US dollars).[11] Smishing attacks in Canada have seen increases as high as 500% in just the first half year of 2023.[12] Many such reports cite specific increases resulting from frauds engineered around the fear and financial obstacles related to the COVID-19 pandemic (Al-Qahtani & Cresci, 2021; Morrison, 2022; Statistics, 2022), and with no signs of decline in the foreseeable future.

A common example of these fraud attempts is the transmission of fake emails, SMS/texts, and/or voice messages purporting to be from the victim's bank, asking the victim to either reply with information directly or click on a link. The email may use logos and wording that reminds the recipient of a prior legitimate communication from the bank. The link will then send the victim to a site that looks legitimate, but is a harvester of PII. Although high-level coding skills are not needed to execute this offense, the fraudster must know how to design such messages or websites so that it looks legitimate to the recipient, and thus effectively fools them into providing PII.

The System of Cyberfraud

One successful cyberfraud attempt can deceive thousands of people into unwittingly providing PII. As discussed in Chapter 2, these attacks are a means through which databases containing millions of customer records can be hacked. Thus, it is often the case that a successful cyberfraud attempt may produce too much PII for one fraudster to use before the company or the customers realize they have been defrauded. Additionally, the individuals with the skills to develop convincing cyberfraud communications are not always the same individuals willing or able to best use the stolen PII to steal money or information. Under these conditions, it is not uncommon for a cyberfraud system to develop where PII is stolen, sold to third parties, and then used by those third parties to steal money or information.

There are at least four roles in this system—coders, fraudsters, brokers, and buyers. Notably with phishing, a model of the relationships between these roles, modified from Konradt and colleagues (2016), is presented in Figure 5.1 (p. 92). The flow of goods moves from coders who produce the fraudulent code, to fraudsters who then deploy the code and accumulate the PII, to brokers who arrange the space for transactions, to the buyers who then purchase the PII. A well-known example of this system was the infamous Silk Road website on Tor, where buyers and sellers of a wide range of illegal goods met to complete transactions. The broker often ensured the transaction—as the money was provided by the seller before the goods were shipped—and received a small percentage of the sale for the service. The flow of cash moved in the opposite direction. The brokers received a

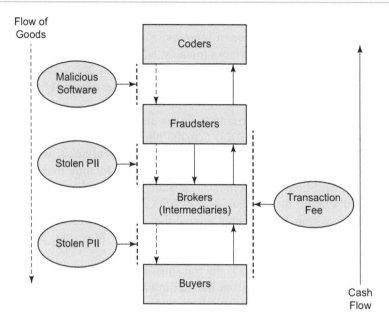

Flow of Goods

Coders

Malicious Software

Fraudsters

Stolen PII

Brokers (Intermediaries)

Transaction Fee

Stolen PII

Buyers

Cash Flow

Figure 5.1   An infographic illustrating the roles and relationships in the system of phishing fraud.

transaction fee for their services, which was a cost of business shared by both fraudster and buyer. For example, a bundle of credit card numbers may sell for $300, plus a transaction fee of 7%, or $21. This fee would be paid by the buyer; however, the fee was considered a "cost" for the fraudster as it increased the overall price of their product (the stolen PII).

Advance Fee Frauds

Advance fee frauds, a particular type of phishing attack, are scams in which a fraudster leads a victim to believe that they will receive a large payment in the future if they perform some present action. The present action is usually the sending of money, hence the label "advance fee." However, in lieu of money, fraudsters may ask for PII instead. For instance, the fraudster may ask the target to supply bank information so that they can wire a large sum of money into the target's account. The money will supposedly then be shared with the fraudster and target.

These frauds are also called *confidence frauds* as the fraudster must create a sense of confidence in the victim that the fraudster is being honest and truthful. These scams are further known as *Nigerian 419 scams*, named after the section of the legal code in Nigeria that it violates. In the early days of the Internet as public domain, English-speaking scammers from Nigeria and other African nations were notorious for sending emails to targets in Western, English-speaking locales. Over time, computer users have become more wary of these scams. Nonetheless, people are still defrauded on occasion and the location of offenders have long since expanded beyond West African countries.

Research done by Onyebadi and Park (2012) identified some common themes of advance fee fraud emails. One theme is that the emails are addressed to an unknown recipient—"Dear Sir/Madam." Onyebadi and Park argue that while this should be a red flag, this is often ignored by victims. Second, the fraudster attempts to establish credibility and engender trust in the target by sharing (false) personal information. This includes contact information such as an email, telephone, or fax number. Third, each message details a circumstance in which a large sum of money is available, but to receive this money help is needed. The money has been gained through illegal dealings, an inheritance, or someone in a troubled circumstance looking to leave the country. Another theme is that the victim is promised a large financial reward for little or no investment. Here is an example of an email provided by Onyebadi and Park (2012):

> From 'Princess Fustina karom': 'I am a female student from University of Burkina faso, Ouagadougou. I am 23 yrs old ... my father died and left I and my junior brother behind. He was a king ... He left the sum of USD 7, 350, 000.00 dollars ... I am ready to pay 20% of the total amount to you if you help us in this transaction and another 10% interest of Annual After Income to you.'

A final theme Onyebadi and Park identified is that the letters are not grammatically correct. At first glance, this would seem to be a clear indicator of the fraudulent nature of the email. However, one explanation provided by the researchers is that while the poor grammar may reveal the real handicaps in the scammer's language, it makes it possible for the victims to assume a sense of superiority: "the poor grammatical construction might be a part of the scammers' strategic deception of their potential victims, especially Europeans, into believing that they (scammers) are naive, uneducated and less intelligent folks who need supposedly wiser benefactors to help them" (Onyebadi and Park, 195).

Romance Scams

Romance scams are acts of fraud in which online profiles and/or communication streams are created and manipulated with the intent of developing a fraudulent romantic relationship with the intended victim. Note here that the creation of an online profile—even a fake one—is not explicitly illegal. While arguably an act of deviance, there are no specific criminal codes prohibiting such acts. However, the usage of such profiles in committing acts of deception or theft definitely is illegal in many countries. The relationship itself is built to extract favors from the victim, usually in the form of monetary payments. In some cases, romance scams can be developed for the purposes of convincing a victim to engage in illegal activity, as in the case of drug trafficking and Sharon Armstrong (see Table 5.5; p. 94).

THE PROCESS OF ROMANCE SCAM VICTIMIZATION

Whitty (2013) used 20 semi-structured interviews with romance scam victims to develop a model of the romance scam victimization process (see Figure 5.2; p. 95). The process begins with need or desire. The strong desire for companionship or love lowers the defenses of a potential victim. While data has been difficult to gather on the subject, most verified knowledge on romance scams suggests older females are the prime target as it is presumed their drive to acquire intimate partners in later years is especially strong. This is likely because as adults age, their romantic opportunities decrease. For women, in

Table 5.5   The Story of Sharon Armstrong

In 2010, Sharon Armstrong, a high-ranking New Zealand government official, met a man named Frank on the dating website Match.com. Over the next six months, she and Frank exchanged over 7000 emails. In 2011, Ms. Armstrong and Frank agreed to meet in London, with Frank asking Ms. Armstrong to stop over in Buenos Aires, Argentina. Ms. Armstrong was to collect some documents in a suitcase from a colleague, a woman named Esperanza.

Ms. Armstrong was arrested by customs officers in the airport. She was transporting five kilograms of cocaine with a street value of over 1 million dollars. Ms. Armstrong was sentenced to four years and ten months in prison in Argentina and was released after two and a half years.

Since her release, Ms. Armstrong has become an advocate for more awareness of online fraudsters. She has written a book describing her experiences entitled *Organised Deception: My Story*. Ms. Armstrong's experiences are not unique, as many people fall victim to romance scams in which they are defrauded of money or asked to traffic drugs for drug cartels.

Source: www.sharonarmstrong.org/

light of some compelling evidence indicating disproportionately greater pressure on them to find romantic partners and/or produce children as they get older (Alexander, 2019; Sprecher & Felmlee, 2021), romance scammers are keen to regularly exploit this audience accordingly.

After a target has been identified, the next steps involve some form of social engineering. For instance, an "ideal profile" is constructed. This profile is what the fraudster believes will attract the greatest number of victims. One of the more interesting aspects of Whitty's study is the sales techniques used by fraudsters. For example, fraudsters often test the waters via so-called "foot-in-the-door" techniques by asking the victim for small, trivial favors. If the victim complies, then favors of greater significance (e.g., larger sums of money) are requested. Fraudsters are also apt to present a crisis in which there is little time to evaluate the validity of the request. This is analogous to salespeople offering a "limited time only" or "buy in the next two hours" sales promotion. These sales techniques can be understood as social engineering.

Another aspect of note is the alternative strategy employed by scammers where they sexually abuse or exploit their victims. Victims are asked to undress or masturbate in front of a camera. This is done for the enjoyment of the fraudster, or for future blackmailing purposes (i.e., sextortion). Whitty's study also illuminates the reason why people remain in scams even when they suspect foul play or become prone to revictimization. She argues that people may be aware that the person they are communicating with is a scammer, but they are willing to play the long odds in the chance that the person is genuine. This is analogous to the person who plays the lottery knowing the odds are exponentially long they will win but is nonetheless willing to risk a dollar or so.

ROMANCE SCAMS AND THE COVID-19 PANDEMIC

In 2020, the Federal Trade Commission (FTC) reported a record high of $304 million in financial losses attributed to romance scams and related acts of fraud and theft (Singletary, 2021). The success of such scammers during this time can be attributed largely to the COVID-19 pandemic, a period of great emotional vulnerability and loneliness resulting

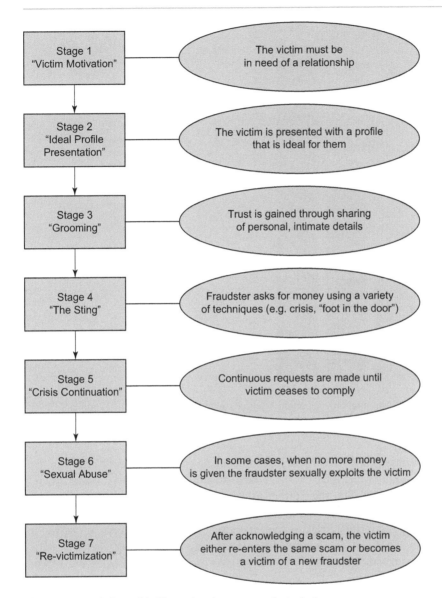

Stage 1 "Victim Motivation"	The victim must be in need of a relationship
Stage 2 "Ideal Profile Presentation"	The victim is presented with a profile that is ideal for them
Stage 3 "Grooming"	Trust is gained through sharing of personal, intimate details
Stage 4 "The Sting"	Fraudster asks for money using a variety of techniques (e.g. crisis, "foot in the door")
Stage 5 "Crisis Continuation"	Continuous requests are made until victim ceases to comply
Stage 6 "Sexual Abuse"	In some cases, when no more money is given the fraudster sexually exploits the victim
Stage 7 "Re-victimization"	After acknowledging a scam, the victim either re-enters the same scam or becomes a victim of a new fraudster

Figure 5.2   An infographic illustrating the process of a typical romance scam.

from prolonged social isolation, health-related stressors and subsequent increases in general online interactions. Along with older female audiences, romance scammers found suitable targets across a great spectrum of demographic profiles (Buil-Gil & Zeng, 2021), and particularly among the elderly (60 and older). They reported losses of $139 million from such scams (Singletary, 2021)—up almost 40% from the previous year. Bear in mind these estimates are likely even higher than what the FBI and FTC captured as such scams are among the more underreported of cybercrime offenses (FBI Houston Media Office, 2022; Parti, 2022).

The pandemic added several unique opportunities to facilitate the subterfuge necessary for romance scams to work. Among them, scammers during this time found success

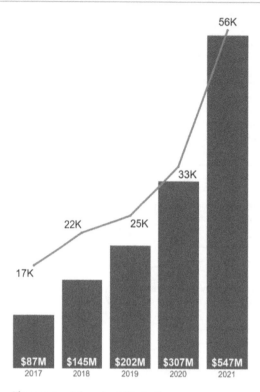

56K

33K

22K 25K

17K

| $87M | $145M | $202M | $307M | $547M |
| 2017 | 2018 | 2019 | 2020 | 2021 |

Figure 5.3 A bar chart illustrating romance scams reported to the FBI Internet Crime Complaint Center (2017–2021).

in connecting with targets who likely had lost someone or knew of someone who had lost a friend or family member due to the virus. Many scammers also found it easier to create excuses for not meeting with their target in person, such as visitation complications resulting from travel and/or health-related restrictions. Another popular scam during this time entailed forging the intimate relationship with the chosen target, then purporting to offer the target valuable financial advice such as cryptocurrency investing (an activity also experiencing upward trending during the pandemic). As of the latest estimates, such fraud was still trending high (Fletcher, 2022; Federal Bureau of Investigations, 2021; Singletary, 2021) (see Figure 5.3).

Selling of Counterfeit Goods

A long-running type of cyberfraud entails the sale of merchandise that purports to be a product of a recognized brand company (e.g., Rolex or Hermes), but is instead a copy or "knock-off." For the fraudster, the selling of counterfeit goods is attractive because of the low levels of perceived risk and potentially high profit to gains (D.S. Wall & Large, 2010). The primary victim in this fraud is usually the purchaser of the counterfeit product. They assume that they are getting an original of the same quality on discount, only to discover when the product arrives that it is of low quality and/or not produced by the brand company. However, there are occasions where the purchaser is aware that the product is a knock-off but are comfortable with the low quality (especially for clothing) if they can convince others that it is the "real deal." Another victim is the company whose products are being counterfeited. They are losing profits because customers are buying knock-offs that take advantage of the name value they have produced.

In this deception paradigm, fraudsters contact victims in at least one of three ways. First, fraudsters may have their own website. Some research suggests that websites selling fakes are often registered in China, and then hosted in Estonia, Russia, or Sweden (Wadleigh, Drew, & Moore, 2015). Interestingly, countries hosting industries often victimized in such counterfeiting schemes are less likely to host counterfeit websites targeting those industries (Wadleigh et al., 2015). For instance, fraudsters in countries like France—a fashion capital—are less likely to host online shops peddling illicit clothing items.

A second means of counterfeiting fraud is through online auction sites like eBay. Sellers can create fake accounts, or accounts not connected to their identity in the physical environment, and attempt to sell counterfeit goods through the eBay marketplace. A third way is through direct emails or spamming. Fraudsters can purchase email lists from email aggregators, and then send email blasts to targets inviting them to purchase their illicit wares online.

Heinonen and colleagues (2012) examined complaints submitted to the Internet Crime Complaint Center (IC3) for 2009 and 2010. They divided all complaints into auction fraud complaints (i.e., being defrauded on sites like eBay) and non-auction fraud complaints. Their study found that most complaints were for non-auction fraud and victims were contacted via email or through a website. Most of the fraudsters were from the US, and most of the victims were male and over 30 years old. While informative, the study is also limited. Only victims from the US and who reported incidents to IC3 were analyzed. Additionally, as with much of the cyberfraud featured in this chapter, counterfeiting of this nature is a worldwide phenomenon and many victims do not report incidents to law enforcement.

Pump and Dump Schemes

Another type of fraud is a stock manipulation scheme commonly called "pump and dump." The scheme begins with a fraudster contacting potential investors to "pump" the stock (provide false and/or incomplete information towards convincing investors of the stock's value). The investors are then conned into purchasing the stock by the misleading claims from fraudsters. The stock may be deemed the "next big thing" or "can't miss." When investors begin bidding for and buying shares of the stock, the price of the stock rises. The fraudsters then sell or "dump"their shares, netting a profit at the inflated value. This flooding of the market causes the value of the stock to fall, and often below the original purchase price.

A traditional approach to pump and dump has been to contact investors by telephone or mail. However, the digital environment has made this scheme easier to execute because fraudsters have more means in which to communicate with investors. Social media platforms such as Twitter and Facebook,as well as online forums like Reddit can be a means through which fraudsters spread false claims about a stock. They can also spam potential investors through email.

Digital Piracy

Digital piracy can be described as "the purchase of counterfeit products at a discount to the price of the copyrighted product, and illegal file sharing of copyright material over peer-to-peer computer networks" (Hill, 2007, 9). More simply, it refers to the illegal acquisition of digital, copyrighted goods. A common example of digital piracy is recording a movie playing in a heatre, and then selling "pirated" copies of the movie. The business can be profitable because, although the quality is often lower, the price of purchasing the pirated copy is a fraction of what it takes to purchase a movie ticket or a legitimate copy of the movie once it has been officially released. Before Internet usage became ubiquitous, pirated movies were often reproduced as physical copies on VHS tapes and.

Today, a modified version of this practice occurs in the digital environment, with pirates making copies of a wide range of content, and then sharing it with millions of computer users through peer-to-peer file-sharing networks. These copies are made through tested methods such as recording movies while in theaters or from heatre copies, but more sophisticated thieves can rip content from subscription services like iTunes or from live TV and on-demand services.

Digital piracy impacts at least three groups. The first group is the content producers. Content producers—the creative talent and support professionals populating mass media content industries—fund their endeavors through selling their products to targeted audiences or advertisers seeking to reach such audiences. While there is some disagreement as to how much digital piracy impacts these sales, there is no doubt that many people elect to download illegal content instead of purchasing it for full price, and the cost to content producers is significant. As far back as 2007, the Recording Industry Association of America estimates the revenue loss for US recording artists at over \$12 billion in total output (Siwek, 2007). The film and television industry, to include streaming content providers of late, show estimates more recently at roughly the same amount due to password sharing alone (Joyce, 2019).

Alongside the producers, content distributors like Netflix, Amazon, Spotify, iTunes and Hulu are also impacted by digital piracy. Initially, the core business model for these distributors was to make content available and deliver that content to paid subscribers; for most, these services are still integral to their base service offerings. However, the cost of piracy (including efforts to try and prevent it) has prompted nearly all such distributors to restructure their service and original content offerings, along with raising subscription prices and employing more rigid credential—sharing restrictions (Joyce, 2019; Kelly, 2022). Here again, there is some disagreement as to how much money content distributors lose and the true amount of piracy occurring. Nonetheless, even conservative estimates indicate many computer users do opt to listen to or watch illegal downloads instead of paying for a subscription. Some estimates allege as much as 95% of downloaded music qualifies as pirated from an original source (Dilmperi et al., 2011), and content services such as Netflix experience as much as one-third of their subscribers sharing their user credentials with non-subscribers (Hayes, 2022; Sutton, 2022).

Finally, legitimate end users are a third group impacted by pirated content distribution and consumption. Indirectly, they already face the aforementioned higher costs and increasing usage restrictions from content distributors responding to digital piracy. However, websites hosting pirated content may also allow hackers to place malware on their sites, and thus increasing the risk of a downloader having their device infected should they download the illegal content (Smith & Telang, 2018). Ransomware and "malvertising" (malware distributed through online advertisements) are an especially popular occurrence in such instances (Chaudhry, 2017).

STATISTICS ON DIGITAL PIRACY

Although piracy is illegal, it carries little stigma. Thus, enough people have willingly reported their piracy behaviors such that several studies have been done measuring the frequency of digital piracy and copyright infringement. For instance, research commissioned by the United Kingdom's Intellectual Property Office in 2022 showed that copyright theft had risen overall in every category since 2016,[13] and was holding steady at 22% of online content consumers on average across all categories tracked since 2019.[14]

Reports from Australia indicate similar rises in the accessing of pirated content, especially post-pandemic. A government-commissioned study estimated that 30% of Australian Internet users age 12 and up consumed at least one item of online content unlawfully in 2021. While this was a decrease from the previous year (34%), it still represents among the higher percentages when compared with other westernized nations.[15]

In the US, most of what we know about digital piracy at a national level comes from businesses or organizations associated with businesses. The Recording Industry Association of America (RIAA), the Motion Picture Association of America (MPAA), and the Business Software Alliance (BSA) routinely produce research showing the costs of digital piracy. These reports need to be read with some skepticism, as these groups have an incentive to produce reports highlighting increases in piracy or new domains in which piracy may take place. The RIAA website's "2023 | Piracy Impact" page reports that that the US economy loses $12.5 billion in total output because of music theft, and $422 million in tax revenues.[16] Similarly, a report from the Global Innovation Policy Center estimated that the worldwide impact of digital piracy of movies and television content on the US economy tops out at nearly $30 billion.[17]

Intellectual Property and Copyright

If someone stakes a claim to a good like a car or a mobile phone, and someone then takes that good, we can see that the good (the property) has shifted possession. The original person who claimed the property no longer has access to it. Or consider someone who has an apple, and that apple is stolen and eaten. The original owner no longer has the potential to use that product. In this sense, the ownership of cars, mobile phones, and even food is competitive in nature. If one person possesses it, no one else can. Economists call this type of good "rivalrous." For *rivalrous goods*, it is easy to identify when a property has been stolen and the original owner has been wronged.

Now consider a song, a movie, or a design that has been digitized and made available online. Or perhaps a software code or an online video game. These are not material goods, but intellectual goods. When ownership is claimed over them, they are intellectual properties. If a copy of these properties is made from the original and shared, the original

Table 5.6   Rivalrous and Non-rivalrous Goods in the Digital Environment

Layer	Description	Type of Good
Human	The ideas that have yet to be coded or digitized	Non-rivalrous
Content	The output from applications such as tweets, posts, audio, video; the digitized output of musicians, visual artists, and writers	Non-rivalrous
Application	The computer code used to produce software like Skype, Pinterest, Facebook; the logos and branding associated with these companies	Non-rivalrous
Operating system	The computer code used to link applications with hardware (e.g., Windows, Linux)	Non-rivalrous
Hardware	The machines that individuals use to enter the digital environment; the design of the machines	Rivalrous/Non-rivalrous
Infrastructure	The connections between machines; the research used to increase data speeds (e.g., fiber-optic cables, Bluetooth)	Rivalrous/Non-Rivalrous

owner still has access to the property. Moreover, the original owner can still benefit from the property, by being entertained or by selling it for a profit. Economists call this type of good *non-rivalrous*. A considerable amount of the products that make up the digital environment have the quality of non-rivalry.

Table 5.6 shows a breakdown of these types of good by layer. The infrastructure and hardware layers are a combination of rivalrous, material properties and non-rivalrous, intellectual properties. Consider the theft of an iPad. The machine itself is a material, rivalrous good. However, its design is intellectual property; it can be copied by someone else and Apple still has possession of the design. All goods above the hardware layer are non-rivalrous. All operating systems and applications are ultimately computer code which can be copied. The content and the ideas in a user's head are also intellectual properties that can be copied.

This understanding of property is important for our interests in cybercrime and digital piracy for at least two reasons. First, it helps explain why people do not see digital piracy as theft. It is easier to rationalize as someone can easily say, "Well, I just made a copy. I didn't actually take the [original] thing." This rationalization would not be available if the good was material and rivalrous. Second, it explains to some extent the ease by which people can commit acts of digital piracy. Compared with physical environments, the logistical barriers to copying and sharing property in the digital environment are low. A few clicks and one has copied a song that can be shared an infinite number of times. The economic barriers are similarly low. There is little difference in price when copying the song once as opposed to one thousand times.

In theory, the property in the digital environment is naturally a non-rivalrous good that is difficult to exclude from others. However, individuals can claim ownership over these non-material, symbolic products via copyright. At its most basic level, a copyright establishes that the holder has the exclusive right to copy, or reproduce, a work. Packard (2013) summarizes the entirety of rights given to a copyright holder:

1 To reproduce the copyrighted work in copies
2 To prepare derivative works based upon the copyright
3 To distribute copies of the work for sale, or transfer ownership of copyright
4 To perform the work publicly
5 To display the work publicly
6 To perform the work by means of digital audio transmission

Copyright infringement, then, is the using of a copyrighted work in one of these six ways without either being the owner of a copyright or getting permission from the copyright owner.

Why So Much Stealing?

To address the matter of why cybertheft has become so prevalent, consider what we know today of consumption. The rise of post-industrialism at the turn of the century saw exponential growths in consumption across most corners of civilization. The digital data landscape is no exception, as illustrated by the commensurate and rapid adjustments in everyday technology to accommodate our vastly changing data and content access demands (the so-called "Internet of Things"; see Chapter 1). Accordingly, so too has risen the attraction for prospective thieves to capitalize on these trends by way of illegal acquisition and distribution of said content. Thus, the stealing of copyrighted content has become widespread and pervasive.

Why so much of it though? What distinguishes digital piracy that might account for the frequency at which it occurs and is projected to for the foreseeable future? One premise worth consideration is that it can be hard for someone who is illegally acquiring and/or sharing files to link their actions to a clearly identifiable victim. Movies, music, and other symbolic products are almost always collaborative efforts, and thus the notion that a single person—the lead actor/actress in the movie, for example—is hurt by piracy can seem implausible to the one pirating. Even when one person can be identified as a clear victim, such as a solo musician, the pirate often rationalizes that the victim is wealthy or famous and the theft of one song does them no significant harm. Smallridge and Roberts (2013) argue that, in addition to traditional techniques, digital pirates have developed piracy-specific tactics. One example identified was "DRM defiance," where digital pirates rationalized their behavior by arguing that they were protesting the digital rights management code that prevents the copying or sharing of music.

In interviews with college students, Moore and McMullan (2009) demonstrated how at least one technique—neutralization[18]—was employed to legitimize the piracy behavior and deny injury:

Artists will benefit from file sharing because my friends and I download music from the file sharing program and then we go out and purchase the CD. I listen to artists' songs off of the file sharing program and then I get more excited about seeing them perform live. I read somewhere that musicians make their money off concerts, so I think file sharing is actually helping the artists.

(Moore & McMullan, 446)

Cryptocurrency and Fraud

In 2009, someone calling themselves "Satoshi Nakamoto" submitted the following message on the codesharing platform, SourceForge: "Announcing the first release of Bitcoin, a new electronic cash system that uses a peer-to-peer network to prevent double-spending. It's completely decentralized with no server or central authority." Nakamoto's invention allowed people to use entries into a database as a medium of exchange. The program made by Nakamoto, *Bitcoin*, quickly became the most well-known cryptocurrency in the world, and simultaneously helped advance global assimilation of the cryptocurrency concept. Today, thousands of cryptocurrencies like Ethereum, Litecoin, and Peercoin join Bitcoin in redefining the nature and function of financial transactions.

UNDERSTANDING CRYPTOCURRENCIES

Essentially, *cryptocurrencies* are entries in a computer database. The database is a computer application that generates a set amount of currency that can then be shared and exchanged amongst everyone who has downloaded the software (or who uses a third party to help them manage the software). The currency, although nothing more than bits of code in a computer, can be used as a medium of exchange because it has nearly all the same qualities as traditional, non-digital forms of money: They are in limited supply, the software prevents people from exchanging the same units twice, the currency is divisible into smaller units (e.g., a person with one bitcoin can exchange to 0.5 bitcoin), and a system of exchange of goods and/or services can be developed around the currency that is consistent and easily interpreted across different actors in the exchange.

We can show how cryptocurrencies are digitized versions of traditional currency by giving an example of one proposed use—aiding transactions in cash-deprived communities:

- Imagine a farmer, John, is ready to harvest his crop. He needs someone to help him harvest before the first frost.
- Another farmer, Ken, has some ability in harvesting this particular crop and purchased newer harvesting equipment recently. Thus, he is willing to provide his services for a fee.
- Notably, both John and Ken live in a remote, rural community that has fallen on harsh economic times. Large businesses are not keen to invest much in their community and financial institutions have been pulling investment out of the community in recent years. Thus, traditional banking outlets are quite limited.
- As an alternative to a traditional cash or credit transaction, John offers Ken 0.30 *smartcoin* (created for the purpose of this example; a type of cryptocurrency structured specifically for farmers) for a day's work. Ken knows about smartcoin and knows that he can take what John is offering and exchange it later for groceries and supplies at the local market later. This is because the market has adopted both cash-based and cashless payment options, and additionally carries software that supports the purchase and trading of smartcoin.
- There is some negotiation as Ken argues that he is better and faster than others at this job; he asks for 0.50 smartcoin instead. They agree on the price.

- After five days of work, John transfers 2.50 smartcoin (5 × .50) to Ken's smartcoin account via his mobile phone.
- Ken then goes to the market and uses his mobile phone to purchase 1.25 smartcoin worth of groceries and supplies, and saves the rest.

Such transactions are possible because digital currencies can work in environments without established financial institutions or stable governments. Citizens in low-income areas may have Internet access, but limited access to traditional hard currency and/or lack trust in conventional banks. In these contexts, digital currencies can be used to exchange goods and services. Though digital currencies do suffer from lack of regulation, and thus comparatively limited formal protection against theft and fraud activity, they are ideal for those concerned with avoiding the cybersecurity threats plaguing formal banks.

FRAUD AND CRYPTOCURRENCIES

Cryptocurrencies and their markets are especially susceptible to fraud. This is largely due to the decentralized nature of cryptocurrencies, along with widespread ignorance about the presence and function of such currencies. The technology underpinning cryptocurrencies is complicated and still unfamiliar to a great number of people. Even individuals with an advanced knowledge of computer technology or economics can misinterpret how these markets work. Moreover, the decentralized nature and lack of regulation characterizing cryptocurrency markets that make them attractive to so many patrons and investors also make them ideal settings for prospective thieves and fraudsters. The fact that a central body is not organizing and regulating who can buy or sell, and a governmental authority cannot legitimate one currency over another, creates more opportunities for advancing deception.

Many cryptocurrencies are introduced to the market with much fanfare during their Initial Coin Offering (ICO). However, after individuals invest in the cryptocurrency by purchasing the currency with legitimate money (dollars, yen, etc.), various forms of deception and/or theft can take shape. A few examples include:

- *Prodeum* purported to be a "blockchain for fruits and vegetables," and consumers could tell where their produce had originated. Environmentalists and green enthusiasts were interested in investing in the technology. After raising only $11, the company vanished. The scammers had used the identities of reputable personalities in the technology industry to legitimate their businesses
- *Confido* had billed itself as being able to guarantee contracts between buyer and seller without the need for an escrow account. In what can be called an "exit scam," the startup disappeared after raising $375,000 from investors
- *Centra Tech* claimed to provide a Mastercard and Visa debit card service that could instantly convert cryptocurrencies to cash. Buoyed by endorsements from celebrities such as the boxer Floyd Mayweather, Jr., the company raised $32 million. However, the company misrepresented themselves to the public and was brought up on charges. Stephanie Avakian, co-director of the SEC's enforcement division said in a statement: "We allege that Centra sold investors on the promise of new digital technologies by using a sophisticated marketing campaign to spin a web of lies about their supposed partnerships with legitimate businesses"

A recent trend in this corner of the cyberfraud landscape is the emergence of various "pump groups." This variation on the pump-and-dump scheme takes advantage of the lack of regulation and the trendiness of cryptocurrencies. Pump groups form in online chat rooms or discussion boards. Group leaders instruct the group when to buy a certain cryptocurrency. The intensity of transactions drives up the price of the cryptocurrency and becomes noticed by investors outside the group. Savvy scammers then pick the appropriate time to sell their currencies at the inflated price.

NFTs and NFT Fraud

Non-fungible tokens, or "NFTs," are essentially digital tags of ownership. Conceptually, owning an NFT is analogous to owning the item that the NFT is connected to. That is to say, when one purchases an NFT, they are actually purchasing the exclusive rights to the asset the NFT represents. Those assets, for example, could be any number of digital creative properties such as digital art, music, literature, and video content. Exclusivity and collectability are key elements with NFTs; such tokens are intended to establish ownership and origin of value for digital content that is deemed worth of acquiring and exists in such a manner that makes it dissimilar from anything else.

The creation and development of value for an NFT is accomplished through a process known as *minting* (encoding a piece of digital content to an NFT, making it available to authorized entities via some secured means of data storage and transfer, and then subsequently "announcing" it on a blockchain server) that formally establishes the NFT as a unique item of finite supply available for acquisition. Quite the opposite of cryptocurrencies like Bitcoin, where one digital unit of currency (e.g., one bitcoin) holds the same value and is interchangeable with an equivalent unit of value on the blockchain, the values between one NFT and another are inherently distinct since they are connected to assets deemed "one-of-a-kind" in value. For instance, NBA Top Shot[19] is a category of NFTs licensed under the National Basketball Association and traded on the Dapper Lab's *Flow* blockchain. Top Shot NFTs are exclusively traded and managed on Flow, and consists of a video clip of some player and a highlight deemed valuable to NBA fans and/or communities that follow NBA fandom (e.g., a game-winning shot by Lebron James in the last game of the NBA Finals). Somewhat similar to sports trading cards, but with video digital content rather than static photos and player details printed on cardstock, Top Shot NFTs derive their transaction prices from value estimations based upon the perceived value of the player featured, the significance of the "moment" they are shown performing, the number of such NFTs minted, and the date when the minting occurred. Notably, higher values are generally assigned to NFTs either lower in volume (thus, rarer to acquire) or carrying a lower "mintage" number (thus indicating it was created earlier than other NFTs in a series). All of these factors dictate the NFTs demand, purchase price, and subsequent resale value on the blockchain.

With some estimates indicating as many as nine million Americans have bought or sold an NFT in 2022 (Vigderman, 2023), the NFT market nonetheless is a foreign concept to many. However, the perceived stability of blockchains like Flow, the security stemming from affiliations with high-profile brands like the NBA, and the growing involvement of known celebrities in either funding or lending their names to NFT minting projects has made NFTs like Top Shot an attractive investment target for prospective owners and sellers alike. Increasingly, NFTs are also gaining expanded utility as a means of identifying and managing ownership of non-digital assets such as real estate and traditional forms of

Victim/target⇨ Main element of the victimization strategy	Creators/owners of NFTs or the actual assets that NFTs represent	Consumers/buyers of NFTs or investors in NFT projects
Technology attacks, such as malware and hacking (mostly in combination with social engineering)	Cell 1 • Attacks targeting digital wallets of NFT creators/owners	Cell 2 • Exploiting security flaws in NFT platforms • Giveaway scams
Purely social engineering and other nontechnological attacks	Cell 3 • Creating fake NFT customer service pages to lure NFT creators/owners • Creating and selling NFTs without the knowledge and consent of the owner of the actual assets that NFTs represent • Tricking artists into paying to mint NFTs of their assets	Cell 4 • Investment scams • Tricking consumers into buying fake NFTs

Figure 5.4 A table illustrating types of NFT scams.

art like sculptures and paintings, where the NFT is used in place of the traditional contract paperwork associated with the transaction of tangible property.

Unfortunately, this also means NFTs have garnered a fair amount of attention from prospective fraudsters seeking to cash in via the market's volatility and general lack of knowledge and/or experience so many have with these commodities. Cyberfraud via NFTs can happen in a number of ways, as Kshetri (2022) illustrated in his summary of the fraud activity common in NFT markets (see Figure 5.4).

Prospective thieves have taken to setting up compromised, counterfeit, or missing content to link with seemingly legitimate NFTs. Some have created NFTs embedded with malware (e.g., ransomware) such that the user's system is compromised once a purchase is authorized. Phishing and related attacks have been facilitated through NFT notifications. NFT fraudsters have been known to generate fraudulent NFTs around stolen content by misrepresenting themselves as legitimate artists—either passing another artist's work off as their own or provide legitimate content under the pretence that the actual artist has authorized the NFT minting. This is especially effective given that neither artist nor buyer ever have to see each other in an NFT exchange. Additionally, aside from the NFT code, blockchain record, and reputation of the minter, there is not much else to verify the authenticity of a piece of content associated with an NFT. In fact, even when those variables are legitimate, the content linked to the NFT could still be fraudulent.

NFT fraud activity is further sparked by the instability of the platforms where they are often traded. Notably, online marketplaces like OpenSea,[20] which allows for NFT minting and distribution without writing to a blockchain, have not as of this date become proactive enough to prevent fraudsters from posting illegitimate NFTs—let alone compensating artists when their work has been so compromised through such fraud. In fact, for most instances, artists themselves must pursue the removal of the fraudulent digital content when detected, and copyright infringement detection techniques on said platforms have yet to match the complexity or volume of NFT fraud efforts.

Conclusion

In this chapter we explored cyberfraud. In the post-industrial reality of the moment, most individuals possess an identity online that can be stolen. Similarly, almost everyone shops, banks, or pays their bills online, and is thus susceptible to auction fraud, counterfeit fraud, and so on. Even in cases where people are vigilant in protecting their identities and are aware of the latest phishing attacks, they may still be susceptible to emotion-based scams such as romance scams and advance fee fraud. Thus, cyberfraud is a category of cyber-crime in which a wide swath of people are potential victims—perhaps more so than cyber-trespass, cyberpornography, or cyberviolence.

CHAPTER 5 CURRENT EVENTS AND CRITICAL THINKING:

The GameStop/Meme-Stock Trading Scandal (Pump-and-Dump 2.0?)[21]

Throughout the beginning of 2021, and particularly January 4th to January 29th, the electronics gaming retailer, GameStop, saw its company stock skyrocket from approximately $17 per share to a high of nearly $500 per share before transactions were halted on various trading platforms. This event was largely prompted by a wave of trading and speculation about the company transpiring amongst investors and other participants on the popular Reddit forum, *r/WallStreetBets* (or *r/WSB*). Trending of GameStop's shares was further facilitated via free online trading apps (e.g., *Robinhood*) that allow for much higher volumes of commission-free trading by private (and in many cases, novice) investors. The unprecedented stock performance sparked by the sharing of news, memes, anecdotes, and stock tips on r/WSB favorable to the perception of GameStop as viable investment fell in stark contrast to the anticipation amongst large hedge fund institutions that GameStop shares would continue falling, or at best hold steady at its previous sub-$20 trading mark from the latter end of the previous year. Notably, as hedge funds saw GameStop as a failing company, many such funds were positioned to "short sale"[22] the company's stock. Thus, the sudden increase in trading activity forced such funds to prematurely re-acquire, and then immediately release the very same purchased shares back to their original owners (a feature of the short selling strategy)—all at massive losses for these funds.

As with many Reddit subgroups, r/WSB was and still is an open social media community. Comprised mostly of individual investors operating outside of the multi-billion-dollar hedge fund community, r/WSB had rapidly grown in user base and influence in the recent years leading up to 2021, and especially during the height of the 2020 pandemic. Its unprecedented influence in inflating the value of GameStop stock led to several significant outcomes:

1. *Some investors made significant profit by cashing out their shares early while the stock was rising in value. One such investor, known by the handle "DeepF**kingValue" on the r/WSB forum, and believed to be the investor that started the initial run on GameStop shares, reportedly cashed out at over four million dollars.*
2. *Trading apps like Robinhood were forced to halt the purchases for GameStop on January 28th after the price went so high as to exceed the company's cash-on-hand necessary as collateral to cover all the transactions.[23]*
3. *Those who did not cash out sooner were left holding large volumes of the stock worth substantially less than what they paid after the market leveled back down to prices more in line with GameStop's true capital value. Thus, many individual investors saw average losses in the thousands.*
4. *The hedge fund community experienced much greater profit losses—literally, billions. A now-infamous example, Melvin Capital Management, lost seven billion in total value throughout the period of trading frenzy.*

A heavily debated subject since these events concerns whether the r/WSB community's actions were a form of cyberfraud (specifically, pump-and-dump). Central to the argument is speculation concerning whether r/WSB members: a) intentionally sought to initiate a wave of major financial losses for hedge funds betting against GameStop's economic viability by driving them to abandon their shorting strategy of the company's shares, or b) genuinely believed GameStop was undervalued and took to social media to voice their "love" for the company, as well as exercise their right to purchase and trade said shares within the rules governing securities exchanges, and all with the hopes of reversing the company's financial outlook. Additionally, it should be noted that despite the various speculations of collusion amongst r/WSB members at the time, no actual evidence has been found that the community was being deceptive or willfully manipulative in their trading activity. Reddit, and subreddits within it like r/WSB, are considered open platforms, and there is no US law against a group of investors taking the same position on a certain stock. Nonetheless, concerns over the community's intentions (for at least some of its members) and the tumultuous stock activity occurring throughout January 2021 remain in light of the many losses suffered by both large- and small-scale investors alike. Clearly, based on these losses at least, some harm was done.

Was the r/WSB subreddit engaging in a digital version of the pump-and-dump scheme? Consider here that the purported (albeit it, again, speculative) intent of some members, revealed during and after the events that unfolded, indicate some collective effort to "stick it to the man"—the man, in this case, being the numerous hedge funds betting on GameStop's downfall by shorting its stock—by artificially pumping the stock solely to force hedge funds to prematurely buy back the shorted stocks at a loss. And all with little-to-no regard for the company's actual business prospects or true capital. Relatedly, can blame for the numerous financial losses be fairly placed on r/WSB or any of its member for merely speculating contrarily with what hedge funds were predicting? What evidence would be needed to conclusively prove some effort to engage in pump-and-dump?

Finally, agree or disagree: The practice of shorting stocks carries the inherent risk that the shorted stock will suddenly jump in value. Thus, hedge funds and other financial institutions that initially shorted the GameStop stock were already assuming the risk that they would lose money if/when the stock suddenly jumped in value. Accordingly, they carry the blame for their losses as a risk of doing business. *For whichever side you argue, provide some justification.*

NOTES

1 Federal Bureau of Investigations Internet Crime Report (2021)
2 https://cybercrew.uk/blog/id-theft-statistics-uk/
3 https://www.cityam.com/identity-theft-driven-data-breaches-costing-brits-close-to-4bn-a-year/
4 https://www.abs.gov.au/statistics/people/crime-and-justice/personal-fraud/latest-release
5 www.bjs.gov/content/pub/press/vit14pr.cfm
6 www.bjs.gov/content/pub/pdf/cv14.pdf
7 www.idtheftcenter.org/
8 www.ic3.gov/Media/PDF/AnnualReport/2021_IC3Report.pdf
9 https://techmonitor.ai/technology/cybersecurity/phishing-attacks-uk
10 https://blog.knowbe4.com/the-number-of-phishing-attack-cases-in-japan-hit-an-all-time-high
11 https://research.checkpoint.com/2023/south-korean-android-banking-menace-fakecalls/

12 https://siliconangle.com/2023/06/21/ups-canada-discloses-data-breach-following-smishing-campaign/; https://www.nsnews.com/highlights/a-tsunami-of-cellphone-scams-is-hitting-canadians-7303370

13 https://www.gov.uk/government/publications/online-copyright-infringement-tracker-survey-12th-wave/executive-summary-online-copyright-infringement-tracker-survey-12th-wave

14 The UK Intellectual Property Office changed the methodology for how infringement was recorded beginning with the 2019 wave of the survey.

15 https://www.infrastructure.gov.au/sites/default/files/documents/consumer-survey-on-online-copyright-infringement-2021-report.pdf

16 https://www.riaa.com/reports/the-true-cost-of-sound-recording-piracy-to-the-u-s-economy/

17 https://www.theglobalipcenter.com/report/digital-video-piracy/

18 For more insight on neutralization, see Chapter 10 – —Cybercriminology.

19 https://nbatopshot.com/

20 https://opensea.io/

21 For the sake of simplicity of this exercise, the reader is asked to consider the events surrounding the stock activity of GameStop at the forefront of the meme-stock trading controversy in 2021. However, we recognize the stocks of several other companies embroiled within the same controversy on meme-stock trading during the same period (e.g., AMC Theatres, the Dogecoin cryptocurrency, Blackberry Limited).

22 Short selling is a practice wherein an investor (short-seller) borrows shares and immediately sells them with the hope of buying them back later at a lower price (called *"covering"*). Once repurchased, the borrowed shares (plus interest) are returned to the initial lender and the short-seller profits from the difference. Notably, short selling is especially prone to sudden price jumps. When this occurs, short-sellers are often forced to prematurely buy back the borrowed stock they sold in order to keep their losses from mounting. This usually results in significant lost earnings for the short-seller—especially if the stock's price continues to jump during the period when the short seller is attempting to re-purchase and give back the borrowed shares.

23 https://www.texasmonthly.com/arts-entertainment/what-everyone-got-wrong-about-gamestop-reddit-robinhood/

REFERENCES

Al-Qahtani, A. F., & Cresci, S. (2021). The COVID-19 scamdemic: A survey of phishing attacks and their countermeasures during COVID-19. *IET Information Security*, 16, 22.

Alexander, E. (2019). Why we need to stop making women over 30 feel pressured to have children. *Harper's Bazaar.* https://www.harpersbazaar.com/uk/culture/a28635150/why-we-need-to-stop-pressuring-women-over-30-to-have-children/

Buil-Gil, D., & Zeng, Y. (2021). . Meeting you was a fake: Investigating the increase in romance fraud during COVID-19*Journal of Financial Crime*, 29(2), 15.

Button, M., Nicholls, C. M., Kerr, J., & Owen, R. (2015). Online fraud victims in England and Wales: Victims' views on sentencing and the opportunity for restorative justice? *The Howard Journal of Criminal Justice*, 54(2), 193–211. doi:10.1111/hojo.12123

Chaudhry, P. E. (2017). The looming shadow of illicit trade on the Internet. *Business Horizons*, 60(1), 12.

Dilmperi, A., King, T., & Dennis, C. (2011). Pirates of the web: The curse of illegal downloading. *Journal of Retailing and Consumer Services*, 18(2), 8.

Fletcher, E. (2022). *Consumer protection data spotlight: FTC reporting back to you* https://www.ftc.gov/news-events/data-visualizations/data-spotlight/2022

Hayes, D. (2022). One-third of U.S. Netflix subscribers share their passwords, survey finds. *Deadline.*

Heinonen, J. A., Holt, T. J., & Wilson, J. M. (2012). Product counterfeits in the online environment: An empirical assessment of victimization and reporting characteristics. *International Criminal Justice Review, 22*(4), 353–371. doi:10.1177/1057567712465755

Hill, C. W. L. (2007). Digital piracy: Causes, consequences, and strategic responses. *Asia Pacific Journal of Management, 24*(1), 9–25. doi:10.1007/s10490-006-9025-0

Investigations, Federal Bureau of. (2021). Internet Crime Report.

Joyce, K. (2019). Streaming companies to see $12.5B in lost revenue by 2024 due to piracy, password sharing: Report. Technology. . https://www.foxbusiness.com/technology/streaming-piracy-password -sharing-lost-revenue-study

Kelly, H. (2022, June 22, 2022). Streamers worry the end is coming for lax password-sharing rules. *The Washington Post.* https://www.washingtonpost.com/technology/2022/06/22/streaming-password-sharing/

Kirk, D. (2014). Identifying identity theft. *The Journal of Criminal Law, 78*(6), 448–450. doi:10.1177/ 0022018314557418

Konradt, C., Schilling, A., & Werners, B. (2016). Phishing: An economic analysis of cybercrime perpetrators. *Computers & Security, 58*, 39–46. doi:10.1016/j.cose.2015.12.001

Kshetri, N. (2022). Scams, frauds, and crimes in the nonfungible token market. *Computing's Economics, 5*.

McAlister, M., & Franks, C. (2021). Identity crime and misuse in Australia: Results of the 2021 online survey (*Statistical Bulletin*, Issue. Australian Institute of Criminology.

Moore, R., & McMullan, E. C. (2009). Neutralizations and rationalizations of digital piracy: A qualitative analysis of university students. *International Journal of Cyber Criminology, 3*(1), 441–451.

Morrison, R. (2022). UK phishing attacks targeting cost of living crisis on the rise. https://techmonitor.ai/ technology/cybersecurity/phishing-attacks-uk

Office, FBI Houston Media. (2022). *$1 billion in losses reported by victims of romance scams.* https://www.fbi .gov/contact-us/field-offices/houston/news/press-releases/1-billion-in-losses-reported-by-victims-of -romance-scams

Onyebadi, U., & Park, J. (2012). 'I'm Sister Maria. Please help me': A lexical study of 4-1-9 international advance fee fraud email communications. *International Communication Gazette, 74*(2), 181–199. doi:10.1177/1748048511432602

Packard, A. (2013). *Digital media law* (2nd edition). Wiley-Blackwell.

Parti, K. (2022). "Elder scam" risk profiles: Individual and situational factors of younger and older age groups' fraud victimization. *International Journal of Cybersecurity Intelligence and Cybercrime, 5*(3), 20.

Singletary, M. (2021). Romance scams cost consumers a record $304 million as more people searched for love online during the pandemic. *The Washington Post, 3.* https://www.washingtonpost.com/business /2021/10/19/dating-apps-rom

Siwek, S. E. (2007). *The True Cost of Sound Recording Piracy to the U.S. Economy* (Policy Report #188).

Smallridge, J. L., & Roberts, J. R. (2013). Crime specific neutralizations: An empirical examination of four types of digital piracy. *International Journal of Cyber Criminology, 7*(2), 125–140.

Smith, M. D., & Telang, R. (2018). Piracy and malware: There's no free lunch. https://techpolicyinstitute.org /publications/privacy-and-security/piracy-and-malware-theres-no-free-lunch/

Sprecher, S., & Felmlee, D. (2021). Social network pressure on women and men to enter a romantic relationship and fear of being single. *Interpersona: An International Journal on Personal Relationships, 15*(2), 16.

Statistics, Office of National. (2022). Phishing attacks – who is most at risk? https://www.ons.gov.uk/peo pleopulationandcommunity/crimeandjustice/articles/phishingattackswhoismostatrisk/2022-09-26

Sutton, K. (2022). A crackdown on streaming service password-sharing is coming. *Morning Brew.* https:// www.morningbrew.com/series/streaming/stories/2022/05/03/a-crackdown-on-streaming-service -password-sharing-is-coming

Vigderman, A. (2023). *2022 NFT Awareness and Adoption Report.* https://www.security.org/digital-security /nft-market-analysis/

Wadleigh, J., Drew, J., & Moore, T. (2015). *The E-commerce market for "lemons": Identification and analysis of websites selling counterfeit goods* (pp. 1188–1197). ACM Press. doi:10.1145/2736277.2741658

Wall, D. (Ed.). (2001). *Crime and the Internet*. Routledge.

Wall, D. S., & Large, J. (2010). Jailhouse frocks: Locating the public interest in policing counterfeit luxury fashion goods. *British Journal of Criminology, 50*(6), 1094–1116. doi:10.1093/bjc/azq048

Whitty, M. T. (2013). The scammers persuasive techniques model: Development of a stage model to explain the online dating romance scam. *British Journal of Criminology, 53*(4), 665–684. doi:10.1093/bjc/azt009

Chapter 6

Policing the Digital Experience

Introduction

In this chapter, we discuss the police work associated with cybercrime, and three broad areas of cybercrime investigations are highlighted. While not exhaustive, these areas encompass the most common points of discussion concerning how formal law enforcement entities and their affiliates address cybercrime investigations. First, we discuss the practice and process of digital forensic analysis. Of the three areas discussed in this chapter, *digital forensics* may be the most well-known (and possibly least understood). Many television shows and movies show law enforcement personnel collecting a computer and handing it to a brainy officer in a computer lab who extracts the evidence needed to apprehend the criminal. However, actual cybercrime investigations and the broader effort of policing digital experiences for computer users are a far cry from this depiction.

Second, investigators also collect data in the form of text, audio, and video that a suspect or victim has left behind—what we describe as "the human presence." We refer to this as *investigating data trails*. This mode of investigating relies on the ability of the officer to understand how people use applications in the application layer (see Chapter 1). The third area, *online undercover investigations*, can be considered a 21st-century version of the classic police stakeout. However, rather than using elaborate disguises, hiding in unmarked vehicles, or perching in inconspicuous buildings, investigators follow a suspect online where they attempt to collect evidence on that suspect. This is often accomplished through subterfuge and impersonation. All three areas require a high level of awareness and knowledge of the technologies that produce the digital environment.

Digital Forensics

Forensic science is the application of science and scientific principles to criminal investigations and law. Popular television shows like *CSI: Crime Scene Investigation* and

DOI: 10.4324/9781003283256-6

Law & Order consistently depict elements of forensic science in a dramatic fashion. For example, the characters in the program may use and show the viewers high-speed ballistics photography to understand what weapon and type of bullet was used to create a bullet wound. The characters may also use DNA profiling to identify a criminal or victim, and often to exonerate someone falsely accused or crack a previously unsolved "cold" case. Digital forensics is a specialization within this larger category, where the techniques focus on digitized evidence. It is the science of identifying, preserving, verifying, and analyzing digital evidence located on computer storage media and presenting this evidence in a court of law or to a client (Crain, Hopwood, Pacini, & Young, 2017; Furneaux, 2006; Holt, Bossler, & Seigfried-Spellar, 2015).

All data on a computer, including text, video, and audio, is stored as binary numbers. For example, the word "Monarch" would be stored as 01001101 01101111 01101110 01100001 01110010 01100011 01101000. Binary notation is cumbersome to display, so most forensic software converts binary notation into hexadecimal notation. And so, "Monarch" would be displayed in hexadecimal notation as 4D6F6E61726368. A full discussion of binary and hexadecimal number systems is beyond the purview of this text. However, readers may use any number of online resources to learn more. One such resource is the Binary Hex Converter (www.binaryhexconverter.com/).

Digital forensic specialists may need to analyze files at this granular level for several reasons. For instance, they may be able to recover data by piecing together file fragments from a block of deleted data. This process, called *file carving*, allows for the recovery of data if it has been deleted, but not yet overwritten by the operating system. A forensic analysis can find such files and "carve" them out for evidence. Another reason for analyzing files at the hexadecimal level is to explore hidden contents of a file. As we discussed in Chapter 2 on cybertrespass, there are types of malware that can be embedded in files such as word documents or audio recordings. These documents may appear to be running normally—when infected by a Trojan, for example—but an analysis at the hexadecimal level will show that the malware is present.

There are many types of forensic software that will automate most of the activities necessary for a digital forensic analysis. They are designed to extract the metadata of a file—the date it was created, modified, and accessed. Such software will also detect and recover files that have been deleted or sift through a collection of files for important keywords. While forensic software can make these tasks easier, the investigator will still need to have the requisite training and experience to judge the relevance of the data extracted to a case.

Although one might think of digital forensics as applying primarily to more technologically advanced cases such as hacking or phishing, the reality is most crimes in the 21st century involve computers or digital content in some way. Computer technology and digitized data are found represented by an ever-wider array of devices. Thus, potential evidence in a case can be found on voice-controlled smart speakers such as Amazon's Echo and Google Home, wearable technologies like Fitbit and Apple watches, and everyday appliances such as televisions and coffeemakers. Nowadays, even commonplace police activities like tracking a suspect's previous whereabouts or the last known location of a missing person often entails "pinging" mobile telecommunications towers to triangulate location estimates from a device the individual has or had on them at a certain time. The ubiquity of digital technology today makes this a very effective technique for such police work.

The Process of Digital Forensics

There are five main steps in the process of digital forensics. While the steps are thought of as sequential, there are often instances in policing procedure of circling back to previous steps (see Figure 6.1) in the process.

1   Identifying evidence—When law enforcement personnel (LEP) arrive on a scene with computer-enabled devices, they must decide what machines to collect. In the simplest sense, all data on a machine is considered an *artifact*—data left after the use of a computer. Not all artifacts have evidentiary value, and LEP on the scene (whenever possible, a dedicated analyst or officer with cybercrime training) must make a judgment as to what artifacts they must collect and invest resources in analyzing.

2   Preserving evidence—In this step, the appropriate evidence is preserved by making a *forensic copy* (also called a forensic image) of the original device where the evidence resides (e.g., a hard drive). A forensic copy is a bit-by-bit copy of the entire hard drive of a device. This is different from more common processes like copying the contents from a thumb drive to a desktop. A forensic copy also contains the drive space that has not been used or has been used but is now ready to be overwritten (i.e., files that have been deleted by the user). It contains all the files and stored data including passwords, applications, user preferences, and log-in files. Often, several forensic copies are made. Then, they and original devices are stored.

Storage of the original devices and forensic copies is an important aspect in the chain of evidence handling and processing in digital forensics. Data and devices

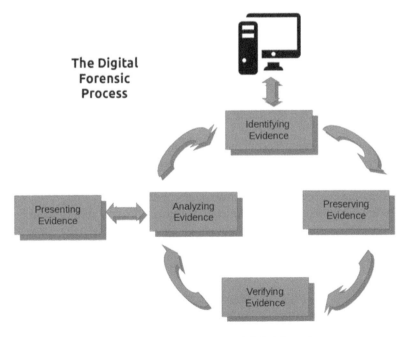

Figure 6.1   An infographic illustrating process of digital forensics.

can be corrupted, stolen, misplaced, or in some other way rendered unusable in the latter stages of the forensic process. For this reason, the devices and copies are kept in a "clean room" whenever possible. *Clean rooms* are separate facilities or spaces within larger facilities dedicated to the storage of sensitive documents or devices. Access to such places is restricted to essential personnel (i.e., the LEPs working the case), are typically heavily monitored, and have several measures in place to control the environment from elements that could cause irreparable damage to digital evidence (e.g., dust/dirt, magnetic devices, extreme fluctuations in temperature, physical mishandling). Additional measures might be taken within these spaces to protect these devices, including multi-layer encryption of storage units housing the devices and the use of RF-signal blocking apparatuses (e.g., Faraday bags and cases).

3 Verifying evidence—Once a forensic copy is made, investigators must verify that the forensic copy is the exact same as the original copy. This is done through a process called hashing. A *hash* is a unique numerical identifier produced by applying a hashing algorithm to a set of data (Konheim, 2010; McKenzie, Harries, & Bell, 1990). The data can be a single file or an entire hard drive. The common algorithms used are MD5 (Message Digest 5) and SHA256 (Secure Hash Algorithm 256). The value of hashing is in the fact that it is practically impossible for any two files to have the same hash, and virtually every piece of data that can be digitized can have a hash value appended. Thus, investigators can produce a hash of the original evidence and then a hash of the copy; if the hashes are the same, the investigators can conclude that their forensic copy is the same as the original.

   Additionally, as with DNA evidence in the tracking of biological connections between humans and trace remains of dead bodies, investigators can use such hash values to identify the origins of a particular piece of digital content and its distribution history across one or more web-based or hardware destinations. Various tools can give investigators a sense of what a hash looks like and (if available) where it has been. They can then work on the copy and present the evidence confidently to a court or a client. For instance, using the website FileFormat.Info,[1] and inputting the text, "Cybercriminology is for the cool kids" (without the quotations) will produce an MD5 hash of "052479b2a7695b330406bef1a8fe6ee9" and an SHA256 hash of "509d4a94e901534ae649258a6abd22ea36744032b9eedc10e1 c952078c333770."

4 Analyzing evidence—The analysis of evidence requires understanding both digital technology and criminal behavior. For example, an investigator may discover a file with an altered extension, such as a file originally entitled "interesting.jpg" now modified to "interesting.doc." The investigator will be able to recognize this by looking at the file at the hexadecimal level or using a forensic tool to identify the file. The investigator's training in the technology and criminal behavior will inform them of the possibility that people possessing and/or distributing illicit digital files (e.g., child sexual abuse material) often hide their files by changing extensions.

5 Presenting evidence—In court, the digital investigator has at least two challenges. One is to appear credible and knowledgeable while presenting in court. The investigator must understand clearly the process by which they have extracted and analyzed their evidence, and convey that effectively throughout the duration

of a courtroom procedure. In fact, communication is the premise of the second challenge: Explaining technical aspects of their analysis to laypersons. A jury or a judge may not understand terminology such as hashing or the purpose of a file extension. The investigator must be able to explain these concepts or risk their analysis not having the appropriate impact in court. This ability to present technical concepts to a lay audience is also important for investigators who work in the private sector.

These are very general steps in the process of digital forensic analysis. Much additional nuance exists based upon case parameters, and entire college courses and majors have developed since the earliest notions of these concepts based upon greater understanding of the digital forensics process. Importantly, however, the core steps remain the same even as these changes have taken shape.

The Tools Used in Digital Forensics

In carrying out the five-step process described, digital forensics professionals must understand computer fundamentals. They must be able to look at a piece of evidence at the binary or hexadecimal level and make judgments about that evidence. They may, in some cases, need to reconstruct a file that has been deleted using bits and pieces of the file found on the hard drive. They must also be knowledgeable in multiple operating systems (e.g., Windows, Linux, Mac OS, Android) to know how to navigate a piece of hardware and where to look for evidence. It is not unusual for digital forensics professionals to take specialized courses in the discipline and earn certificates and degrees to establish and advance their knowledge of the subject. Table 6.1 lists a few certificates that signify a digital forensic analyst's expertise. Some of these certificates verify one's ability to work with certain software in forensic analysis, while others verify one's competence in the general forensic analysis process. Increasingly, some certificates are oriented towards a particular occupation such as law enforcement or the military.

As more tools become available to make digital forensic analysis easier, both highly specialized professionals and LEPs with minimal specialized training can conduct a

Table 6.1 Digital Forensic Analysis Certifications

- AccessData Certified Examiner (ACE)—certifies that the examiner has proficiency in the Forensic Toolkit software
- Certified Computer Examiner (CCE)—a general certification administered by the International Society of Forensic Computer Examiners
- Certified Forensic Computer Examiner (CFCE)—a general certification administered primarily for local and federal law enforcement administered by the International Association of Computer Investigative Specialists
- Defense Cyber Investigations Training Academy (DCITA)—a general certification primarily for military personnel and administered by the Department of Defense
- Encase Certified Examiner (ENCE)—certifies that the examiner has proficiency in the EnCase forensic software
- Global Information Assurance Certified Forensic Examiner (GCFE)—a general certification administered by the testing company Global Information Assurance Certifications

forensic analysis with effective results. The following are a few such types and their basic function within a policing/investigative context:

- Write blocker—When a computer is powered on, the operating system immediately begins writing new information to the hard drive. If a computer is seized in the powered off state, it will need to be powered on for a forensic copy of the hard drive to be made. Any changes to the original state of the hard drive can be used to question the validity of future analyses. A write blocker is used to prevent an operating system, once turned on, from writing new information to its hard drive.
- Disk imager—Disk imagers create forensic copies to be analyzed by a forensic tool. As mentioned previously, a forensic copy is a bit-by-bit copy of a drive that includes unused space and deleted items. There are many tools available for making disk images. These include FTK Imager[2] and Paladin.[3] A free version is Win32 Disk Imager. One of the most common files is the "E01," or "expert witness" format. Others include "AFF" (advanced forensic format) and "DD" (raw evidence format).
- Digital forensic analysis software—Digital forensic analysis software will automate the process of identifying relevant files and will present evidence by producing user-friendly output. Law enforcement agencies that routinely work with digital evidence may purchase forensic analysis software for their officers. Three of the more well-known are EnCase,[4] Forensic Explorer,[5] and Magnet Axiom[6] A well-known free and open-source software is Autopsy.[7]
- Big Data analysis software—Just as Big Data is used in developing algorithms for law enforcement decision-making, it is also recognized as a vital resource in engineering alert protocols from which many cybercrime investigations begin. As discussed in further detail later in Chapter 8, Big Data analysis software is especially adept at rapid processing of large amounts of digital data. An investigation can often entail dealing with terabytes or more of data at a time. This is especially so in investigations like those concerning online sexploitation, sextortion, and theft of personal data via phishing attacks, where the amount of data to be processed can represent a few hundred to several million victims at a time. Powerful software is needed to process such massive amounts of data (Big Data) in order to help LEPs prioritize cases to pursue and discern specific pieces of critical evidence for those cases. For instance, Foundry—a software suite custom designed and managed by Palantir[8] to assist the National Center for Missing and Exploited Children (NCMEC) and LEPs alike—greatly reduces the processing time to prioritize high value cases and associated evidence from the millions of reports NCMEC receives weekly.

Investigating Data Trails

Investigating cybercrime does not always require the analysis of evidence at the binary level or training in specialized digital forensics. Law enforcement can also investigate crimes by analyzing the "digital footprints" or "digital breadcrumbs" of a suspect (Weaver & Gahegan, 2010). Within a cybercrime context, we prefer to use the term *data trail* as it connotes following someone or retracing the path of a suspect or victim. By data trail, we simply mean the evidence of human presence in a digital environment. This evidence can be interactions with others such as likes and retweets, web searches, text messages, and posts on forums. It can also be the action of signing up for a web service, logging into an account, or completing documentation for a warranty. It can even be the information collected by devices that someone owns such as GPS coordinates.

Consider the case of Andrew Saunders, from Wales, UK. Saunders, according to *BBC News*, searched for "information on how to make a pipe bomb, how to rig a car to explode when started, how to illegally buy a gun, and how to inflict knife injuries."[9] These search queries were extracted by Welsh authorities and later used as evidence in Cardiff Crown court to convict Saunders, who stabbed his ex-girlfriend and her new partner outside of a department store.

It is increasingly difficult for people not to leave a data trail. Even individuals who decide to go "off the grid" by logging out of their social media accounts and turning off their mobile phones still may go online to check their bank account or pay a bill or drive their cars to and from work—all activities that increasingly entail digital access, and thus a data trail. The increasing likelihood and expanse of leaving data trails in everyday life is a by-product of the so-called Internet of Things that characterizes society at present, and will for years to follow. Very few objects entailing human interaction remain untethered from the Internet without human operators specifically disabling such features, and even then a true decoupling is not always possible.

Additionally, a digital investigation is not exclusively about following data trails stemming from forensic work on devices or networks. Often, traditional detective work is just as relevant. Cybercrime investigators can uncover important leads by "pounding the pavement" via traditional interviews and observations with suspects and targets alike in the physical environment. Particularly with underage audiences, online activity of a deviant

Table 6.2 Data Trails in the Digital Environment

Type of Layer (Public or Private Domain)	*Description*	*Example of Evidentiary Data*
Human (Public)	The connections and communications between users	Social networks online and offline (parent-to-offspring, employer-to-employee, followers-to-those followed)
Content (Public)	The information produced and shared in the digital environment (i.e., the Internet)	Information on social media accounts—text, links, likes, photos, etc.; publicly available videos and audio productions
Application (Private)	Programs that allow users to perform operations in the digital environment	The subscription and log-in information for an application (e.g., Skype, Discord, Netflix)
Operating System (Private)	The software that manages the operation of applications in the digital environment	Boot-up records on a device; records of files written/re-written on a device
Hardware (Private)	The machines that compute and manipulate data	Warranty information for hardware and peripherals; serial numbers; history of OEM vs. after-market parts for a device
Infrastructure (Private)	The technologies that transmit data between devices	Internet connection records between IP addresses; WiFi logins,

or criminal nature is often associated with factors stemming from their households (e.g., parenting rules, screen time allowances, digital device supervision) and/or interactions within peer groups (e.g., peer pressure, discord within friendship circles). Thus, in such instances, when keen observation and purposive interviews reveal these case nuances, the likelihood of successfully closing an investigation is that much greater.

In fact, because there is so much data available for law enforcement to collect, it is useful to consider the data sources by layers of the digital environment (see Table 6.2; p. 117).

Search Warrants and Intermediaries

Starting with the application layer, data in these layers are generally considered private domain and protected by the Fourth Amendment of the US Constitution; American citizens can, in the language of the amendment, "be secure in their persons, houses, papers, and effects, against unreasonable searches and seizures" without probable cause. Once a degree of probable cause is established, law enforcement can request data from the intermediaries that have provided services to the user. *Intermediaries* are entities that facilitate the communication between users in the digital environment. They are usually companies or organizations specializing in a service and produce a profit through the selling of that service, or through the advertisements connected to that service. Facebook, Skype, Dropbox, and your local ISP are all examples of such intermediaries (Perset, 2010).

Intermediaries collect data on their subscribers, and can provide a detailed account of the when, the where, and in some cases even the why in an investigation. Consider the data that is collected by the intermediary, Pinterest:[10]

- Name
- Email address
- Phone number
- Profile photo
- Pins and Comments
- Location data on Pins and Comments
- Payment information if a purchase is made (what was bought, credit card information, addresses, delivery details)
- Information from Facebook or Google if Pinterest is linked to these accounts
- Internet Protocol address at log-in
- The address of and activity on websites you visit that incorporate Pinterest features
- Web searches
- Browser type and settings
- The date and time of your request
- Cookie data
- Device data
- If you install Pinterest's "save" button, then more information is also collected when this button is used on certain sites

Other social media websites reflect Pinterest in what they collect. Much of this data, as mentioned previously, is not publicly available and law enforcement must compel social media websites to provide this data. In the US, the primary legislation that governs this process is the *Electronic Communications Privacy Act* (ECPA). The ECPA was passed in 1986 to protect the electronic communications of individuals. It prohibits the interception or attempted interception of an aural, wire, or electronic communication by a device. Wiretapping a phone line, for example, is prohibited by the ECPA. Hacking an Internet connection and intercepting the communications between computers—for example "packet sniffing"—can also be a violation of the ECPA. The ECPA also regulates the type of content that law enforcement can collect on a suspect and can be summarized with three processes that are progressively more invasive and require progressively more justification, as per Tables 6.3 and 6.4.

The process that requires the least amount of justification is a subpoena, which can be obtained in both civil and criminal cases. A subpoena allows law enforcement to collect such specific subscriber info as the name associated with the account, IP address at the time of registration, and time stamps for when a user signs in. This information can be considered *metadata* since it does not allow law enforcement to read the content of a person's communications—only the data about that data (Baca & Getty Research Institute, 2016; Donohue, 2013; van der Velden, 2015). Examples of metadata include:

- The "tags" associated with a piece of content uploaded to a social media site
- The date that a document was last opened or modified
- The permissions on a document (i.e., can it be modified or is it read only?)
- The geolocation data
- The type of machine that produced the content (e.g., what camera took the picture, what device was used to browse the web)

Table 6.3 ECPA Using Google Services as an Example

Legal Process	*Description*	*Gmail*
Subpoena (Civil and criminal cases)	Basic subscriber info	Name, account creation information, associated email addresses and phone numbers, time stamp, IP address at registration
Court Order (Criminal cases)	Transactional info	Email header information (to and from); IP addresses from where a person is using their account
Warrant (Criminal cases)	Content of messages	Email content

Table 6.4 ECPA Using YouTube as an Example

Legal Process	*Description*	*YouTube*
Subpoena (Civil and criminal cases)	Basic Subscriber Info	Subscriber registration info; Registration IP addresses and time stamps
Court Order (Criminal cases)	Transactional Info	Video upload IP address and time stamp
Warrant (Criminal cases)	Content of Messages	Copy of a private video and video info; Private message content

A court order requires more justification, and specific details about an investigation must be presented and approved by a judge or magistrate. A court order allows the agency to collect transactional info, including the user accounts and IP addresses that have communicated with the account, and places and times where a user has logged in. The most intrusive, a warrant, requires the highest level of legal justification. The requesting agency must present to a judge or magistrate "probable cause" that within the content to be searched is evidence relevant to the case at hand. Upon the granting of a warrant, law enforcement can then collect restricted access data such as emails or private videos associated with a suspect's account.

The ECPA, first ratified in 1986, was written at a time before the explosion of Internet usage. As a result, many of its provisions are outdated. Among the provisions most concerning to civil liberties organizations is that the legal processes discussed earlier are only applicable if the communications are less than 180 days old. Within this period, a user's data is protected. After the six months, law enforcement only needs a subpoena to collect all information from a user's account. In 1986, this was not an issue as most information sent through email was downloaded from computers and removed from the digital environment. Now, however, people store a lifetime's worth of private information in emails, social media accounts, and cloud services. All this information can be obtained with little justification after 180 days, and as a result many lawmakers and advocacy groups are working to modify these provisions.

Online Undercover Investigations

A third way in which cybercrime is investigated is through law enforcement performing undercover or "sting" operations (Grant & Macleod, 2016; Mitchell, Wolak, Finkelhor, & Jones, 2012; Tetzlaff-Bemiller, 2011). These investigations are done to witness someone in the act of committing a crime online. Sting investigations are also conducted to collect evidence about an ongoing criminal activity, with the focus usually being on identifying the offending patterns and likely targets of a suspected offender, or the network structure of a criminal enterprise and discovering who the most important members are. Once enough evidence is gathered, investigators may then request a search warrant of the suspect's hardware or digital accounts.

One type of criminal activity that is routinely investigated through sting operations is online child exploitation (Grant & Macleod, 2016). Online predators use the anonymity of the digital environment to manipulate children, and often including sexual exploitation—either through direct sexual contact for the purposes of producing child sexual abuse material or other illicit sexual activities. These offenders employ a variety of trust-building and manipulation techniques, collectively known as *grooming*, to gain the trust of their young targets and prepare them for the subsequent victimization. Grooming can last from a few weeks to several years and may never catch the attention of investigators until significant damage has already been done. Thus, an online undercover investigation where, for example, police may pose as a minor on a website or discussion forum popular among child predators can be extremely helpful in proactively meeting the predator where they operate and taking full advantage of the same anonymity the predator enjoys.

A parent or guardian may identify the communications their child is having online with another individual as being predatory and contact the police. More commonly, however, such information will make its way to agencies deputized under the Internet Crimes Against Children Task Force Program[11] via anonymous reports generated through NCMEC. Once alerted, the law enforcement entity authorized to work the case may then contact the respective hardware manufacturer and/or online service provider mentioned in the report to obtain additional information towards identifying a suspect, and inevitably an arrest warrant. Where more sensitive and/or restricted data is needed, we again see the benefit of undercover investigations.

During an undercover investigation, the investigator(s) can take over the account of the child referenced in a report and pose as the child to collect personally identifiable information from a suspected predator (e.g., name, address, phone number, username). The police may further proceed in collecting evidence showing that the adult is making overtures to the minor, and subsequently ask the adult to meet them in a specific location. If the adult appears at the location, they are apprehended; note that this stage still requires the acquisition of a proper arrest warrant before apprehending the suspect in person.

A second criminal activity amenable to sting operations is the trade of illegal goods and services in online marketplaces. There are numerous such marketplaces that sell illicit wares like drugs, firearms, malware, and stolen credit card information. Child sexual abuse material is also traded in such settings. To identify the buyers and sellers in these markets, law enforcement must become buyers or sellers themselves. Many high profile "take downs" of websites on the *darknet*—the version of the worldwide web containing websites owned and operated by private individuals or user groups, and accessible through specialized browsers (i.e., The Onion Router aka TOR;[12]; Hyphanet[13])—were aided by information collected in undercover operations. The infamous online drug marketplace, Silk Road, was busted through an online undercover operation where the FBI kept tabs on the owner of the website, Ross Ulbricht, until enough evidence was collected to authorize an arrest warrant.[14]

In another example, Artem Vaulin allegedly owned and operated Kickass Torrents, or KAT—a commercial website that enabled users to illegally reproduce and distribute hundreds of millions of copies of copyrighted motion pictures, video games, television programs, musical recordings, and other electronic media circa 2008–2016. According to a criminal complaint filed in the U.S. District Court of Chicago in 2016, KAT was collectively valued at more than $1 billion and was the 69th most popular site on the Internet at the time. Vaulin was charged with:

- One count of conspiracy to commit criminal copyright infringement
- One count of conspiracy to commit money laundering
- Two counts of criminal copyright infringement

This case is instructive for the cybercrime student due to several innovative ways in which officers collected evidence to charge Vaulin:

- Investigators used the "Wayback Machine" website at "www.archive.org" to view the historical content of the KAT website (Murphy, Hashim, & O'Connor, 2007). The domain had been moved several times because the website had been seized or blocked by authorities in each country. Using the Wayback Machine, investigators could chart and document the movement of KAT (see Table 6.5; p. 122).
- To establish that Vaulin was indeed making money from copyright infringement, an undercover IRS Special Agent sent a request to the email address "pr@kat.cr"

Table 6.5   The Domain History of KickAss Torrents

Date Range	Domain
November 2008 through April 2011	kickasstorrents.com
April 2011 through June 2013	kat.ph
June 2013 through December 2014	kickass.to
December 2014 through February 2015	kickass.so
February 2015 through June 2015	kickass.to

(an email account listed on KAT's website for "press") on November 2015 inquiring about advertising. In a later correspondence, a KAT representative agreed to provide advertising at $300 per day. The agents bought advertising on KAT on two separate occasions.

- In order to pay for advertising, undercover agents were given two bank account numbers. One of which was to a bank in Latvia under the Mutual Legal Assistance Treaty. Law enforcement was able to establish some sense of the scale of the operation, with the account showing a total of approximately €28,411,357 in deposits between roughly August 28, 2015 and March 10, 2016. This is quite a large sum and this was only one of the banks used.

Undercover sting operations like what was used to catch Vaulin and shut down KAT are necessary for investigating cybercrime. Many cases require investigators to "follow the breadcrumbs" or to link several offenders and organizations together. This requires time and a degree of subterfuge. However, there are more specific concerns with undercover sting operations. The Center for Problem Oriented Policing (C-POP)[15] identifies several; we list some here:

- <u>They may not significantly reduce or prevent recurring crime problems</u>. If the criminal activity is a repeated one, such as human trafficking or drug selling, then an undercover operation may not reduce overall rates of such crime. An individual offender may be apprehended, but the root causes remain.
- <u>They may increase crime</u>. Baits and decoys provide new opportunities for criminal behavior. For example, to establish trust or evade suspicion, an undercover officer may need to participate in the criminal enterprise, such as the buying or selling of malware on an online market.
- <u>The government may overreach</u>. To apprehend criminals, law enforcement may be creating conditions for the behavior. As per Graeme Newman's C-POP report (2007), "Is it the government's role to construct enticements and situations that encourage all citizens to commit a crime?" If, for example, a federal agency established a fake online forum soliciting for stolen movies and other illegally acquired entertainment content, wouldn't the very existence of the forum serve to stimulate the illicit trading of such content? (Newman, 2007)
- <u>There are entrapment issues</u>. Offenders can argue that law enforcement tricked them into committing the crime. However, courts have standards for determining entrapment; often a jury must decide if the offender was entrapped.
- <u>They are expensive</u>. Undercover operations often require the use of props. For example, an undercover officer may need to have in his possession drugs to be sold online. Alternatively, the officer may need money to purchase goods on the

illegal market. Just as importantly, a considerable amount of time may need to be invested in an undercover operation; such operations can take months or even years to yield conclusive results.

Pluralized Policing in the Digital Environment

Policing the digital experience is often characterized by *pluralized policing*, where several non-state actors aid formal law enforcement in the investigation of a crime (Loader, 2000; McCahill, 2008; O'Neill & Fyfe, 2017). By non-state actors, we mean businesses, non-profit organizations, advocacy groups, and even private individuals. These actors have an interest in reducing crime, and help law enforcement by collecting data, identifying potential criminals and/or locations of criminal activity, crafting legislation, and publicizing the crimes.

Pluralized policing is a common characteristic of modern societies. However, non-state actors can have a greater influence on cybercrime investigations. First, many cyber-crimes are technologically sophisticated, and thus their investigation requires a degree of expertise that may not be present in many law enforcement agencies. Second, while the severity of cybercrimes have come to be regarded on par with many crimes offline, law enforcement spending (especially concerning street crimes) still focuses manpower and material resources towards preventing the offline criminal activity. Cybercrime investigations, therefore, are often outsourced to non-state actors out of necessity. Additionally, given the advantage of heightened expertise and more nuanced resource allocation parameters, non-state actors can often serve to enhance the investigative efforts of law enforcement. This is demonstrated by the aforementioned partnership between NCMEC and Palantir to streamline the review of CyberTipline[16] reports to aid LEPs in prioritizing which cases to investigate.

Another prominent non-state actor is the Internet Watch Foundation, or IWF.[17] The IWF's mission is to remove "child sexual abuse content hosted anywhere in the world," and "non-photographic [fantasy] child sexual abuse images hosted in the UK (2013)." The IWF provides a host of services to law enforcement and content providers. Among other things, they compile a hash list of images that content providers can use to quickly identify illegal images. They also operate a hotline where computer users can report instances of child pornography. In this way, the IWF performs many of the functions that have been traditionally associated with state law enforcement agencies.

Yet another example is Romancescams.org. *Romance scams* are the type of cyber-crimes that are difficult to investigate and receive less priority than other types of crimes. Romancescams.org performs the function of informing the public in the way that a local police precinct may hold community meetings about street crime. The website is organized by dating site genre, and lists articles by genre as well.(Foundation, 2013)

Open-Source Intelligence

Open-source intelligence (OSINT) refers to both a category of data and a set of procedures by which the data is acquired and implemented. In the broadest sense, it encompasses publicly accessible information on the identity and activities of individuals and organizations active on the Internet. These information sources generally require little-to-no special tools or privileges beyond basic access to the worldwide web. However, OSINT is truly defined by its application. The data alone is simply data; once it is applied in an information-gathering effort to gain insight for a specific intelligence objective, that is when we observe OSINT in full form.

For example, an Instagram account holder creates digital data once their account becomes active. They continue creating data as they interact with the account (e.g., posting photos, sending messages, visiting other Instagram pages). This data is ever-present and exists in perpetuity until the user or Instagram does something to remove the information. However, a prospective employer seeking to hire the account holder might decide to perform a background check. In such an instance, the aforementioned Instagram account (particularly if unrestricted) could be included as part of the investigation of the user, and thus becomes a form of OSINT.

Information from social media websites like Instagram is just one example of OSINT; there are many others (far too numerous to fit within this book). However, in the effort to safeguard the digital user experience from deviant and criminal behavior, law enforcement agencies and supporting institutions regularly rely upon a variety of OSINT data and resources. Residential address history, e-mail accounts, phone numbers, and court actions are just some of the many data points that can be acquired through OSINT means. Michael Bazzell, a leading authority on OSINT sources and investigative techniques, summarizes a wide array of OSINT material. Among the more common ones are as follows (2021) (see Table 6.6).

Table 6.6 Examples of OSINT Data Types and Search Tools[18]

OSINT Data Types	*Common Search Tools*
Search Engines	google.com, bing.com, yandex.com
Social Networks	facebook.com, instagram.com, X.com (formerly Twitter)
Online Communities	reddit.com, 4chan.com, tiktok.com
E-mail Addresses	mail.google.com, mail.yahoo.com, mail.bing.com, mail.yandex.com
Usernames	knowem.com, checkusernames.com, whatsmyname.app
People Search Engines	truepeoplesearch.com, fastpeoplesearch.com, nuwber.com
Telephone Numbers	freecarrierlookup.com, twilio.com/lookup, opencnam.com, truecaller.com
Online Maps	maps.google.com, bing.com/maps, zoom.earth
Documents	docs.google.com, docs.microsoft.com, aws.amazon.com
Images	images.google.com, bing.com/images, tineye.com, yandex.ru/images
Videos	youtube.com, google.com/videohp, videos.bing.com, yandex.com/video
Domain Names	viewdns.info/_____*, whoxy.com, whosiology.com
IP Addresses	viewdns.info/_____*, iplocation.net, thatsthem.com
Government and Business Records	blackbookonline.info, publicrecords.onlinesearches.com, pacer.gov**
Virtual Currencies	blockchain.info, bitcoinwhoswho.com, blockchair.com

The View DNS domain provides a range of embedded search tools depending upon what the user puts after the backslash (/). For instance, to view the IP address history for a domain name, the user would put "viewdns.info/iphistory/." A full list of the tools can be found at the "viewdns.info" website.

***PACER = Public Access to Court Electronic Records**

The broad scope and increasing popularity of OSINT in formal investigative practice is much of the reason for its inclusion in this chapter. The implementation of OSINT in criminal investigations by both LEPs and non-government actors has advanced greatly in recent years. Some of the best examples have been observed in criminal cases pertaining to terrorism/anti-terrorism (Lakomy, 2021; Tierney, 2017), sexual abuse investigations involving minors (Acar, 2018; Rajamaki et al., 2022), and investigations of human rights violations (Deutch & Habal, 2018; Hogue, 2023; Meyer & Shelley, 2020; Murray et al., 2022).

OSINT techniques are valuable to LEPs when direct physical access to data in an investigation (e.g., suspect/eyewitness/victim interviews, on-site analysis of a physical crime scene) is not possible, or when the nature of the evidence is primarily or exclusively online. OSINT also carries the benefit of not (usually) requiring special permissions to acquire or execute. Therefore, a wider array of talent can be employed in the effort—a feature undergirding the recommendation from scholars like Kemal Acar (2018) to enhance law enforcement investigative efforts with crowdsourced and carefully vetted surrogate investigators (Bazzell, 2021).

A great deal of OSINT work can be executed using quotation marks or special commands called *operators*. Regarding the former, most search engines and tools with

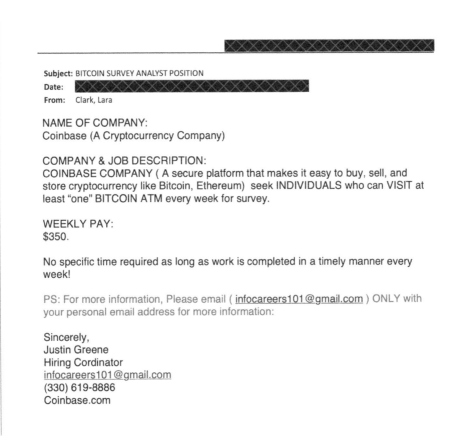

Figure 6.2 A sample e-mail illustrating a phishing attempt.

searchable functions allow for specificity by placing quotation marks ("") around the terms. If one wanted to, for instance, investigate the sender of a suspected phishing e-mail, operators can be useful. Consider Figure 6.2 (p. 125).

The figure represents a phishing e-mail one of the authors received not too long ago. Suppose the author wanted to determine the legitimacy of the e-mail and/or identity of the sender. Here are the results when the author attempted to run a search[19] on the supposed sender—Justin Greene—of the e-mail both with and without quotations marks:

- Justin Greene (without quotes): 37,500,000 hits
- "Justin Greene" (with quotes): 79,000 hits
- "Justin Greene" with "Coinbase.com" added: 3,190 hits

Note how the search results grew increasingly more precise when quotes were added, followed by additional information indicating who the sender purportedly represents (Coinbase.com). At the point where 3,190 hits were acquired, the author concluded that each hit represented a webpage where the words "Justin" and "Greene" appear consecutively with one another, and where the website "Coinbase.com" is also mentioned. While still not an exact determination of legitimacy or identity, this simple OSINT technique increased the chances of determining the answers sought by narrowing the search field online a great deal. In fact, employing the same technique for an additional piece of information, the e-mail address "infocareers101@gmail.com", yielded the most important information of all: Six total hits all referencing phishing scams incorporating the e-mail address.

Granted, this particular e-mail had a number of other obvious indicators of illegitimacy (i.e., inconsistent fonts, grammatical errors, disagreement between sender name and closing signature). Nonetheless, using quotations and operators in such ways can be powerful and simple OSINT resources for the criminal justice profession and private citizens alike, and is just one of a diverse and growing field of tools available to the criminal justice community in dealing with cybercrime offenses. With that said, there are important challenges to also consider with the usage of OSINT, and more broadly running investigations in digital settings.

Law Enforcement Challenges

Law enforcement has developed many techniques for investigating crime in the digital environment. However, there are unique challenges that make these investigations difficult. One problem is the differentiated levels of digital technology education and training available for law enforcement. This is especially problematic at the local level in less populated, geographically isolated, and/or impoverished communities as police departments there tend to lack adequate funding and opportunity for such training. In such instances, police officers typically will not seek out additional training in cybercrime investigative techniques unless prompted to do so. If they do request such training proactively, they often must seek out programs and funding sources on their own.

Although there are numerous out-of-box tools for performing digital forensic analyses, personnel must still be trained on those tools and increase their computer and communication technology acumen to some degree. Concerning following data trails, performing online investigations, identifying possible types of data that can be used as evidence in cybercrime cases, and writing warrants for those cases—tasks requiring comparatively less computer expertise than the actual forensic work—training and experience is still needed.

The number of available training programs across countries with first-tier technology infrastructure and government support is less of a problem. Consider, for instance, in the US nearly every state host at least a few collegiate institutions and state agencies offering certificates or degrees in either cybercrime or cybersecurity training (several with emphasis in criminal investigations). Many such programs offer enrollment options for in-person, online, and hybrid (in-person and online coursework) applicants. However, funding sources aside from out-of-pocket options continue to prove elusive for many LEPs. Table 6.7 illustrates some of the more well-known resources available as of this publication specifically geared towards cybercrime and/or cybersecurity training.

Concerning the previous discussion of OSINT, the challenge of training access and funding presents itself in a unique way. While there is OSINT training available for law enforcement and private citizens alike, the latter need not be specifically deputized in order to learn and implement OSINT techniques. As such, a fair amount of amateur sleuthing takes place absent the purview of law enforcement, and with troubling outcomes. One such instance in 2021 saw a woman exposed to online shaming and ridicule following

Table 6.7 Federal Grants with Allotments for Cybercrime Education[20]

Grant Name	2020	2019	2018	2017
DHS* State Homeland Security Program	$415,000,000	$415,000,000	$402,000,000	$402,000,000
DHS Urban Area Security Initiative	$615,000,000	$590,000,000	$580,000,000	$580,000,000
DHS Tribal Homeland Security Grant Program	$15,000,000	$10,000,000	$10,000,000	$10,000,000
DOJ** Edward Byrne Memorial Justice Assistance Grant	$547,200,000	$423,500,000	$415,500,000	$403,00,000
DOJ Community Oriented Policing Services	$303,500,000	$304,000,000	$276,000,000	$222,000,000
DOJ Paul Coverdell Forensic Science Improvement Grants Program	$30,000,000	$30,000,000	$30,000,000	$13,500,000
Economic, High-Technology, White Collar, and Internet Crime Prevention National Training and Technical Assistance Program	$8,250,000	$8,570,000	$10,400,000	$8,681,000
DOJ Program for Statistical Analysis Centers	$5,000,000	$4,594,000	$5,500,000	$4,650,000
DOJ Intellectual Property Enforcement Program	$2,400,000	$2,400,000	$2,400,000	$2,400,000
Student Computer and Digital Forensics Educational Opportunities Program	$0	$1,800,000	$0	$0

*Department of Homeland Security
**Department of Justice

digital vigilantes uncovering and exposing the woman's identity following viral video of her ignoring nationwide masking mandates. Unfortunately, the woman—Tuhina Singh—was the victim of mistaken identity (Sherman, 2021). Internet sleuths fingered the wrong person, and though this fact was later revealed, the damage to her reputation and mental health was already done.

At times when formal investigations run concurrent with amateur OSINT work, scholars like Dekker and Meijer (2021) note how the amateur investigations can result in compromising the efforts of formal casework, undermining the authority of police investigations, and breaching ethical conduct. The expanse of social media, along with the advent of powerful tools like facial recognition, satellite imaging, and Big Data extraction of public records create a landscape for online communities of private citizens to engage in a brand of digitized detective work that potentially impedes the criminal justice process. Accordingly, most LEPs would prefer high levels of pluralization in OSINT investigative efforts out of concern that non-professionals might misuse any data they come across or misinterpret the meaning/value of evidence encountered. Prosecutorial steps like search warrants and indictments are also more likely to stick when law enforcement can demonstrate that an OSINT investigation has adhered to the ethical and practical standards held by any other investigation.

Additionally, given the volume of data potentially available through OSINT, the opportunity for *paralysis-by-analysis* is another obstacle for law enforcement. With so many information types publicly available, and obviously no shortage of cybercrime, it can be quite a challenge determining what information is useful, when and how. Excluding literature and online resources from scholars such as those already discussed in this chapter, there are few guides for how to navigate OSINT written strictly for the criminal justice community.

Yet another challenge stems from the expanding variety of international locations of many cybercrimes. In one example, concerning CSAM, consider the Internet Watch Foundation's claim that in 1996 the UK hosted 18% of the world's known online child sexual abuse material, but now less than 1% of such content today.[21] This may be debatable, but current estimates nonetheless indicate consumers of CSAM are simply finding the material in another countries. As per the NCMEC CyberTipline Reports for 2022, the following countries rank among the highest in reported CSAM complaints (see Table 6.8; p. 129).

As explained further in the next chapter, organized crime activities online demonstrate the propensity for criminal organizations to leverage the Internet's everyday advantages of anonymity and data transference across great physical distances. Many such organizations engaged in such offenses as identity theft, ransomware extortion, cyberterrorism, and distribution of illicit goods and services (including CSAM) operate in "cells" across multiple locations within the same country or separate nations. It even becomes necessary to do so often times to allow for the organization to continue operation even if one or more cells are taken down by law enforcement.

Thus, it is only through coordinated efforts that law enforcement can truly address the challenges presented by such crimes. Institutions like the IWF must work with other international organizations (e.g., the European Financial Coalition against Commercial Sexual Exploitation of Children Online, the Internet Governance Forum Dynamic Coalition on Child Online Protection, and the aforementioned NCMEC). FBI offices throughout the US regularly coordinate with international counterparts like the European Union Agency for Law Enforcement Cooperation (EUROPOL), the Public Security Intelligence Agency (Japan), and the National Crime Agency (Great Britain). Cybercriminals may live in one

Table 6.8 2022 CyberTipline Reports by Country[22]

Country	Number of Reports (% of total N: 32,059,029)
Algeria	731,167 (2.3)
Bangladesh	2,145,098 (6.7)
Brazil	611,230 (1.9)
Egypt	431,044 (1.3)
India	5,675,324 (17.7)
Indonesia	1,878,011 (5.9)
Iraq	905,883 (2.8)
Mexico	815,792 (2.5)
Pakistan	2,059,884 (6.4)
Philippines	2,576,182 (8)
Saudi Arabia	602,745 (1.9)
Thailand	525,932 (1.6)
United States	1,562,616 (4.9)

* United Kingdom: 316,900 (1)

country, route their Internet activity through a second, and then victimize a user in a third. Thus, the international nature of cybercrimes means that coordination is essential between non-state, local, and national agencies across many borders.

Conclusion

In this chapter we explored aspects of policing in the digital environment. We focused on three broad areas—digital forensics, exploring data trails, and online undercover investigations. These three separate areas are mainly for teaching purposes. The reality of investigations is that these three areas comingle, and many cases require a combination of forensic analysis, collecting information from intermediaries, and doing undercover work to collect more evidence.

National trends suggest that the number of crimes in the physical environment is decreasing. Indeed, aside from some minor deviations, the number of street and property crimes has been steadily decreasing since the late 1980s–early 1990s. Meanwhile, because so many human activities are occurring in the digital environment, the number of cybercrimes is increasing. Given these trends, it is imperative that current and future professionals be trained in cybercrime investigations.

CHAPTER 6 CURRENT EVENTS AND CRITICAL THINKING:

The New Model of Cybercrime Policing?

Blade Runner. Minority Report. I-Robot. Robocop. Popular media entertainment is just one area where the intersection between policing and advanced technology has been pondered extensively. As we discuss later in Chapter 8, law enforcement has made great strides in incorporating such technology via artificial intelligence for the purpose of predictive policing and similar efforts. More broadly, the face of cybercrime policing has been reimagined to some extent in the wake of rapid development and adoption of the latest technology for prospective offenders and potential target alike.

Consider the recent success in efforts from an international consortium of law enforcement agencies to shutdown the ransomware syndicate, Hive, as well as the FBI's takedown of the botnet, Cyclops Blink (Vicens, 2023). In both instances, law enforcement professionals acted with emphasis on disabling the infrastructure and functionality of the cybercrime networks behind the offending activity and cutting off connections to additional targets and offending opportunities. This approach radically downplays the conventional focus in policing on investigations, apprehending criminals, and presenting them to a state-sponsored formal criminal justice system to receive some measure of commensurate retribution. In a nutshell, rather than pursuing the criminal organization and those operating within it, we see in these activities a model with enhanced focus on addressing victims through disruption of cybercrime offending patterns and reducing victimization risk over.

What do you think about this model shift? Is it practical for law enforcement to focus less on pursuing and prosecuting the cybercrime offender and more on cutting off opportunities for him/her to reach intended targets? Why/why not?

How might this model shift look in other areas of criminal justice (i.e., sentencing, corrections, post-incarceration reentry into society)?

What of the opinion that such a model equates to "giving up on trying to stop the bad guys" with respect to cybercrime and deviance in the digital environment? Is such an opinion valid? Why/why not?

NOTES

1   www.fileformat.info/tool/hash.htm
2   http://marketing.accessdata.com/ftkimager3.4.2
3   https://sumuri.com/software/paladin/
4   https://www.opentext.com/products/encase-forensic
5   https://getdataforensics.com/product/forensic-explorer-fex/
6   https://www.magnetforensics.com/products/magnet-axiom/
7   https://www.sleuthkit.org/autopsy/
8   https://www.palantir.com/platforms/foundry/
9   www.bbc.com/news/uk-wales-south-east-wales-39100854
10 https://policy.pinterest.com/en-gb/privacy-policy
11 https://www.icactaskforce.org/
12 https://www.torproject.org/
13 https://www.hyphanet.org/pages/about.html
14 http://theconversation.com/end-of-the-silk-road-how-did-dread-pirate-roberts-get-busted-18886
15 http://theconversation.com/end-of-the-silk-road-how-did-dread-pirate-roberts-get-busted-18886
16 CyberTipline = NCMEC's centralized system for reporting the online exploitation of children; considered the leading resource in the US for filing reports of suspected abuse of minors via the digital environment.
17 www.iwf.org.uk/
18 Adapted from *Open Source Intelligence Techniques* (Michael Bazzell, 8th edition)
19 Facilitated via Google Chrome 114.0.5735.198
20 https://www.thirdway.org/report/follow-the-money-few-federal-grants-are-used-to-fight-cybercrime

21 https://www.iwf.org.uk/policy-work/
22 https://www.missingkids.org/content/dam/missingkids/pdfs/2022-reports-by-country.pdf

REFERENCES

Acar, K. V. (2018). OSINT by crowdsourcing: A theoretical model for online child abuse investigations. *International Journal of Cyber Criminology, 12*(1), 22.

Baca, M., & Getty Research Institute (Eds.). (2016). *Introduction to metadata* (3rd edition). Getty Research Institute.

Bazzell, M. (2021). *Open source intelligence techniques: Resources for searching and analyzing online information* (8th edition). Michael Bazzell.

Crain, M. A., Hopwood, W. S., Pacini, C., & Young, G. R (Eds). (2017). Digital forensics. In *Essentials of forensic accounting* (pp. 301–339). New York: American Institute of Certified Public Accountants, Inc. doi:10.1002/9781119449423.ch11

Dekker, R., & Meijer, A. (2021). Citizens as aides or adversaries? Police responses to digital responses to digital vigilantism. In *Introducing vigilant audiences*. D. Trottier, R. Gabulhakov, & Q. Huang (Eds). Open Book Publishers. https://doi.org/10.11647/OBP.0200

Deutch, J., & Habal, H. (2018). The Syrian archive: A methodological case study of open-source investigation of state crime using video evidence from social media platforms. *State Crime, 7*(1), 29.

Donohue, L. (2013). Bulk metadata collection: Statutory and constitutional considerations. *Harvard Journal of Law and Public Policy, 37*(3), 757–900. doi:10.2139/ssrn.2344774

Foundation, Internet Watch. (2013). *IWF welcomes progress in the fight against online child sexual abuse content.* https://www.iwf.org.uk/news-media/news/iwf-welcomes-progress-in-the-fight-against-online-child-sexual-abuse-content/

Furneaux, N. (2006). An introduction to computer forensics. *Medicine, Science and the Law, 46*(3), 213–218. doi:10.1258/rsmmsl.46.3.213

Grant, T., & Macleod, N. (2016). Assuming identities online: Experimental linguistics applied to the policing of online paedophile activity. *Applied Linguistics, 37*(1), 50–70. doi:10.1093/applin/amv079

Hogue, S. (2023). Civilian surveillance in the war in Ukraine: Mobilizing the agency of the observers of war. *Surveillance and Society, 21*(1), 5.

Holt, T. J., Bossler, A. M., & Seigfried-Spellar, K. C. (2015). *Cybercrime and digital forensics: An introduction.* Routledge.

Konheim, A. G. (2010). *Hashing in computer science: Fifty years of slicing and dicing.* John Wiley & Sons, Inc. doi:10.1002/9780470630617

Lakomy, M. (2021). Mapping the online presence and activities of the Islamic State's unofficial propaganda cell: Ahlut-Tawhid Publications. *Security Journal, 34*, 26.

Loader, I. (2000). Plural policing and democratic governance. *Social & Legal Studies, 9*(3), 323–345. doi:10.1177/096466390000900301

McCahill, M. (2008). Plural policing and CCTV surveillance. In M. Deflem & J. T. Ulmer (Eds.), *Sociology of crime law and deviance.* (Vol. 10, pp. 199–219). Emerald (MCB UP). doi:10.1016/S1521-6136(07)00209-6

McKenzie, B. J., Harries, R., & Bell, T. (1990). Selecting a hashing algorithm. Software: *Practice and Experience, 20*(2), 209–224. doi:10.1002/spe.4380200207

Meyer, L. F., & Shelley, L. I. (2020). Human trafficking network investigations: The role of open source intelligence and large-scale data analytics in investigating organized crime. *International Journal on Criminology, 7*(2), 13.

Mitchell, K. J., Wolak, J., Finkelhor, D., & Jones, L. (2012). Investigators using the Internet to apprehend sex offenders: Findings from the Second National Juvenile Online Victimization Study. *Police Practice and Research, 13*(3), 267–281. doi:10.1080/15614263.2011.627746

Murphy, J., Hashim, N. H., & O'Connor, P. (2007). Take me back: Validating the wayback machine. *Journal of Computer-Mediated Communication, 13*(1), 60–75. doi:10.1111/j.1083-6101.2007.00386.x

Murray, D., McDermott, Y., & Koenig, K. A. (2022). Mapping the use of open source research in UN human rights investigations. *Journal of Human Rights Practice, 27.*

Newman, G. R. (2007). *Negative features of sting operations* (Problem-Oriented Guides for Police — Response Guides Series). United States Department of Justice.

O'Neill, M., & Fyfe, N. R. (2017). Plural policing in Europe: Relationships and governance in contemporary security systems. *Policing and Society, 27*(1), 1–5. doi:10.1080/10439463.2016.1220554

Perset, K. (2010). The economic and social role of Internet intermediaries (OECD Digital Economy Papers No. 171). doi:10.1787/5kmh79zzs8vb-en

Rajamaki, J., Lahti, I., & Parviainen, J. (2022). OSINT on the dark web: Child abuse material investigations. *Information & Security, 53*(1), 10.

Sherman, R. (2021). The dark side of open source intelligence. https://www.codastory.com/authoritarian-tech/negatives-open-source-intelligence/

Tetzlaff-Bemiller, M. J. (2011). Undercover online: An extension of traditional policing in the United States. *International Journal of Cyber Criminology, 5*(2), 813–824.

Tierney, M. (2017). Spotting the lone actor: Combating lone wolf terrorism through financial investigations. *Journal of Financial Crime, 24*(4), 5.

van der Velden, L. (2015). Forensic devices for activism: Metadata tracking and public proof. *Big Data & Society, 2*(2), 1–14. doi:10.1177/2053951715612823

Vicens, A. (2023). To combat cybercrime, US law enforcement increasingly prioritizes disruption. *Cyberscoop.* https://cyberscoop.com/doj-cybercrime-disruption-ransomware/

Weaver, S. D., & Gahegan, M. (2010). Constructing, visualizing, and analyzing a digital footprint. *Geographical Review, 97*(3), 324–350. doi:10.1111/j.1931-0846.2007.tb00509.x

Organized Cybercrime, State Crimes, and Cyberterrorism

Introduction

The chapters to this point have focused primarily on individuals or uncoordinated groups committing criminal or deviant acts. However, organizations can also commit criminal or deviant acts. Indeed, the most sophisticated crimes will require an investment in money and personnel that usually only an organization can provide.

When people hear Organized Crime, they probably think about street gangs, crime syndicates, drug cartels, or the various iterations of the Mafia. Indeed, many of these groups have shifted some of their activities into the digital environment—either by committing cybercrimes or more commonly using digital technologies to help facilitate crimes they have traditionally committed offline (racketeering, sex trafficking, gambling, prostitution). In this chapter we will focus less on traditional Organized Crime groups and more on describing the structure and practices of Organized Crime groups that originated specifically to commit cybercrimes.

We also expand our discussion to organizations that state crimes and cyberterrorism under the premise that states and terrorist groups are also stable organizations. States can commit or sponsor crimes against their own citizens, other states, and the citizens of other states. In this chapter, we will narrow our focus to state crimes that (1) occur in the digital environment and (2) crimes that states commit against other states. Similarly, terrorist groups motivated by religious or political ideologies can commit crimes and potentially harm citizens through cyber-attacks.

Organized Cybercrime

There has been a debate within the social sciences about how to conceptualize organized crime. The debate revolves around the term "organized" (Finckenauer, 2005, 64). Almost any crime can be committed by a group working together as co-conspirators. For example,

DOI: 10.4324/9781003283256-7

individual juveniles may make temporary alliances to commit an armed robbery. Or disgruntled associates in a retail business may work together to embezzle money. These are certainly "crimes that are organized." The offenders must work together and coordinate their activities to attain their goals. They will likely have some type of rudimentary leadership structure and assigned roles—even if the structure is simply the boss and two henchmen. However, their lack of sophistication and permanence constrains the scale of their activities. Once the "crime that is organized" has been committed, the group may dissolve and not attempt to build on its success or further develop its infrastructure.

To distinguish between crimes committed by temporary groups, and crimes committed by stable, sophisticated organizations, Hagan (2006) designates the latter as a proper noun. We do the same here. A few juveniles working together to rob someone's home is a crime that is organized. We can even call it organized crime (lowercase). But groups like the Mafia and drug cartels participate in Organized Crime (proper noun).

Social scientists have explored what makes a collection of individual criminals an Organized Crime group. Finckenauer identifies four dimensions (2005, 75–76):

- Criminal sophistication—The degree of planning used in carrying out a crime, how long the commission of a criminal act takes, and how much skill and knowledge is required to carry out the crime. Consider the degree of planning and skill required in a successful drug trafficking enterprise. The group members will be required to coordinate the negotiation and acquisition of contraband from entities outside of the country, secure safe passage of that contraband, distribute it to sellers in the most advantageous locations, monitor the sellers' sales, and maintain that supply chain for customers, all while evading law enforcement.
- Structure—The degree to which a division of labor defines authority and leadership, and the degree to which the structure maintains itself over time and across crimes. As with all large groups, a stable group structure is needed for individuals to work together efficiently. Organized Crime groups tend to have relatively large group structures with several levels of authority. Consider the well-known organization of the Italian American Mafia crime families. Each family has a "Boss" or "Don" at the top who leads the organization, followed by a second in command or "Underboss." The Don is advised by a counselor, or consiglieri, who is usually third in command. Under these leaders are "Capos" who lead a crew of "Soldiers." At the bottom of the organization are "Associates" who may not be official family members but assist in criminal activity.
- Self-identification—The degree to which individuals in the group see themselves as being a part of an organization: there are examples of group connections such as the use of colors, special clothing, special language, and tattoos. The individuals in Organized Crime groups self-identify as being members of a group. In street gangs, drug cartels, and the mafia an erstwhile member may need to undergo some type of initiation, often involving committing a crime. There will also be certain customs, beliefs unique to the group that a person who identifies with this group will adopt. Members may also share an argot, or specialized language.
- Authority of reputation—The degree to which the organization has the capacity to force others to do what it dictates through fear and intimidation, without resorting to violence. Organized Crime groups can intimidate civilians and law enforcement and defend their zone of criminal activity through their reputation.

Previous acts of violence precede Organized Crime groups, such that potential rivals, concerned citizens, and even law enforcement are less likely to interfere with current or future crimes. This reputation develops over time and speaks to a permanence and stability that Organized Crime groups have, that individuals committing crimes that are organized do not.

These dimensions are good theoretical tools for analyzing a group and determining if it can be sufficiently categorized as an Organized Crime group. However, it is important to note that these dimensions are only guideposts, and groups will vary in the degree to which they fall on any given dimension. Ultimately labelling a group as an Organized Crime group is a matter of informed judgment.

We will use these dimensions to construct a working definition of Organized Crime for this chapter. *Organized Crime groups are defined as hierarchical and structured organizations conducting sophisticated criminal activities in which the members develop their own inner culture, and the group develops a reputation for criminality.* Our next task is to import this definition into the digital environment and explore the ways Organized Crime—now we can say Organized Cybercrime is conducted online.

The Unique Characteristics of Organized Cybercrime

Organized Crime can occur offline and online. Groups that have historically operated in the physical environment can use digital technologies to help facilitate traditional crime, and they can expand their criminal activities to include cybercrimes. However, a new class of criminals emerged during the Internet Age—hackers and others interested in using computer technology to commit crime—are primarily online based. We can think of these groups as Organized Cybercrime groups. Organized Cybercrime has different characteristics than traditional Organized Crime groups.

One difference is that crimes are coordinated over greater distances. Communication between different members can occur via text or instant messages, with the two parties being in different countries or continents. Moreover, the targets of these crimes are often in different countries. Most of the cybercrime attacks we have discussed in this text are such that the attacker is in a different country to the victim.

Another difference is that this coordination can potentially occur amongst a greater number of people. In the research for his famous ethnography *Gang Leader for a Day* (2008), Sudhir Venkatesh comments on how the gang leader J.T. had to find places for his gang to meet. As the leader, he had to identify and secure places large enough and secret enough for upwards of 100 gang members. This is no small task when law enforcement is attempting to monitor your movements. The digital environment greatly reduces this difficulty. Group members do not need to meet physically to coordinate activities.

There are some disadvantages to being exclusively online. For one, it is harder to establish a reputation of fear and intimidation when your members operate from computers, their primary focus is financial institutions and governments, and the crimes committed are usually cyberfraud. There have been several Organized Cybercrime groups that have gained the attention of companies and authorities for their ransomware attacks or data breaches. However, the public response seems to be one of anger or even fascination, not fear and intimidation.

Second, being online—often anonymous, does not lend itself to developing a sense of identity with the group. It is not impossible (we will discuss some research on an Anonymous cell in Quebec later in this chapter illustrating identity building), but it appears to be more difficult. Group identity develops through social interaction and shared experience. Organized Cybercrime Groups are less likely to have these shared experiences.

LEUKFELDT'S ORGANIZED CYBERCRIME TYPOLOGY

Leukfeldt and colleagues (2017) have provided a typology of organized cybercrime, derived from a study of 18 phishing criminal investigations in Denmark. According to these scholars, organized cybercrime networks can be divided into three types based upon the sophistication of technology used and the degree of victim–attacker interaction:

- Type 1: Low-tech attacks with a high degree of victim–attacker interaction—The attacker sends a phishing email to a victim stating that their account is not secure. The victim supplies banking information when clicking on the link. An attacker then contacts the victim by phone and gains more information that can be used to steal monies from the victim's account
- Type 2: Low-tech attacks with a low degree of victim–attacker interaction—These attacks are more sophisticated and find ways of extracting necessary information without the use of a phone call. A phishing email may be designed such that a victim inputs all the necessary information via the email
- Type 3: High-tech attacks with a low degree of victim–attacker interaction—These attacks are the most sophisticated and rely on various types of malware to infect and control a computer. Once this occurs, the criminal network can manipulate the bank transfers of the victim

Although this is a typology specifically describing phishing groups, it can aid our understandings of how to investigate a criminal network. For example, questions can be asked as to what kind of offenders are more likely to associate with a given organized network. The offenders who migrate to low-tech, high-interaction crime networks are likely more comfortable with human interaction in the physical environment and may branch off to other traditional types of con-artistry. They may be "script kiddies" who are only temporarily focusing on cybercrime. Meanwhile, offenders operating in high-tech, low-interaction networks may be classic "black hat hackers" who write malware for crimes solely in the digital environment. These criminals may continue working in Organized Cybercrime groups.

DIVISION OF LABOR IN ORGANIZED CYBERCRIME NETWORKS

Carding gangs (or carding crews) are groups whose primary criminal activity is the theft of credit card information. The process of carding involves finding ways to steal credit card information from individuals or credit card companies and extracting cash from that information through cashing out the cards, buying goods, or selling the credit card information in a market. In this context, Broadhurst et al., (2014) summarizes the ten roles in Organized Cybercrime carding networks:

1. Coders or programmers—They create the malware and exploits. The creation of malware and exploits is not in itself criminal
2. Technicians—They maintain the supporting technologies, such as servers, ISPs, and encryption
3. Distributors or vendors—They trade and sell stolen data in carding markets (carding markets are online forums where stolen credit card numbers are bought and sold)
4. Hackers—They search for vulnerabilities in applications, systems, and networks
5. Fraud specialists—They develop and employ non-technical social engineering schemes
6. Hosts—They provide facilities—servers and sites—for the storing and sharing of illicit content
7. Cashers—They control drop accounts and provide those names and accounts to other criminals for a fee; they also manage individual cash couriers, or "money mules"
8. Money mules—They transfer the proceeds of frauds to a third party for further transfer
9. Tellers—They assist in transferring and laundering illicit proceeds through digital currencies and national currencies
10. Executives—They select the targets, and recruit and assign members to the above tasks. They also manage the distribution of criminal proceeds

Like the organized phishing network example above, these roles are specific to the crime of carding, but also speak a general characteristic of organized cybercrime networks—their complexity. They can grow large and sophisticated. Of course, not all networks will have a person or persons that fulfill each of these roles. Given the media reports, most organized cybercrime networks are composed of a tight-knit group of hackers, who then build temporary connections with individuals and groups to perform other tasks. However, as an organized cybercrime network grows larger and undertakes a wider range of activities it will need individuals to permanently take on these roles. It is also the case that one person can fulfill several of these roles. For example, one person may perform the roles of coder, technician, and hacker as they require a similar skill set. Meanwhile, another person may handle all the "human contact" skills, such as being a distributor or fraud specialist.

THE ACTIVITIES OF ORGANIZED CYBERCRIME IN THE DIGITAL ENVIRONMENT

Organized Cybercrime can entail any of the crimes discussed within the four categories of cybertrespass, cyberpornography, cyberviolence, and cyberdeception. However, certain crimes are more effectively done using the infrastructure and resources of Organized Crime groups. Grabosky (2007) discusses several of these crimes, and we highlight four of these here—digital piracy, forging official documents, money laundering, and cyberter-rorism. We also add a fifth—wide-stroke attacks.

- Digital piracy—Digital piracy, as discussed in a previous chapter, is common-place in society. Most computer users who illegally download or share material do not consider their activities criminal. Indeed, there is little incentive for content creators, content distributors, or law enforcement to pursue digital piracy cases because an individual person's copyright infringement has little impact on the industry. However, Organized Crime groups pirate content on a large scale and cost industries millions of dollars. They have the financial resources to purchase the hardware to copy digitized content on compact discs. They also have the con-nections and infrastructure to deliver pirated materials to marketplaces
- Forging official documents—Organized Cybercrime groups participate in the digital reproduction of official documents, especially passports. The forging of official documents is itself a crime. But as Grabosky argues, it is also a crime facilitator. Fraudsters use driver's licenses to open bank accounts for the deposit-ing of stolen money. Criminals of all stripes may wish to cross borders to evade law enforcement and can use false passports to do so
- Money laundering—Governments monitor cash transactions, making it difficult for criminals to conceal the origins of their cash. However, the infrastructure of Organized Cybercrime makes it possible for money to be "cleaned." For example, the Organized Cybercrime group may have built a ledger of accounts in sev-eral countries and can route monies across many jurisdictions making it diffi-cult for funds to be traced. Another strategy is to use people as mules to deposit cash below the threshold of surveillance. Yet another strategy is to coordinate a phantom sale on an online auction website, where stolen cash is deposited in an account disguised as monies from a sale. What is important here is that these types of activities require a level of coordination and depth of infrastructure found in Organized Cybercrime groups.
- Cyberterrorism—Cyberterrorism can be described as "an intentional act, com-mitted via computer or communication system and motivated by political, reli-gious, or ideological objectives, against information, data, or computer systems/programs, intended to cause severe harm, death, or destruction to civilians" (Kremling & Parker, 2018, 131). Cyberterrorist activities are not usually labelled as Organized Cybercrime. But as Grabosky (2007) writes, "Most terrorist activ-ity is certainly organized. And it is usually, if not always, criminal. Moreover, one sees examples of terrorist organizations engaging in more traditional criminal activity in order to raise revenue" (153).
- Wide-stroke attacks—In addition to the crimes already listed, Organized Cybercrime groups supervise the mass deployment of malware, or what can be called wide-stroke attacks. These attacks include the collection of person-ally identifiable information (PII) sometimes needed to deploy the malware, the extraction of money or information, and the laundering of that money. Individual hackers or temporary groups can also perform these activities. However, organ-ized crime groups can better organize the collection of monetizable data and the laundering of money stolen. Moreover, because many examples of cybertrespass require social engineering, Organized Cybercrime groups can better recruit and deploy individuals with the right linguistic skills and social intelligence.

AN EXAMPLE OF ORGANIZED CYBERCRIME IN THE DIGITAL ENVIRONMENT—THE CARBANAK/COBALT GROUP

One example is the Russian Organized Crime group called Carbanak/Cobalt. The group has been in operation since 2013, and the name derives from the two pieces of malware—Carbanak and Cobalt—used to steal over 1.3 billion dollars during that time frame. Carbanak was the name of the first penetration tool used, and Cobalt followed. The group has attacked over 100 financial institutions across 14 European countries, including Britain, Russia, Spain, and the Netherlands.

The attacks follow a general pattern. First, the group deploys the malware through a spear phishing attack. Emails are sent to company employees, asking them to click on a link. Once one computer is infected, the malware spreads throughout the financial institution's network, eventually infecting the servers and ATMs. Next, criminals use money mules to extract cash. One way this is done is by inflating the balance of bank accounts and then having a money mule withdraw cash. Another is for the money mule to be at a specified ATM at a time when cash is automatically ejected. Next, the money is laundered by purchasing goods on black markets or converting the cash into cryptocurrencies.

The Carbanak/Cobalt gang has many of the characteristics of an Organized Cybercrime group. The crimes are complex and sophisticated, with the production of specialized malware deployed across a range of countries, and the need for a variety of co-conspirators working together. The organization exhibits a structure, with hackers and money mules being the two known roles. There is also a recognized leader. In 2018, the leader of Carbanak/Cobalt, called "Denis K" was arrested along with three other members of the group.

The two other characteristics of Organized Crime we introduced—self-identification and authority of reputation—are likely present. One indirect way of assessing reputation is to look at how much resources are dedicated to investigating and stopping the crime. The arrest of "Denis K" required the work of the Spanish National Police, Europol, the FBI, the Romanian, Moldovan, Belarussian, and Taiwanese authorities, and private cyber-security companies.

Arresting the leaders of mafias and street gangs will slow down and destabilize an Organized Crime group. However, these groups can often reorganize after a shuffle of roles and responsibilities within the group structure. After the arrest of "Denis K," the Carbanak/Cobalt group is still active.

ORGANIZED CRIME MYTHS

Many scholars are critical of the public's understanding of Organized Crime. They believe that the media sometimes over-hypes an instance of crime by describing it as organized, and therefore more dangerous. Lavorgna (2018) argues that explaining instances of activities that are organized as Organized Crime is a rhetorical tool to attract more resources to law enforcement agencies. In a study of UK news reports from 2010 to 2016, Lavorgna found consistent evidence that reports linking cybercrime with Organized Crime were "moral panics." The term moral panic refers to an exaggerated public concern that a group or trend is damaging society. News stories painted hyperbolic and exaggerated pictures of the prevalence and threat of Organized Cybercrime.

Similarly, Leukfeldt, Lavorgna, and colleagues (Leukfeldt, Lavorgna, et al., 2017) argue that many countries, such as the United Kingdom, link the seriousness of a crime to Organized Crime. A hacking activity that creates a large data breach, like the ones discussed in Chapter 2, may be considered an instance of Organized Crime simply because of the amount of money stolen. These crimes may indeed be sophisticated. But their lack of structure, lack of self-identification amongst those who participated in the crime, and the lack of reputation suggests that a collection of temporary co-conspirators committed these crimes, and not a stable group of organized criminals.

Caution is required when making a judgement about organized crime because the digital environment makes it easy for collections of individuals to come together and commit crime, and the labelling of these networks as Organized Crime may be premature. Because organized crime investigations are challenging and time-consuming, much-needed resources in time, money, and intellectual energy may be wasted on the wrong criminal activities.

State Cybercrime and State Digital Deviance

State crimes are criminal acts committed by or sponsored by governments in violation of international or domestic law. State crime occurs when a person acting on behalf of a state (government official, member of an intelligence agency, etc.) commits a criminal activity or when the state sponsors a criminal activity. With respect to sponsoring, Maurer (2018) suggests three ways this can occur (as summarized in Mannan (2019)):

- Delegation—The state selects agents to act on their behalf based on their expertise, in a "principal-agent" relationship. The state has only marginal control over the agent (non-state actor). But they try to screen their agents and monitor their actions closely. An example used by Maurer is the hiring of private contractors by the United States government.
- Orchestration—The state selects agents to act on their behalf and then support them with knowledge and materials. Maurer gives the example of the Iranian government, who cultivated and now supports a group of hackers to increase its cyber capabilities. In the orchestration model, the state has more direct control over the non-state actor, deploying them to complete specific tasks.
- Sanctioning—The state does not actively provide support or guidance but tolerates the behaviors of the non-state actor. In this model, the state has little control over the activities of the non-state actor. The state may choose to take this approach, according to Maurer, for several reasons. One reason is because the non-state group is popular within its national borders and cracking down on them would lead to citizen unrest. Another is because successful activities of the non-state actor may allow the state to project a veneer of power. Or the state can enjoy the benefits of the actors activities in a more internationally palatable way. Meaning that allowing a group to continue their cybercrime activities is not seen as negatively as activity funding and supporting that group. Maurer cites Russia as an example of a nation using the sanctioning model.

Most documented state crimes appear to be state sponsored and are hard to attribute to a government. The problem of attribution—knowing who is ultimately responsible for the act—is one of the unique problems with cybercrimes in general, and especially with state cybercrime. Is it the state itself to blame, like their intelligence agency or branch of their military? Is it a state-sponsored entity, like a hacker organization financed by the state? If it is a state-sponsored entity, to what degree should a state be held accountable? Or is it a group that has no real connection to the state but nonetheless wishes to support the state in some way, like a nationalist paramilitary organization?

The victim of a state cybercrime is usually another state, and the motive tends to be "the need to identify and to neutralize perceived national security threats, or to give one's nation a strategic advantage" (Grabosky, 2015, 11). To put it another way, when the computer systems of a company, government agency, or person are targeted, the ultimate purpose is for the offender state to gain some sort of advantage over the victim state. For example, in 2022 Meta, Facebook's parent company, removed a network of Russian accounts impersonating European news outlets. The fake news outlets spread disinformation about the Russian invasion of Ukraine in early 2022. While the victim was Facebook in terms of exceeding unauthorized access (the terms of service were violated), the ultimate purpose of the campaign was to weaken Ukraine. According to a threat analyst at Facebook:

> *You can actually sum up everything it was saying in ten words: 'Ukraine's bad. Russia's good. Stop the sanctions. Stop supplying weapons'.*
>
> (Bond, 2022)

This example also illustrates the problem of attribution. Russia benefits from the disinformation campaign, but who was the offender? Were the group of accounts acting alone, funded by the Russian government, or was it the Russian government itself? This is the problem of attribution.

Disinformation campaigns are a well-known way a state may act criminally in the digital environment. Scholars and news agencies have identified several other activities that can qualify as state cybercrime:

- Espionage—Spying to gain access to sensitive information. The objective of espionage is most often to obtain sensitive information for strategic or political purposes. For example, a Pakistan-based hacking group called "Transparent Tribe" have conducted a series of attacks on the Indian military. The two countries have had a historically hostile relationship. The operation has been dubbed "Operation Sidecopy" by cybersecurity researchers (Dogra, 2020). The operation's aim is to steal sensitive information from the Indian military.
- Theft—Unlawfully taking the property of another state. As in the chapter on cyberfraud, theft in the digital environment is usually of intellectual property (IP) or money. Theft differs from espionage (which can be thought of as the theft of sensitive information) primarily in the objectives and targets. The objective of espionage is often to gain a strategic advantage militarily or during negotiations with that other country. Thus, the targets are military or government officials. The objective of theft is to acquire Intellectual or economic assets that benefit the country committing the crime. Thus, the targets are financial institutions or corporations. For example, it has been reported that North Korean hackers stole

approximately 3 billion US dollars from corporations and financial institutions worldwide. Much of the money, it is reported, is being used to fund their ballistics program (McMillan & Volz, 2023).

- Sabotage—Damaging infrastructure and technologies. Critical infrastructure—what is it and its importance, is frequently discussed when exploring aspects of state cybercrimes. We will explore critical infrastructure later in this chapter. But briefly, critical infrastructure is the systems a nation relies on to function. Most modern states use computer networks to operate these systems—subways, airports, electrical grids, water filtration systems, banking systems. Critical infrastructure is a prime target for states. For example, a state directly (or more likely sponsor) the hacking into another state's passenger rail line and infecting it with ransomware.
- Surveillance—The monitoring of individuals and entities. Generally, when state surveillance is discussed, the focus is on monitoring individuals, although it is possible for entire corporations or government agencies to be surveilled.

Cyber Privateers

During the period when naval ships dominated international trade and were a primary tool for the prosecution of war, what is called the "Age of Sail," states would authorize private individuals and groups to engage in acts of piracy against enemy ships. They were not understood as pirates because the government granted them commissions to carry out their activities, and they kept a percentage of the profits from the goods they pirated. Privateering was a legal and legitimate state activity for many centuries. Several scholars have wrestled with whether state-sponsored cybercriminals should be understood as "cyber privateers" (Gregg & Scott, 2006; Egloff, 2022; Martin & Whelan, 2023).

Martin and Whelan (2023) examine two state-sponsored ransomware groups—Darkside and REvil—and argue that these groups should be understood as "cyber privateers." DarkSide was responsible for the attacks on the Colonial Pipeline—a main artery supplying oil to the United States East Coast. Meanwhile, REvil attacked JBS Foods, a Brazilian multinational food company. Both groups were working within Russia's borders and are viewed as being sanctioned by the Russian state.

They argue that the Russian state and criminal networks are intertwined, creating a dynamic different from that found in many Western nations:

> *The extraordinary degree of integration between the Russian state and domestic criminal networks ensures that no criminal industry of any size or significance escapes the notice of state representatives who, it is argued, are not concerned in the administration of law enforcement and justice per se, but rather in state control and the steady flow of illicit profits all the way up to the Kremlin.*
>
> (Martin & Whelan, 2023, 16)

They argue that the Russian state follows the sanctioning model proposed by Maurer (2018), allowing these groups to operate freely as long as they do not target Russian-owned or affiliated computer networks.

Dwan et al. (2022), working from an international law perspective, are less sure that the privateer analogy for state-sponsored hackers is appropriate. Their argument rests on the illegality of actual privateering. The Paris Declaration Respecting Maritime Law, signed in 1865 by many countries, including the two dominant naval powers England and France, prohibited privateering. Since privateering is illegal, they reason, non-state actors do not have legal cover for sponsoring criminal activities. A state cannot then give non-state actors legal permission to conduct hacking activities against another state. Despite their critiques of the analogy, the cyber privateers analogy will likely continue to be used to describe state-supported hacking groups.

AN EXAMPLE OF STATE CRIME: APT41

APT41 (Advanced Persistent Threat 41) is a hacking group associated with the Chinese government. According to the Council on Foreign Relations, the group has conducted both espionage and financially motivated activities:

> *This threat actor has, since 2014, conducted operations backed by the Chinese government, including targeting the health-care and high-tech sectors and conducting espionage against political dissidents. It has simultaneously conducted its own for-profit illicit activity in the video games industry, amassing millions of dollars in digital currency to be sold to gamers on the black market.*
>
> (APT41, n.d.)

APT41 has been a prolific and long-standing state-sponsored organized crime group. Members of the group are on the United States Federal Bureau of Investigation's Most Wanted List on several charges including Unauthorized Access to Protected Computers, Aggravated Identity Theft, and Money Laundering.

APT41 illustrates what makes organized crime under the cover of state support so dangerous. The group is enduring, being in operation since at least 2012. Because its base of operations is within a state that sanctions their activities, law enforcement agencies in other countries cannot bring the group to justice. Moreover, the group has the resources and tools to undertake complex operations. According to the cybersecurity firm Mandiant, "APT41 leverages an arsenal of over 46 different malware families and tools to accomplish their missions, including publicly available utilities, malware shared with other Chinese espionage operations, and tools unique to the group" (APT41, n.d.).

Cyberwar

According to Singer and Friedman (2014):

> *Defining cyberwar need not be so complicated. The key elements of war in cyberspace all have their parallels and connections to warfare in other domains...Whether it be war on land, at sea, or in the air, or now in cyberspace, war always has a political goal (which distinguishes it from crime) and always has an element of violence.*
>
> (121)

Singer and Friedman identify three key elements in cyberwar—it occurs in cyberspace (or as we term it here in this text the digital environment), there is a political goal, and there is an element of violence.

We add one other element to their definition. Cyberwar occurs between two states or territories governed by a political unit. This stipulation seems necessary for several reasons. First, suppose military theorist Carl von Clausewitz is correct that war is a "continuation of politics by other means." In that case, cyberwar is an attempt to enact policy through armed conflict when other, non-violent means have failed. War ends with the signing of enforceable treaties between political units. If the armed combatants in the war did not commit war crimes—an action carried out during the commission of a war that violates agreed upon rules of war, then they are allowed to return to their lives with no penalty. Second, the international community has developed conventions of war over the years that govern how states conduct a war to some degree. For example, the protocols from the various Geneva Conventions held over the years are meant to protect people who are not directly participating in an armed conflict—citizens, journalists, and medical professionals. Theoretically, states conducting warfare may wish to avoid the sanctions that come with violating the rules of war. The war will end, and they will want to participate in international trade and scientific collaboration. Of course, there are exceptions to this, but almost every nation has adopted some or all the convention protocols.

Consider hacktivists or extremist groups. They may wish to attack another nation, have political goals, and use violence. Their attacks would be similar in form to those conducted by nation-states—targeting critical infrastructure, for example. So, are they participating in cyberwar? Not likely. There is no treaty to sign because the groups are not the government of a territory and people. As such, the actions of these groups are best understood as criminal or as terrorism.

Levinson (2020) argues that there are two types of cyberwar—micro-cyberwar and macro-cyberwar. Macro-cyberwar is "when one nation takes over another's infra-structure, including, at its worst, the nation's health care, transport, and/or nuclear facilities" (171). Meanwhile, micro-cyberwar is when a state targets a specific person—their devices and the files they may possess. He argues that macro attacks are more hypothetical, while micro attacks have been documented more frequently.

The Difference Between State Crime and Cyberwarfare

A question may be asked: What is the difference between state crimes and cyberwar? Hacking into a foreign officials computer and stealing information (espionage or theft), for example, is a violation of domestic law (state crime) and can be an act committed when two countries are in conflict (cyberwarfare). One the one hand, the distinction between the two seems a matter of context. During peacetime, when states are expected to abide by international and domestic laws, these acts are state crimes. During war time, when there is no expectation that two nations in conflict will respect each other's laws, these are acts of cyberwarfare.

While this is a general rule, some cyberwarfare acts may be considered war crimes by international governing bodies. For example, during the Russo-Ukrainian War, Ukranian officials have argued that the cyberattacks from Russia on their country's critical infrastructure are war crimes (we will discuss critical infrastructure in the section below on cyberterrorism). For example, Victor Zhora, a top cybersecurity official said in a 2023 interview:

> *When we observe the situation in cyberspace we notice some coordination between kinetic strikes and cyberattacks, and since the majority of kinetic attacks are organized against civilians — being a direct act of war crime — supportive actions in cyber can be considered as war crimes.*
>
> (Van Sant, 2023)

We will return to this idea of cyberwarfare as war crime in the critical thinking section at the end of this chapter.

Cyberterrorism

A good working definition of cyberterrorism, provided by Kremling and Parker (2018), is "an intentional act, committed via computer or communication system and motivated by political, religious, or ideological objectives, against information, data, or computer systems/programs, intended to cause severe harm, death, or destruction to civilians" (131).

Kremling and Parker do not include in their definition terrorist groups using digital technologies to support their goals. The authors focus solely on direct terrorist acts committed by computer. But certainly terrorist groups can use computer technologies to facilitate or aid in their goals. For example, terrorist groups can use social media to spread their ideology. They can recruit new members in online chat rooms. They can defraud people online or steal money to finance their activities. And they can use computers or mobile phones to coordinate physical attacks. But these activities in support of terrorism are not the same as using the digital environment to directly inflict harm on civilians.

Some scholars believe that these supporting activities should also be understood as cyberterrorism. However, the authors of this textbook agree with Kremling and Parker in separating acts of cyberterrorism that directly harm individuals from activities in the digital environment that support future cyberterrorism. This is because implied in the notion of terrorism is terror, or fear. Cyberterrorist groups using the digital environment to recruit members or communicate their ideology to the public do not generally instill fear in a population.

One of the main ways in which experts theorize cyberterrorism will occur is through attacks on critical infrastructure. We have mentioned critical infrastructure briefly above and will discuss more detail here. Critical infrastructure refers to the systems and the computers that facilitate their operation that are so vital to a state that if they were to be disrupted or incapacitated the citizens in that country could face serious physical or psychological harm. Examples of critical infrastructure include:

- Financial institutions
- Communication networks
- Transportation systems
- Power grids
- Water supply systems
- Healthcare facilities

If cyberterrorists gain unauthorized access to the computers or networks that support critical infrastructure they could cause tremendous damage. Disrupting or halting the operation of a power grid, water supply system, or transportation system in the country could halt daily life. Lack of power, water, and transportation would lead to economic losses for businesses, increased crime and chaos, and will likely lead to deaths of citizens. Moreover, suppose citizens become aware that the cause of the problem was a cyberattack from a terrorist group. In that case, the public will become fearful and lose trust in the ability of their government to protect them from outside threats.

WHY NO CYBERTERRORISM?

If we use Kremling and Parker's definition, then there have been no recorded acts of cyberterrorism. Even though there has been much discussion of cyberterrorism in the media, no political, religious, or ideological group has yet inflicted direct harm, death, or destruction on civilians through the digital environment. Why not? Jacobsen (2022) offers four reasons:

1. *Cyberterrorism is more difficult to produce than terrorism by physical means.* It requires more than good hacking skills. Jacobsen (2022) writes "cyberterrorists must 'weaponize' the targeted computer in such a way that it enables it to cause material destruction or bodily harm. As a result, the cyberterrorist must have in-depth knowledge, not only about how to access, read, find vulnerabilities and write computer code, but also possess specific knowledge about the technical processes that can cause destruction in the selected target" (63). If a cyberterrorist wanted to stop a subway line from operating, they need to have knowledge not just of computer networks but also how the subway line they want to derail works. Cyberterrorists could hire hackers with the required expertise, but Jacobsen argues that this is unlikely. One of the reasons for this is that other types of cybercrimes are more lucrative and are less likely to draw the attention of federal law enforcement agencies.
2. *Cyberterrorism does not produce a media spectacle.* If a subway line is shut down because of a cyberattack, it will certainly instill fear in the population and depending upon when and how the line was halted it may cause loss of life. But most types of cyberattacks will not generate the type of attention a terrorist group needs to publicize their cause. Cyberterrorism would not usually be fear inducing or cause a nation to focus their attention on the perpetrator of the crime (ask yourself, have you heard of any of the Organized Cybercrime gangs before you read this text?). Compare the visuality of a suicide bomber or planes flying into buildings, with a water filtration plant being shut down for several days. For this reason, terrorist groups will choose the former and not the latter.
3. *Hackers with the skills to commit cyberterror are simply not as interested in physical violence.* Jacobsen argues that radicals become ready for violence by mimicking or performing the life of an extremist. In the case of Jihadists, "walking, talking, training and even producing fake reenacted beheading videos is transforming the subject and its violent capacities" (Jacobsen, 2022, 65). Far-right domestic terrorist Anders B. Breivik, who in 2011 killed 78 people in Norway, practiced shooting skills on *Call of Duty* and bought a uniform to pose in with medals. Meanwhile, hackers are invested in the thrill of solving puzzles and spend most of their time looking at computer code.

4. *Cyberterrorism often requires collaboration, and it is hard to generate trust online.* People who are skilled enough to produce a cyberattack are so few—especially given reasons 1 and 3—that it is unlikely that these individuals will be found in a shared physical space (e.g. same city). Thus, if a terrorist group wants to recruit hackers they must do so through online forums and social media. However, because of the anonymity of online spaces, terrorist organizations cannot easily vet the people they may communicate with, making them vulnerable to infiltration by counterterrorism groups. These factors discourage collaboration.

Conclusion

In this chapter we explored organized crime as it operates in the digital environment. We discussed some of the difficulties in defining and describing what makes Organized Crime different than "crimes that are organized." While acknowledging that there are other ways of defining the phenomena, we settled on a definition incorporating the elements of sophistication, structure, self-identification, and reputation. Organized Crime in the digital environment is characterized more by network connections, and we discussed two typologies developed by social scientists. We suggest that as life becomes more digital, Organized Crime, like street and property crimes, will continue to migrate into the digital environment. We see this already with traditional mafia groups moving their operations online.

We next moved to state cybercrime and cyberwar. While these two phenomena are similar, the former violates international or domestic law, and the latter are actions done during the commission of an armed conflict. Cybersecurity researchers have documented many instances of state-sponsored cybercrimes, where a state delegates, orchestrates, or sanctions the activities of a non-state actor. The world is also witnessing acts of cyberwarfare in the Russo-Ukranian War.

We ended this chapter with a discussion of cyberterrorism. While there has been much discussion about terrorist groups harming civilians through actions in the digital environment, it has not happened yet. However, that does not mean that it won't, and cybersecurity and military professionals will need to be vigilant in protecting its citizens from extremist groups.

CHAPTER 7 CURRENT EVENTS AND CRITICAL THINKING:

Is Attacking Critical Infrastructure a War Crime? Is it Moral?

A war crime can be defined as an action carried out during the commission of a war that violates agreed-upon rules of war. War crimes can be committed against civilians, prisoners of war, and other non-combatants. Some examples of war crimes include:

- Targeting civilians: Deliberately causing harm to civilian populations (bombing, air strikes)
- Massacres: Deliberately killing of large numbers of unarmed civilians without due process
- Torture: Inflicting severe pain or suffering on soldiers, detainees, or civilians

- Sexual violence: Using sexual violence—rape, forced prostitution, and sexual slavery—as a tactic in war
- Attacking protected objects: Intentionally attacking objects protected under international law such as cultural, religious, and historical monuments, hospitals, schools, and places of worship
- The use of Biological, Chemical, and Nuclear Weapons: Using weapons that inflict unnecessary suffering or have indiscriminate effects on civilians, such as biological, chemical, or nuclear weapons
- Denial of humanitarian aid: Preventing organizations that provide aid to civilians in need, such as OXFAM and the Red Cross, from delivering that aid

Some of these war crimes can be committed through a cyberattack. Which ones, and how? Should nations be seen as morally wrong if they commit a war crime through a cyberattack? Why or why not? Should countries sign a rule of war agreement prohibiting attacks on critical infrastructure? Why or why not?

REFERENCES

APT41: A dual espionage and cyber crime operation. (n.d.). *Mandiant*. Retrieved July 23, 2023, from https://www.mandiant.com/resources/blog/apt41-dual-espionage-and-cyber-crime-operation

Bond, S. (2022, September 27). Facebook takes down Russian network impersonating European news outlets. *NPR*. https://www.npr.org/2022/09/27/1125217316/facebook-takes-down-russian-network-impersonating-european-news-outlets

Broadhurst, R., Grabosky, P., Alazab, M., & Chon, S. (2014). Organizations and cyber crime: An analysis of the nature of groups engaged in cyber crime. *International Journal of Cyber Criminology*, 8(1), 20.

Dogra, S. (2020, October 4). Pakistani hackers blamed for cyber attacks on Indian defense forces, says report. *IndiaTimes*. https://www.indiatimes.com/technology/news/pakistani-hackers-cyber-attacks-indian-defense-forces-524059.html

Dwan, J. H., Paige, T. P., & McLaughlin, R. (2022). Pirates of the cyber seas: Are state-sponsored hackers modern-day privateers? *Law, Technology and Humans*, 3(2). https://doi.org/10.5204/lthj.1583.

Egloff, F. J. (2022). *Semi-state actors in cybersecurity*. Oxford University Press.

Finckenauer, J. O. (2005). Problems of definition: What is organized crime? *Trends in Organized Crime*, 8(3), 63–83. https://doi.org/10.1007/s12117-005-1038-4

Grabosky, P. (2007). The Internet, technology, and organized crime. *Asian Journal of Criminology*, 2(2), 145–161. https://doi.org/10.1007/s11417-007-9034-z

Grabosky, P. (2015). Organized cybercrime and national security. In R. G. Smith, R. C.-C. Cheung, & L. Y.-C. Lau (Eds.), *Cybercrime risks and responses* (pp. 67–80). Palgrave Macmillan UK. https://doi.org/10.1057/9781137474162_5

Gregg, D. G., & Scott, J. E. (2006). The role of reputation systems in reducing on-line auction fraud. *International Journal of Electronic Commerce*, 10(3), 95–120. https://doi.org/10.2753/JEC1086-4415100304

Hagan, F. E. (2006). "Organized crime" and "organized crime": Indeterminate problems of definition. *Trends in Organized Crime*, 9(4), 127–137. https://doi.org/10.1007/s12117-006-1017-4

Jacobsen, J. T. (2022). Cyberterrorism: Four reasons for its absence—So far. *Perspectives on Terrorism*, 16(5).

Kremling, J., & Parker, A. M. S. (2018). *Cyberspace, cybersecurity, and cybercrime* (1st edition). SAGE Publications.

Lavorgna, A. (2018). Cyber-organised crime. A case of moral panic? *Trends in Organized Crime*. https://doi.org/10.1007/s12117-018-9342-y

Leukfeldt, E. R., Kleemans, E. R., & Stol, W. P. (2017). A typology of cybercriminal networks: From low-tech all-rounders to high-tech specialists. *Crime, Law and Social Change, 67*(1), 21–37. https://doi.org/10.1007/s10611-016-9662-2

Leukfeldt, E. R., Lavorgna, A., & Kleemans, E. R. (2017). Organised cybercrime or cybercrime that is organised? An assessment of the conceptualisation of financial cybercrime as organised crime. *European Journal on Criminal Policy and Research, 23*(3), 287–300. https://doi.org/10.1007/s10610-016-9332-z

Levinson, P. (2020). Micro-cyberwar vs. macro-cyberwar: Towards the beginning of a taxonomy. *Digital War, 1*(1–3), 171–172. https://doi.org/10.1057/s42984-020-00020-z

Mannan, S. H. (2019). Projecting power: How states use proxies in cyberspace. *Journal of National Security Law & Politics, 10*(2), 445–461.

Martin, J., & Whelan, C. (2023). Ransomware through the lens of state crime: Conceptualizing ransomware groups as cyber proxies, pirates, and privateers. *State Crime*.

Maurer, T. (2018). *Cyber mercenaries: The state, hackers, and power.* Cambridge University Press.

McMillan, R., & Volz, D. (2023, June 11). WSJ News Exclusive | How North Korea's hacker army stole $3 billion in crypto, funding nuclear program. *Wall Street Journal*. https://www.wsj.com/articles/how-north-koreas-hacker-army-stole-3-billion-in-crypto-funding-nuclear-program-d6fe8782

Singer, P. W., & Friedman, A. (2014). *Cybersecurity and cyberwar: What everyone needs to know.* Oxford University Press.

Van Sant, S. (2023, January 9). Kyiv argues Russian cyberattacks could be war crimes. *POLITICO*. https://www.politico.eu/article/victor-zhora-ukraine-russia-cyberattack-infrastructure-war-crime/

Venkatesh, S. A. (2008). Gang leader for a day: A rogue sociologist takes to the streets. Penguin Press.

Algorithms, AI, and Big Data

Introduction

In this chapter, we look at how the criminal justice system is using Big Data, algorithms, and artificial intelligence to investigate and prosecute crimes. Big Data is used to train algorithms that help professionals in law enforcement make decisions. The police, the courts, and correctional institutions have embraced algorithms. They promise a more efficient and impartial means of accomplishing the goals they have as institutions. However, these new technologies are not beyond criticism. Many advocacy groups question the use of algorithms and allege that they are violating civil liberties and can be biased against minority groups.

Society is entering the age of artificial intelligence (AI). AI refers to computer systems that perform tasks that require human intelligence. AI is not human intelligence *per se*, but mimics the outputs of human intelligence. The relationship between algorithms, Big Data, and AI is straightforward: Big Data provides the raw material, and algorithms are the instructions used to derive outputs from that material, and when those outputs mirror human intelligence, we call that system AI.

Artificial intelligence represents a step forward in the use of Big Data and algorithms. Many of the examples we discuss below end with a human taking the output from algorithms and making a decision. *However, AI computer systems make decisions themselves or perform actions without the direct guidance of humans.* As of this writing, few examples of AI are used in this way within our criminal justice system. However, we expect law enforcement agencies, correctional facilities, and courts to begin using AI more in the future. As such, we will use some examples from AI usage in cybersecurity to think about how AI can potentially be used in the criminal justice system.

DOI: 10.4324/9781003283256-8

Understanding Big Data

Big Data refers to large quantities of information produced by and stored on computers (Kitchin & McArdle, 2016). The number of discussions surrounding Big Data lends support to the notion that modern societies are in the "age of Big Data." Organizations and governments are developing ways of collecting and organizing massive amounts of data generated by computers. "Data analytics" has become a profession and a college major. "Chief Data Scientist" or "Chief Information Officer" are executive positions that are well paid and hold a high degree of status. A question one can ask is, why has Big Data become so important? There are several reasons.

First, computer hardware has become more powerful. As computer hardware is only ever an information-producing machine—taking inputs and producing outputs—more powerful machines mean potentially more data produced. An oft-cited example is that a modern smartphone is more powerful than the computers used in the original Apollo space mission.

Second, software applications, and the algorithms powering those applications, have become more sophisticated. As we will discuss later, computer programmers and mathematicians have developed algorithms that can read handwriting, recognize speech patterns, and learn a language.

Third, more of life's activities have migrated into the digital environment. This means that more data can be collected. In *Everybody Lies: Big Data, New Data, and What the Internet Can Tell Us About Who We Really Are*, data scientist Seth Stephens-Davidowitz (Stephens-Davidowitz, 2017) uses Google search data to answer questions about racism, abortion, and pornography among other things. Google collects the searches of users and makes this data available publicly. Stephens-Davidowitz uses this data to show, for example, that a large proportion of young men are attracted to elderly women, and men search for ways to perform oral sex on themselves as often as they search for pleasuring the opposite sex. He also found that areas of the United States that showed the most support for Donald Trump made the most Google searches for the racial epithet "n-----." These types of insights would be unavailable if people chose not to conduct these activities online.

While we can talk about Big Data in shorthand as large quantities of information, scholars and writers have identified specific characteristics that identify data as "Big":

- Volume—The sheer amount of information. Organizations are often manipulating data that are many terabytes or petabytes in size. For comparison, someone may carry a flash drive that stores 10 gigabytes (GB) of data, or their personal computers store 500 GBs of data. This is enough storage for most people for all their videos, music, and files. A terabyte (TB) is approximately 1,000 gigabytes, and mid to large size organizations have databases and servers housing several terabytes of data. A petabyte is even larger and is applicable mainly to government databases or the largest organizations. One petabyte is 1,000 terabytes or 1,000,000 gigabytes. Some organizations like the United States military and social media companies have several petabytes (PB) of data stored on their machines.

- Velocity—The speed at which new data is produced. Some databases are relatively static, meaning that once data is collected, it remains relevant for months and even years. An example would be the United States Census, which can be downloaded via an Excel file. One can change their copy, but the original information is meant to remain a permanent record of value for generations to come. As such, the data analysis will occur at a slower speed and remain relevant to the organization for a longer period. However, with Big Data, new information is constantly being added to databases and necessitates a much quicker data analysis. Organizations that analyze data from social media applications to gauge public opinion must revise their conclusions based on this new information.

- Variety—The number of sources and formats in which data is retrieved. Organizations must analyze data in the form of raw numbers, video, audio, and text. Moreover, this information can come from a variety of sources. For example, facial recognition technology uses at least two streams of data—the video feed from CCTV along with the images, text, and numerical data from a state license database. The technology must extract meaningful information from both streams to match an image with a license, and then present this information to law enforcement.

It is important to note that there are degrees of Big Data. Any particular use of information will vary on levels of volume, velocity, and variety. For example, the data used in law enforcement for predictive policing is likely lower in volume, less dynamic, and has less variety than the data used by large technology companies. However, it is still "Big" relative to the types of data historically used in policing.

There can be other characteristics of Big Data. Many scholars include veracity—the accuracy of the data collected—as an important characteristic. Veracity can be important, as valid conclusions cannot be drawn if the data collected is not accurate. Consider the problems that can be caused if police reports did not record actual events or biased events in favor of officers. This would mean that any algorithms applied to the data will produce erroneous conclusions.

Some scholars also include volatility. This is similar to velocity. However, velocity refers to the speed at which new data is produced and collected, while volatility refers to the relevance of that data over time to the organization. Consider a rapid response team during a hurricane using an application that places help requests on a map and plots the most efficient rescue path. This information is highly volatile, as the number of people needing rescue and their locations will change by the hour.

Understanding Algorithms

An algorithm is a sequence of instructions used to solve a problem. The algorithm takes input in the form of data, performs a set of instructions, and produces an output. In her book *Hello World: Being Human in the Age of Algorithms*, Hannah Fry (Fry, 2018) organizes the real-world tasks of algorithms into four categories:

- Prioritization—The ordering of data regarding importance. Examples of prioritization include the ordered search results on a webpage, the list of results presented by a Google search, and a list of homes a user is likely to buy or rent.
- Classification—Placing data into meaningful categories. Organizations want to place entities into categories they deem important so that they can make decisions about what content to provide or what actions they should take. A risk assessment

algorithm classifies offenders into "high risk" and "low risk." When inappropriate content is removed from YouTube, a classification algorithm has scanned videos and placed them into "appropriate" and "inappropriate."

- Association—Finding relationships between data. When someone sees "You might like this" on a software application, an association algorithm may be at the core of the suggestion. An association algorithm connects two or more pieces of data from databases in the past and assumes that similar pieces of data will be connected in the future. And so, because so many users who bought a pair of sneakers in the past also bought an activity tracker, a person buying a new pair of running shoes will get a suggestion for Fitbit models.
- Filtering—Removing data deemed unimportant. Software applications that aggregate content for users, such as Facebook or Twitter, use algorithms that filter out unimportant news stories, tweets, and posts. Filtering algorithms present a more pleasant experience for the user, as content that he or she may find boring or unpleasant is removed. However, some scholars have found fault with these algorithms when used to filter out news stories.

Most computer applications and institutions must accomplish all four tasks to produce their products or services. As with many examples in this text, we simplify to explain the underlying concepts. And so, Fry writes:

> *Take UberPool, for instance, which matches prospective passengers with others heading in the same direction. Given your start point and end point, it has to filter through the possible routes that could get you home, look for connections with other users headed in the same direction, and pick one group to assign you to—all while prioritizing routes with the fewest turns for the driver, to make the ride as efficient as possible.*
> (2018, 10)

ALGORITHMIC OUTPUTS AS SOCIAL CONSTRUCTIONS

There may be a tendency to assume that the values produced by an algorithm are unbiased and neutral, and therefore can be trusted (Lee, 2018; O'Neil, 2016). Indeed, in most professions, the data produced through computer applications are rarely questioned by those who use them. One reason for this is that algorithms appear to have a sense of objectivity because a computer makes the decisions. If a computer says that a black offender is more likely to be a recidivist, then this is seen as being more trustworthy than if a judge makes the same claim based on her experience. People may view the judge as being biased because of stereotypes, but not the computer. Another reason is that those who are using the data produced by algorithms are not aware of how the data is produced (Burrell, 2016). If police are told to patrol in a certain area because it is a high crime area, they may not be aware of what inputs were used to produce the "high crime area" output.

But algorithms and their outputs are what social scientists call "socially constructed." Individuals make decisions as to what phenomena are important and worthy of their time developing algorithms for. They determine what data are used as inputs. They make decisions as to what procedures or formulas are used to produce outputs. And they make decisions about how those outputs are used. All those decisions are contingent upon our constructed world and what individuals and groups have decision-making power. This understanding means we should not accept the use of algorithms uncritically and should always hold them up to scrutiny (Mittelstadt et al., 2016).

The Impact of Big Data and Algorithms in the Criminal Justice System

In 2016, Georgetown University's Center on Privacy & Technology Law produced a report entitled The Perpetual Line-up: Unregulated Police Face Recognition in America (Garvie et al., 2016). The report stated that:

> *16 states let the FBI use face recognition technology to compare the faces of suspected criminals to their driver's license and ID photos, creating a virtual line-up of their state residents. In this line-up, it's not a human that points to the suspect—it's an algorithm.*

Along with the FBI, at least 26 states allow their law enforcement personnel to use facial recognition technology, and over 117 million American adults are affected. Facial recognition matches images from an established database holding personal information, such as a driver's license database, with images collected from the web, public cameras, or law enforcement taking pictures on the spot. The technology sifts through the collected images and matches them with the established database. The algorithm provides a probabilistic answer based upon certain characteristics, including the distance between the eyes, the width of the nose, and geometric proportions of the face. Because a person's facial image can be collected anywhere and everywhere as they walk or drive through a town and post images of themselves online, it is possible to identify and monitor a person without them knowing it.

The report highlighted several aspects of facial recognition technology that threaten civil liberties. Agencies do not need a warrant to search a database of images. It can be argued that this violates citizens' Fourth Amendment protection from illegal search and seizure. People can be searched without their consent, and this monitoring can be done without reasonable suspicion. The use of the technology can also threaten a citizen's First Amendment rights to free speech and freedom of assembly. Because anonymity is often necessary for people to speak their minds or express themselves, facial recognition technology threatens this fundamental civil liberty. Individuals may hesitate to join protests, and law enforcement may target an individual simply because they attended a protest.

Another problem is that the algorithm may better detect some phenotypes than others. According to the report:

> *algorithms developed in East Asia performed better on East Asians, while algorithms developed in Western Europe and the U.S. performed better on Caucasians. This result suggests that algorithms may be most accurate on the populations who developed them—a concerning effect given that software engineers in the United States are predominately Caucasian males.*

Because algorithms are probabilistic, a collected image can fit many possible matches in a database. If the algorithm is more inaccurate for racial minorities, then a greater proportion of innocent non-white people may be approached by law enforcement.

The use and misuse of facial recognition software illustrate the importance of understanding the impacts of Big Data and algorithms. Individuals and institutions use the outputs of algorithms to make critical decisions. The decision by law enforcement to approach and question a person could set off a series of life-changing events. If these algorithms are consistently inaccurate, they can negatively affect an entire group of people. This logic can be extended to other domains of life. One's credit score is based on an algorithm. The tests given to potential new hires are also algorithmic in nature. Insurance companies decide premiums based upon algorithms, and so on. Because Big Data and algorithms impact people's life chances, they must always be held up to scrutiny. There are also legal implications to algorithms. As the Center on Privacy & Technology Law argues, both the First Amendment (free speech) and Fourth Amendment (protection from illegal search and seizure) are threatened by facial recognition technology.

BIG DATA AND ALGORITHMS IN POLICING

One way in which algorithms have become a part of law enforcement practices is through predictive policing (Bennett Moses & Chan, 2016; Chan & Bennett Moses, 2016; Hunt et al., 2014; Mantello, 2016). Predictive policing can be defined as *"the application of statistical methods to identify likely targets for police intervention (the predictions) to prevent crimes or solve past crimes, followed by conducting interventions against those targets"* (Hunt et al., 2014, iii). Data and statistical analysis are at the heart of predictive policing. However, there is more involved. As Chan and Bennett Moses (2016) write, predictive policing is a process, "which consists of a cycle of activities and decision points: data collection, analysis, police operations, criminal response, and back to data collection" (2). We describe this process below.

DATA COLLECTION

The first decision point in the cycle of predictive policing is the collection of data. Data has been collected on crime rates by local and federal law enforcement since the early 20th century. For example, the Federal Bureau of Investigation has administered the Uniform Crime Reports program since 1929. The Uniform Crime Report is a compilation of crime statistics reported by local agencies. These crimes include murder, rape, robbery, arson, and more.

In the era of predictive policing local agencies have become more purposeful in their data collection and often collect a wider range of data specific to their locality. Most police precincts input data into a records management system (RMS). Police RMSs are relatively standardized in that they are databases that can be manipulated using Structured Query Language (SQL). A crime analyst can then retrieve relevant data using SQL and present crime data to police or management. Placing data into a standardized RMS also facilitates the extraction of that data by third-party software for crime mapping or predicting future high crime areas (forecasting).

The collection of data is not an objective process where crimes happen and are then recorded. The data that end up in a database depend on people. As such, it is fraught with human-related issues. For example, if police have historically policed one area of a city, then they will have more data on that area. Similarly, if police are more likely to take notice of a person of color, they are more likely to stop that person (the infamous "driving while black" phenomenon) and are more likely to find and record some type of infraction.

ANALYZING DATA

At this stage of the cycle, some type of algorithm is applied to the collected data. As mentioned above, law enforcement agencies use third-party computer software to draw conclusions about their collected data. One well-known example is Predpol predictive software. Predpol uses three data points to make predictions about crime—the type of crime, the location of the crime, and the date/time of the crime.[1] These data points are retrieved from the law enforcement agency's database. Predictions for high-risk areas are visualized on a map. One of the more interesting aspects of Predpol is the rationale behind the algorithm used. The software's designers theorized that crimes might emanate from an initial crime like aftershocks occur after an initial earthquake. Predpol applies a formula that is used to model earthquake aftershocks to predict these future crimes.

The software and algorithms applied in the process of predictive policing have been questioned by scholars and civil liberties organizations. One reason is that the algorithms used are not oriented towards the underlying causes of crime. With the Predpol software, police will be able to anticipate and arrest the "aftershocks" from initial crimes. However, this does not mean that they will be in any better position to address the underlying causes of crimes.

POLICE OPERATIONS

Police use the outputs from algorithms to inform them on how they should use their resources. Algorithms are used to inform who is targeted, where, and when. For example, the Chicago police department uses a "heat list" (Ferguson, 2017). As described by Ferguson:

> the heat list uses 11 variables to create risk scores from 1 to 500. The higher the score means the greater risk of being a victim or perpetrator of gun violence. Who gets shot? The algorithm knows … Using the heat list, police have prioritized youth violence to intervene in the lives of the most at-risk men.
>
> (2017, 37)

Person-based policing allows law enforcement to be more proactive by identifying potential victims and perpetrators. They can monitor those who are "at-risk" and possibly prevent crimes.

This same rationale underlies the use of algorithms to determine where to police. Place-based policing, also called hot-spot policing, places personnel where crime is likely to occur. Predpol, as discussed, is an example of an algorithm that helps police anticipate the places where crime is likely to occur.

A third way that algorithms affect police operations is by altering decisions in real time. An example of this would be law enforcement using facial recognition technology on a suspect while on the scene. The response from the technology—"likely a match," "not likely a match," will determine the next actions of the officer. Another way in which real-time decisions are made is with automated license plate readers (ALPRs). These devices can be mounted on police cars or at strategic locations in a city. The ALPRs then scan license plates and match them to the records associated with those license plates such as the owner of the vehicle, traffic or parking violations, the number of times the vehicle has been seen in the area, and more. This information can then be sent in real time to law enforcement.

For all these algorithmically informed operations, law enforcement must balance the efficiency of these operations with the potential harms they may cause in communities. For example, place-based policing can lead to an increase in police shootings and animosity from citizens. "In the targeted areas, police may feel additional license to investigate more aggressively. Because the areas have been designated as more dangerous, police may respond in a more aggressively protective posture" (Ferguson, 2017, 79). Similarly, suppose police officers are more likely to investigate marginalized communities or communities of color. In that case, they are more likely to collect license plate data and facial images from the people in those communities. This may help with their investigations, but it also means that the people in those communities are more likely to have their civil liberties violated.

CRIMINAL RESPONSE AND NEW DATA COLLECTION

The predictive policing process is an iterative cycle. If the operations adopted by the police are successful, criminal patterns will change in response to these operations. Potential offenders learn who is being targeted, where, and when. If, for example, police learn of an open-air drug market and deploy units in those spaces, drug dealers will migrate to another space. This will then require new data and then a new response.

Even if criminals are not aware of the technologies brought to bear on their behavior, the effectiveness of predictive policing as a general practice must be repeatedly evaluated. Does predictive policing lead to a reduction in the number of crimes committed in the locality in which it is applied? There is some debate as to the effectiveness of predictive policing. This debate is complicated by several factors. All types of predictive policing are not the same. When evaluating effectiveness, distinctions need to be made between place-based policing, person-based policing, and real-time policing. Moreover, even when comparing the same type of predictive policing, the context and culture of a locality may matter. Place-based policing may have a different impact in a dense urban metropolis like Chicago than in a less dense, mid-sized city like Virginia Beach, Virginia. Another factor that must be considered is the perceptions of the community. If people feel that their rights are being violated, then even if crime is reduced, they may want police practices to change. Police may need to balance the objective decreases in crime with a more subjective but no less real increase in public animosity.

Big Data and Algorithms in Sentencing

Sentencing involves deciding what punishment, or penalty, to levy on a convicted offender. The penalties are usually prison time, a fine, or community service. The next decision is the intensity of the penalty. There are often wide ranges in the amount of prison time or fines for any given guilty sentence. For example, under the Computer Fraud and Abuse Act, the penalty for giving an unauthorized person a password to a computer network ranges from a minimum of one year to a maximum of ten years.

The primary function of algorithms during the sentencing process is predicting the risk of recidivism. A high risk of recidivism means that a judge may wish to imprison that offender for longer periods of time. There are many companies that provide risk assessments for courts. One major company is COMPAS (Correctional Offender Management Profiling for Alternative Sanctions).

A notable case with regards to algorithmic sentencing and COMPAS is State v. Loomis in 2016. Eric Loomis was arrested for driving the vehicle during a drive-by shooting and pleaded guilty to the charges. The court requested and received a risk score report from COMPAS. COMPAS classified Loomis as high risk for recidivism. Considering this score, the presiding judge sentenced Loomis to six years in prison and cited his COMPAS score as one of the factors in determining the sentence.

Loomis challenged the sentence. He argued that the algorithm violated his Sixth Amendment right to a fair trial. Specifically, the algorithm is proprietary, and the formula used to generate the risk scores is hidden. Loomis could not, then, confront his accuser or the evidence presented against him publicly. Wisconsin's State Supreme Court rejected Loomis's argument and ruled that proprietary algorithms could be used as supplemental information in sentencing but could not be the only criterion.

PRE-TRIAL DETENTION AND RELEASE

States have recently pushed to use algorithms to determine if an accused person should be released before trial or put in jail. A primary reason for using an algorithm during pre-trial is to save the state money. At a pre-trial court appearance, a judge must determine if an accused individual is a flight risk—not returning for trial, a risk to the community—and thus needs to be jailed until their trial or are non-violent and low risk—and can be released.

On some rare occasions, people can be released on the good faith that they will re-appear at the upcoming trial, what is called "personal recognizance." On most occasions, however, people must post bail money to ensure they will return for their court date. Unfortunately, many defendants cannot post bail and must stay in jail awaiting trial. The housing of people in jails awaiting trial costs the state money. There is also a human cost of housing people before a trial, often for months, for minor offenses. A person in jail cannot work, pursue their interests, or be with their family. An algorithm that can determine risk may allow courts to be confident that individuals will return for their court date without requiring them to post bail.

The United States state of New Jersey has eliminated traditional bail proceedings and now relies heavily on the use of an algorithm that determines flight risk. An article written in The Economist ("Replacing Bail with an Algorithm," 2017) states:

> *Defenders of New Jersey's experiment [pre-trial algorithms] point to a dramatic decline in the state's jail population, driven by a reduction in the number of poor, non-dangerous offenders who are incarcerated while awaiting trial for no other reason than their inability to pay bail. In September 2017 New Jersey's jails held 36% fewer people than they did in September 2015.*

Other states are also considering or have adopted some form of pre-trial algorithms, including Arizona, Kentucky, and Alaska.

In 2013, former Attorney General for the State of New Jersey Anne Milgram gave a TED Talk on using data in the criminal justice system (TED, 2014). "We weren't using data-driven policing. We were essentially trying to fight crime with yellow Post-it notes," Milgram said in her talk. Milgram went on to describe the project she led to introduce algorithms and Big Data into an important decision—should a person who has been arrested be detained and put into jail before trial or released on bail. People who are likely to not return for trial or commit another violent act while awaiting trial must be detained. On the other hand, it is costly to taxpayers to detain someone who is not violent or a flight risk. According to Milgram, 50% of people currently in jail and awaiting trial are non-violent and low risk. To address the issue, Milgram and her researchers developed an assessment tool to judge pre-trial risk. Using data from 1.5 million cases across the United States, Milgram and her team developed a universal risk assessment tool based on nine factors. The tool gives a judge a score, based on an algorithm, that shows (1) the likelihood of committing a new crime, (2) if the person will commit an act of violence if not put in jail, and (3) if the person will appear in court for trial if released.

Although algorithms like the one explained by Milgram appear to be a fairer approach to pre-trial sentencing, some groups may be unhappy with their use. If New Jersey is indicative of other states, then states that use pre-trial algorithms may have more people released pre-trial. Citizens in those localities may feel unsafe, and there is a real possibility that although an algorithm may label a person "low risk," it does not mean that the person will not commit a crime while awaiting trial. And so, the savings gained by local and state governments may be matched by the emotional costs of people who now feel less safe.

Big Data and Surveillance

Some scholars have argued that we live in a "surveillance society," meaning that we now live in an age when governments and corporations routinely identify and monitor individuals (Lyon, 2007). In the past, an individual or a group needed to be suspected of criminal activity to justify resources devoted to their surveillance. However, two factors have reduced the barriers to surveillance. First, people live online, and gathering information in the digital environment is easier. All Internet traffic must travel through a series of intermediaries such as an ISP or social media company's server. These intermediaries make it possible to collect information on a person not by following them but querying the intermediary. Second, it has become much easier to store information in terms of space and money. It is possible to store all the possible information collected on a person on a thumb drive that costs less than $10. Moreover, that information is stored on a microchip the size of an adult fingernail. Contrast this with an analog world, where reams of paper, rows of bookshelves, and hundreds of square feet could be dedicated to one person.

In an article published in the *Yale Law Journal*, Bankston and Soltani (Bankston & Soltani, 2014) show in stark detail the investments in US dollars that the United States Federal Bureau of Investigations must make to monitor a suspect (see Figure 8.1; p. 160). Their analysis shows that surveilling someone through digital means is much less costly. Therefore, agencies can be much less discriminating in whom they monitor. If they so wish, they could participate in "dragnets," where they monitor a wide range of people without sufficient probable cause.

Method	1 day		1 week		28 days	
	Estimated cost	Cost per hour	Estimated cost	Cost per hour	Estimated cost	Cost per hour
Foot Pursuit	$1,200.00	$50.00	$8,400.00	$50.00	$33,600.00	$50.00
Car Pursuit	$2,520.00	$105.00	$17,640.00	$105.00	$70,560.00	$105.00
Covert Foot Pursuit	$6,000.00	$250.00	$42,000.00	$250.00	$168,000.00	$250.00
Covert Car Pursuit	$6,600.00	$275.00	$46,200.00	$275.00	$184,800.00	$275.00
Beeper	$2,720.00	$113.33	$17,840.00	$106.19	$70,760.00	$105.30
IMSI Catcher or "Stingray"	$2,520.00	$105.00	$17,640.00	$105.00	$70,560.00	$105.00
GPS	$240.00	$10.00	$240.00	$1.43	$240.00	$0.36
Cell Phone (AT&T)	$125.00	$5.21	$275.00	$1.64	$800.00	$1.19
Cell Phone (T-Mobile)	$100.00	$4.17	$700.00	$4.17	$2,800.00	$4.17
Cell Phone (Sprint)	$30.00	$1.25	$30.00	$0.18	$30.00	$0.04

Figure 8.1 A table illustrating the average costs of different surveillance methods.

For example, the cost of surveilling someone through foot pursuit would cost the agency approximately $1,200, with the average agent costing the agency $50 per hour, and surveillance being for the entire 24-hour period. The cost of foot pursuit becomes quite costly, with 28 days costing the agency over $33,000 to follow one person. The costs are even higher in a covert car pursuit—where four cars (four agents) must work together to surveil a suspect. A covert car pursuit costs the agency approximately $6,000 for one day and $184,800 for one month.

Now contrast these costs with following someone using the GPS on their phone. The FBI must pay an intermediary, for example Sprint, $30 per person, to collect the suspect's data. Unlike foot or car pursuits, this cost does not compound over time. Indeed, because it is a one-time fee, the overall cost of surveillance *decreases* the longer a person is surveilled—from $1.25 per hour for a day's surveillance to 4 cents per hour for a month's surveillance! This is a powerful incentive for law enforcement agencies, even if there is not yet a strong case supporting the surveillance.

DATAVEILLANCE

We have already discussed how suspected criminals are monitored. In this section, we focus on surveillance as it relates to non-offenders. Van Dijck (2014) has called this type of surveillance dataveillance "a form of continuous surveillance through the use of (meta) data" (198). Metadata refers to data about data. Metadata could be, for example, the GPS coordinates embedded in a picture taken with a digital camera and uploaded to a social media site. It could also be the time stamp on an email or the last modified date on a word processing document. Another form of metadata would be the people that you have friended on a social media account or the people you have text messaged or emailed.

Unlike the more focused surveillance via predictive policing, dataveillance is more diffuse but also more pervasive. Almost every citizen in some form or other has metadata attached to them that governments and businesses can collect. Our rationale for highlighting these types of surveillance is that many scholars and activist organizations have argued that law enforcement and corporations have overstepped their bounds in collecting and using metadata, and they must be tightly regulated to preserve civil liberties. In other words, these organizations assert that governments and corporations have committed transgressions against individuals and violate the social contract between government and citizen.

Artificial Intelligence and Cybercrime

As mentioned in the introduction, artificial intelligence, or AI, refers to computer systems that perform tasks that mimic human intelligence. And so, the technology is not "thinking" as a human would, but it can accomplish activities that a human brain can accomplish. An approach to understanding AI was posited by English Mathematician Alan Turing. He argued that if a machine acted in ways that were indistinguishable from a human, we can call that machine intelligent. He posited an experiment to test for this intelligence:

> *a remote human interrogator, within a fixed time frame, must distinguish between a computer and a human subject based on their replies to various questions posed by the interrogator. By means of a series of such tests, a computer's success at 'thinking' can be measured by its probability of being misidentified as the human subject.*
> (Turing Test | Definition & facts | Britannica, 2023)

Even though this test has been widely critiqued, the "Turing Test" is arguably the most well-known understanding of AI. Its popularity is in part because Alan Turing was a hero for the Allies during World War II. Turing's work help break the military codes of the Axis powers. He is also considered one of the founders of modern computing.

CRIME AND AI

Artificial intelligence is a technology that, like all technologies, can be leveraged for good and evil. Hayward and Maas (2021) organized three ways in which criminals may use AI:

AI as a tool—Cybercriminals can build artificial intelligence technologies in order to commit crimes. An example given by Hayward and Maas is equipping drones with facial recognition software and small explosive charges, and then deploying them. Governments, including the United States, Libya, and Israel, have already developed and deployed this technology. However, this technology could also be used by non-state actors. Another example given is "DeepPhish." DeepPhish is an AI algorithm that learns how to create effective phishing attacks. The algorithm was created by using over 1 million phishing URLs collected in 2017 from the database website Phishtank (*PhishTank | Join the Fight against Phishing*, n.d.). The URLs were tested against a phishing detection software. The algorithm used the text from URLs that successfully evaded the detection software to create new URLs which were even more effective at evasion.

Crimes on AI—AI computer systems are attack surfaces, and hackers can "exploit and reverse-engineer system vulnerabilities in a bid to fool or 'hypnotise' AI systems." (Hayward and Mass 2021, 216). For example, AI is widely used in healthcare. One use is to predict health outcomes for patients and estimate treatment costs. If this system is compromised, hackers can commit insurance fraud by tricking the AI into giving an inaccurate diagnosis. Another example cited is the algorithm "TextFooler" (Jin, 2019/2023). TextFooler strategically changes the text that an AI system reads, thus altering the decision made by that system. A *Wired* article gives an example of how "TextFooler" works (Knight, 2000). This sentence was classified by a movie review algorithm as a negative review: "The characters, cast in impossibly contrived situations, are totally estranged from reality." TextFooler changed the sentence to "The characters, cast in impossibly engineered circumstances, are fully estranged from reality." Now the algorithm classified the review as positive. "The demonstration highlights an uncomfortable truth about AI—that it can be both remarkably clever and surprisingly dumb," writes *Wired* author Will Knight.

Crimes by AI—AI can be used as an independent criminal intermediary. In 2015, a shopping robot called "Random Darknet Shopper" was created for an art installation exploring the dark web (Kasperkevic, 2015). The robot was given 100 bitcoin in which to purchase items by its creators the Swiss art group !Mediengruppe Bitnik. Once released online, the robot made all types of purchases from fake Diesel Jeans, cigarettes, a fake Louis Vuitton handbag, a *Lord of the Rings* e-book collection, and ten ecstasy pills. The bot (or rather the computer in which the bot was housed) was confiscated for a time by Swiss police. In this example, the AI was not *specifically* designed to commit crimes, however it eventually did.

Another example is a market-based trading AI learning profitable trading strategies, then manipulating the market in illegal ways. Hayward and Mass (2021) write:

> *In a 2016 experiment, computer scientists showed that AI trading agents can discover and learn to execute profitable strategies that amount to market manipulation. Using reinforcement learning, an 'artificial agent' explored the space of actions it could take on the market, and found that placing deceitful false buying orders was a profitable strategy.*

(217)

CYBERSECURITY AND AI

The cybersecurity industry has readily adopted artificial intelligence, especially machine learning. In machine learning, a computer is trained on a set of data to recognize patterns, identify relationships, and make predictions based on those patterns or relationships. In the simplest sense, this training involves programming the computer with what the "right" answer is based on previous data, and then having the computer look for that right answer in new data. A right answer could be signs of someone hacking into a computer, sending a phishing email, or attempting to install malware on a computer. The training and prediction process is iterative, where the computer learns to become more accurate in its predictions as it takes in more data. In this way, the system "learns." Machine learning is being used in cybersecurity for a variety of purposes, including malware detection, spam detection, phishing detection, and intrusion (hacking) detection.

THE TRUST PROBLEM

Using artificial intelligence, especially machine learning, to enhance cybersecurity holds much promise. However, it is not without problems. One major problem is how well the users of an AI system understand how the system operates. This is the "trust" problem inherent in artificial intelligence. Imagine a decision made by machine learning software, categorizing an application or block of code as malware. The human user must trust that this is the right decision without knowing how the machine learning software made this categorization.

This lack of trust also extends to consumers. A survey done by the World Economic Forum showed that 50% of those surveyed said they trusted companies that used AI as much as they trusted other companies (Myers, 2022). Kay Firth-Butterfield, Head of Artificial Intelligence and Machine Learning at the World Economic Forum, remarked "In order to trust artificial intelligence, people must know and understand exactly what AI is, what it's doing, and its impact. Leaders and companies must make transparent and trustworthy AI a priority as they implement this technology."

ARTIFICIAL INTELLIGENCE ETHICS

The use of artificial intelligence introduces many moral issues. As such, professionals who deploy AI technologies need to develop ethical standards for the use of AI. Ethics are morals in a specific context, such as professions or industries that develop and deploy AI. A working definition for AI ethics is "a set of values, principles, and techniques that employ widely accepted standards of right and wrong to guide moral conduct in the development and use of AI technologies" (Leslie, 2019, 3). Professionals and scholars must identify the potential ethical concerns, and then develop guidelines for addressing those concerns.

The developers of AI must collect large amounts of data for testing and training. This raises issues of privacy and confidentiality of data. Privacy and confidentiality are similar but point to different phenomena. Privacy is the right to keep data from becoming public, while confidentiality is about ensuring data is only viewed by authorized parties. Data collection also raises concerns about anonymity. Activity collected by applications can identify users by collecting location data, phone numbers, health information, and bank account information.

Consider Amazon's Alexa device. Each time a user speaks to an Alexa device, their commands are collected and stored on Amazon's servers. The company can use this data to refine and improve its Alexa service. The company also allows third-party developers to create "skills" for Alexa—the equivalent of an app on a mobile phone. A study done in 2021 found that 23.3% of the 1,146 skills that requested access to sensitive data raise privacy concerns (Lentzsch et al., 2021). For example, the study noted that Amazon does not fully verify the developers of skills. As such, a developer could be anyone, including someone with malicious intent. Another concern raised by the study was that developers could change the code of their skills once Amazon approved them. This opens the door for bad actors to follow privacy rules initially, but then violate them once they are in Amazon's ecosystem. The study was done in 2021, and it is likely that the company has addressed many of these issues. What is important here is that these potential issues of privacy, confidentiality, and anonymity issues be identified and addressed so that data can be collected and used ethically.

Another ethical concern, briefly mentioned earlier, is bias. Suresh and Guttag (2021) identify six ways in which bias enters an AI system. These six ways are described below with examples:

- *Historical bias*—Data is collected to train AI, but the data collected reflects harmful historical patterns we wish not to repeat. The research example was the Google image search for "CEO." Women make up a small number of CEOs in Fortune 500 companies, and an image search reflected this historical pattern (men are shown as CEOs). However, this historical pattern is partly rooted in sexism and is not consonant with the values we currently have in society. It may be unethical to reproduce this pattern in image searches. As such, Google changed its image search results to show a higher percentage of women.
- *Representation bias*—The data collected does not include enough of an important population. This then biases the AI being developed, and it may underperform when applied to those populations. The example they provide is the ImageNet database (https://www.image-net.org/), which at the time of their research had 1% and 2.1% of the images coming from China and India, respectively. But these two countries are home to about 17% of the world's population each.
- *Measurement bias*The measures used, or the labels given to measured phenomena are inappropriate. For example, the algorithms used in predictive policing software often use arrests as a proxy measure for crime. However, minority communities are often overpoliced and are arrested at higher rates than other communities. Thus, the proxy measure of arrest is not equivalent to actual crime. Police are then directed by the algorithm to minority communities based on an incorrect measure.
- *Aggregation bias*—Occurs when distinct populations are inappropriately combined. A "one size fits all" model is produced, which can harm subpopulations. Suresh and Guttag (2021) argue that a one size fits all AI model for predicting diabetes complications would be inaccurate because of the differences in how diabetes manifests itself in different ethnic populations. The model may be accurate for ethnic groups with higher instances of diabetes but be harmful to others.
- *Evaluation bias*—Occurs when the evaluation data for an algorithm doesn't represent the target population. In other words, the algorithm is deemed successful. However, it is successful for one population but not others. An example given is the poor performance of some facial recognition software for dark-skinned individuals. The software was evaluated as effective, but this evaluation was based on its success with lighter-skinned individuals.

- *Deployment bias*—After an AI model is developed, it is deployed in inappropriate ways. Consider risk assessment tools. They are meant to help a judge determine the risk of recidivation or committing a crime while awaiting a trial. However, they could also be used also determine the *length* of a sentence, with a judge deciding that a high-risk person should be incarcerated longer.

Although these types of biases are described here as if they are distinct, they are often present together in the development and deployment of AI. As with privacy, confidentiality, and anonymity concerns, the challenge for those working with AI is to recognize when bias may be entering into the systems they are working with and address those biases.

GENERATIVE AI AND THE PRODUCTION OF DEVIANT CONTENT

Generative AI refers to artificial intelligence that creates new content that is indistinguishable from the human-generated content it was trained on. Generative AI can produce new text, images, audio, and video. One of the five challenges of cybercriminology is understanding the new laws and policies pertaining to cyber phenomena. Generative AI is a paradigmatic example of this. Industries and governments are scrambling to understand how to regulate AI and the consequences of that regulation. For example, if AI creates a new song by being trained on a series of songs by an artist—is that a copyright violation? Most countries have not yet addressed this issue. Generative AI also raises concerns for disinformation, as it can produce fake news stories or fake social media accounts spreading false information.

What about the use of generative AI in the production of pornographic material? Like other forms of creativity such as music and photography, there are going to be copyright concerns. But other concerns go far beyond the economics of copyright.

Suppose generative AI uses the likeness of a person and synthesizes it with a pornographic scene to create a "deepfake" where it looks as if the person is performing a sexual act? There can be deepfakes of limitless types of scenarios, but the vast majority of deepfakes are pornographic in nature (Simonite, 2019). Deepfake technologies are not morally ambiguous. Most people would consider creating content that looks like a person performing sexual acts without their consent to be at minimum violating decency and honesty norms. An audience is led to believe that an actual person is doing something they are not. While the creator of the content may argue that this is artwork and not intended to harm (although often they are created to abuse women), there is little denying that deepfakes can cause psychological and emotional distress to the person faked. As of this writing in 2023, most nations have yet to pass laws regulating the production of deepfakes.

Another concern is generative AI producing pornography that, while not using the likeness of others, is depicting sexual acts that are problematic or illegal. For example, imagine an AI generated pornographic scene in which a female character is the victim of sexual violence from several male characters? One the one hand, depictions of rape and other instances of sexual violence can be just that—depictions, and are found in movies and television shows to narrate unfortunate events in society. On the other hand, pornographic material can be more graphic (showing vaginal and anal penetration), young people can more easily obtain and consume this material, and there is a potential for there to be vast quantities of this material available. As such, society may be concerned that a proliferation of generative AI porn could have an adverse effect on young people.

Conclusion

In the early 1990s, New York City policeman Jack Maple purchased a computer from Radio Shack to help the department map crime. This one idea slowly developed into a system of mapping and analyzing crime statistics called alternatively Compare Statistics or Computer Statistics, or more commonly known as CompStat. Maple and his fellow officers were unaware that they were at the cusp of a revolution in policing. Since the 1990s, computers have become more ubiquitous and powerful, producing massive quantities of Big Data. Computer programmers, mathematicians, and social scientists have developed more efficient and accurate ways of producing actionable intelligence from this data—algorithms. We now live in an age where computers are essential to an effective criminal justice system.

As we have discussed, relying solely on data collection and mathematical formulas for processes that often require nuanced human judgment can be problematic. The indiscriminate use of algorithms can lead to bias towards racial minorities and violations of civil liberties.

Thus, it is important that social scientists explore the societal implications of the use of algorithms and Big Data in the criminal justice system. On the other hand, a wealth of social science research, along with a glance at national headlines, shows that individual police and the criminal justice system was dealing with race and class biases before the advent of algorithms. Moreover, predictive policing and algorithmic sentencing have been shown to make elements of the criminal justice system more effective. Big Data and algorithms are here to stay in policing, the courts, and correctional institutions.

Big Data and algorithms are foundational components of an AI system. Many examples we give in this chapter use Big Data and algorithms to produce outputs that humans can use in their decision-making. However, AI systems make decisions themselves or perform actions without the direct guidance of humans. Cybersecurity researchers use AI, specifically machine learning, to automate cybersecurity tasks. Law enforcement agencies have not yet deployed AI to the same degree as the cybersecurity industry. This will likely change in the future.

For both cybersecurity professionals and law enforcement, AI introduces ethical issues that must be addressed. Data collection used to train algorithms introduces privacy, confidentiality, and anonymity issues. AI systems can be developed with bias, causing harm to populations. Generative AI can also raise problems. Deepfakes can cause emotional distress to people whose likeness has been used in the fake, and a proliferation of pornography depicting sexual violence raises questions about its impact on society.

CHAPTER 8 CURRENT EVENTS AND CRITICAL THINKING:

If the Person is Made Up, is it a Crime?

Most cybercrimes in this textbook come with definitional, legal, and moral ambiguities associated with them. Individuals can disagree over the phenomena in question, should it be prohibited, and the justness of the penalties associated with laws.

Child pornography may be the only cybercrime that lacks most of these ambiguities.

Law enforcement agencies devote considerable resources to investigating cases and apprehending child pornography offenders. Non-profit organizations like Polaris and Thorn develop technologies to combat the presence of child pornography. The activities of law enforcement and non-profits are generally supported by society.

Being labelled as a paedophile will incur severe informal negative sanctions. The different motivations for producing, distributing, and consuming child pornography, as well as the distinctions between discussing sex and gender with young people, consuming images of children, and the pursuance of physical contact with children are ignored if the label is successfully applied to a person or group. As such, individuals may apply the label to individuals and groups they have disagreements with, knowing that it will cause those individuals and groups reputational damage.

But this universal condemnation is because there are children who are victims. But generative AI makes it possible for the production of life like sexualized content of children.

Should the production of child pornography through AI be illegal? Why or why not? If you say that it should be illegal, then who are the victims? If you say that it should not be illegal, then what are the possible negative consequences to making this available?

NOTE

1 www.predpol.com/how-predictive-policing-works/

REFERENCES

Bankston, K. S., & Soltani, A. (2014). *Tiny constables and the cost of surveillance: Making cents out of* United States v. Jones. *Yale Law Journal Online.* https://www.yalelawjournal.org/forum/tiny-constables-and -the-cost-of-surveillance-making-cents-out-of-united-states-v-jones

Bennett Moses, L., & Chan, J. (2016). Algorithmic prediction in policing: Assumptions, evaluation, and accountability. *Policing and Society*, 1–17. https://doi.org/10.1080/10439463.2016.1253695

Burrell, J. (2016). How the machine 'thinks': Understanding opacity in machine learning algorithms. *Big Data & Society*, 3(1), 205395171562251. https://doi.org/10.1177/2053951715622512

Chan, J., & Bennett Moses, L. (2016). Is Big Data challenging criminology? *Theoretical Criminology*, 20(1), 21–39. https://doi.org/10.1177/1362480615586614

Ferguson, A. G. (2017). *The rise of Big Data policing: Surveillance, race, and the future of law enforcement.* New York University Press.

Fry, H. (2018). *Hello world: Being human in the age of algorithms* (1st edition). W.W. Norton & Company.

Garvie, C., Bedoya, A. M., Frankle, J., Daugherty, M., Evans, K., George, E. J., McCubbin, S., Rudolph, H., Ullman, I., Ainsworth, S., Houck, D., Iorio, M., Kahn, M., Olson, E., Petenko, J., & Singleton, K. (2016). Unregulated police face recognition in America. *Perpetual Lineup*, 151.

Hayward, K. J., & Maas, M. M. (2021). Artificial intelligence and crime: A primer for criminologists. *Crime, Media, Culture: An International Journal*, 17(2), 209–233. https://doi.org/10.1177/1741659020917434

Hunt, P., Saunders, J. M., & Hollywood, J. S. (2014). *Evaluation of the Shreveport predictive policing experiment.* RAND Corporation.

Jin, D. (2023). *TextFooler* [Python]. https://github.com/jind11/TextFooler (Original work published 2019)

Kasperkevic, J. (2015, April 22). Swiss police release robot that bought ecstasy online. *The Guardian.* https:// www.theguardian.com/world/2015/apr/22/swiss-police-release-robot-random-darknet-shopper -ecstasy-deep-web

Kitchin, R., & McArdle, G. (2016). What makes Big Data, Big Data? Exploring the ontological characteristics of 26 datasets. *Big Data & Society*, *3*(1), 205395171663113. https://doi.org/10.1177/2053951716631130

Knight, W. (2000, February 23). This technique uses AI to fool other AIs / Wired. https://www.wired.com/story/technique-uses-ai-to-fool-other-ais/

Lee, M. K. (2018). Understanding perception of algorithmic decisions: Fairness, trust, and emotion in response to algorithmic management. *Big Data & Society*, *5*(1), 205395171875668. https://doi.org/10.1177/2053951718756684

Lentzsch, C., Shah, S. J., Andow, B., Degeling, M., Das, A., & Enck, W. (2021). Hey Alexa, is this Skill safe?: Taking a closer look at the Alexa Skill scosystem. *Proceedings 2021 Network and Distributed System Security Symposium*. Network and Distributed System Security Symposium, Virtual. https://doi.org/10.14722/ndss.2021.23111

Leslie, D. (2019). Understanding artificial intelligence ethics and safety: A guide for the responsible design and implementation of AI systems in the public sector. *Zenodo*. https://doi.org/10.5281/ZENODO.3240529

Lyon, D. (2007). Surveillance, security and social sorting: Emerging research priorities. *International Criminal Justice Review*, *17*(3), 161–170. https://doi.org/10.1177/1057567707306643

Mantello, P. (2016). The machine that ate bad people: The ontopolitics of the precrime assemblage. *Big Data & Society*, *3*(2), 205395171668253. https://doi.org/10.1177/2053951716682538

Mittelstadt, B. D., Allo, P., Taddeo, M., Wachter, S., & Floridi, L. (2016). The ethics of algorithms: Mapping the debate. *Big Data & Society*, *3*(2), 205395171667967. https://doi.org/10.1177/2053951716679679

Myers, J. (2022, January 5). *5 charts that show what people around the world think about AI*. World Economic Forum. https://www.weforum.org/agenda/2022/01/artificial-intelligence-ai-technology-trust-survey/

O'Neil, C. (2016). *Weapons of math destruction: How Big Data increases inequality and threatens democracy* (1st edition). Crown.

PhishTank | Join the fight against phishing. (n.d.). Retrieved July 24, 2023, from https://phishtank.org/

Replacing bail with an algorithm. (2017, November 23). The Economist. https://www.economist.com/united-states/2017/11/23/replacing-bail-with-an-algorithm

Simonite, T. (2019, October 7). Most Deepfakes Are Porn, and They're Multiplying Fast. *Wired*. https://www.wired.com/story/most-deepfakes-porn-multiplying-fast/

Stephens-Davidowitz, S. (2017). *Everybody lies: Big Data, new data, and what the Internet can tell us about who we really are* (1st edition). Dey St., an imprint of William Morrow.

Suresh, H., & Guttag, J. V. (2021). A framework for understanding sources of harm throughout the machine learning life cycle. *Equity and Access in Algorithms, Mechanisms, and Optimization*, 1–9. https://doi.org/10.1145/3465416.3483305

TED (Director). (2014, January 28). *Anne Milgram: Why smart statistics are the key to fighting crime*. https://www.youtube.com/watch?v=ZJNESMhIxQo

Turing Test | Definition & facts | Britannica. (2023, May 11). https://www.britannica.com/technology/Turing-test

Van Dijck, J. (2014). Datafication, dataism and dataveillance: Big Data between scientific paradigm and ideology. *Surveillance & Society*, *12*(2), 197–208. https://doi.org/10.24908/ss.v12i2.4776

Chapter 9

Cybervictimization

Introduction

Cybercrime victimization, or simply *cybervictimization*, has been tracked consistently in the United States and abroad since the early 2000's. Most research underlines the general premise that worldwide proliferation of Internet usage across the past several decades has resulted in increased cybervictimization across several audiences. Young people, the elderly, and populations of specific vulnerability are particularly prone to victimization experiences online, with noteworthy examples abundant in nearly every country employing some means of consistently tracking such experiences (Alhaboby et al., 2023; Luo et al., 2023; Rodriguez-Enriquez et al., 2019; Sakellariou et al., 2012).

In 2013, the FBI Internet Crime Complaint Center (*IC3*) recorded approximately 262,000 victims and 780 million dollars in financial losses due to cybercrime (Federal Bureau of Investigations, 2017). Within just half a decade, the number of victims reporting skyrocketed to five times that amount, and total losses increased sevenfold (Investigations, 2017) (see Figure 9.1; p. 170).

Yet, as rates and damage continue to climb, there is still much to answer concerning what cybervictimization entails, the types of harms resulting from cybercrime offenses, and the results of such harms. This chapter introduces these topics and offers some clarity on the relevance of traditional victimization theory in consideration of the harmful experiences encountered in digital settings.

The Concept of Cybervictimization

In many ways, the digital world is best thought of as an extension of the physical world with respect to social interaction. One might say the Internet "augments real-world social life rather than providing an alternative to it (Shirky, 2008)." With respect to victimization in both the cyber- and physical sense, this seems to hold true. Accordingly, some scholars

DOI: 10.4324/9781003283256-9

2013	2014	2015	2016	2017	1,420,555
262,813	269,422	288,012	298,728	301,580	TOTAL COMPLAINTS

2013	2014	2015	2016	2017	$5.52 Billion
$781.8M	$800.5M	$1,070.7M	$1,450.7M	$1,418.7M	TOTAL LOSSES

Figure 9.1 A table illustrating five years of cybercrime complaints and recorded losses. *Courtesy of the FBI ICC Center's 2017 Internet Crime Report.*

contend the two phenomena need not be regarded as totally exclusive of one another; cybercrime and physical, conventional crime are not so distant from one another conceptually (Yu, 2014). Thus, to better understand cybervictimization, it stands to reason an understanding of the general concept of victimization is necessary.

In theory, every crime has a victim (Quinney, 1972). The core definition of a crime entails that a deviation from prevailing social construction, for which laws have been created to preserve, has occurred that brings about some type of harm. For harm to be determined, there must be at least one entity carrying the end result of the deviant act in such a way that a general understanding of inflicted harm can be reached. Even within the scope of so-called *victimless crimes*—criminal acts for which there is either no true victim, or for which one has not been or cannot be determined—social institutions prohibiting the activity would argue that the victims are not so much absent as they are unknown and/or inconsistently acknowledged.

Dating back to some of the earliest developments in victimization studies, the act of victimization can be understood from at least three perspectives: 1) the formal identification/definition of the victimization act, 2) the events or circumstances that cause one to experience the victimization act, and 3) the outcomes resulting from such victimization. Consider, for example, phishing scams. In cybervictimization, we first must see that such an act results in a victim. Even though a piece of legislation might define phishing as illegal, it does not come to be recognized as cybervictimization until a clear definition of what phishing entails is established. We must know and be able to define what the victim experienced. We must then also see and understand the events leading up to, during, and following the phishing experience for the victim. That is, there must be a series of events connected to their experience such that we can dismiss the notion that the phishing act experienced was simply an act of chance and not intentional. Finally, we must see that the phishing act caused a clear (and negative) outcome to occur (e.g., PII was stolen, money was lost, mental/emotional anguish wrought).

To further clarify, we acknowledge that formally recognizing an act of victimization comprises several considerations. First, what "wrongful" act was committed? For the idea of victimization to crystalize, there needs to be a firm understanding that something wrong occurred. Importantly, this may or may not constitute an actual crime—an act for which there is specific legal identification and precedence for sanction. We know that formal legal systems do not always align with what is actually deemed a wrongful act in the broader social context. Rather, if the act is determined to have produced a harm, and especially if that determination has originated and/or is supported by the ruling class/es of said context (Quinney, 1972), then indeed we can say a wrongful act has occurred.

Presuming that a wrongful act has been determined, the next consideration is the target. Specifically, who is/was the target upon which the wrongful act was inflicted? In order for there to be victimization, it stands to reason there must be an entity upon which a wrongful act was committed. Granted, the extent of victim identification can and does vary, and it is certainly possible to conceive of a victimization event where victim identification is problematic (e.g., crimes like sexual assault, for which the victim/s are reluctant to come forward and identify themselves). Nonetheless, identification of at least one victim—versus none—goes a long way towards cementing whether or not victimization has occurred and the nature of it.

Upon establishing the presence of a wrongful act and a target, we arrive at the issue of identifying harm done and the extent of damage caused. Any firm determination of victimization must clearly state how and to what extent the identified target was harmed. Ideally, this harm would be measurable, but criminology often teaches that many harms are not so. For instance, in the Bernie Madoff fraud scandal, the amount of money Mr. Madoff embezzled and the number of investors connected to those sums has been calculated to within a fair degree of accuracy; thus, the quantitative harm was measurable. However, the psychological and emotional trauma Madoff's scheme wrought upon said victims would be more difficult to calculate.

Finally, what precursory elements led to the victimization event? What factors influenced the likelihood of the victimization event taking shape? Numerous demographic, behavioral, and status triggers impact victimization. Prominent among these factors are age, gender, race/ethnicity, family dynamics, relationship statuses, wealth, and extracurricular activities. Many of these same factors—notably, age and gender—are preconditions for cybervictimization experiences as well.

For example, we know that cybervictimization is especially prevalent and pernicious among those on polar ends of the age spectrum. On one hand, and to little surprise given the comparatively higher concentration of Internet usage among audiences aged 34 and under (Dutton et al., 2013), many online victims skew on the young side (Bernat & Godlove, 2012; Campbell & Moore, 2011). Some rationale for this points to online victims demonstrating too little experience with notions of criminal behavior, unawareness of their own legal rights when navigating digital space, and/or lack of agency to advocate for themselves if they do become aware of their own victimization.

On the senior end of the spectrum, several scholars have found older Internet users become more susceptible to online information theft and fraud when such victimization targeting centers around higher incomes and/or financial activity, and in combination with greater online shopping activity or inexperience with the threats associated with such activities (Jorna, 2016; Reyns, 2013; Williams, 2016). Ironically and unfortunately, as illustrated in Campbell and Moore's study of cyberstalking (2011), it is often these naïve and vulnerable population segments that carry the burden of initially diagnosing if they have fallen victim to some manner of cybercrime.

Concerning gender, men and women have long been known to vary in some notable ways with respect to online victimization (Henson et al., 2011; Popovic-Citic et al., 2011). Despite some indications of nearly identical amounts of Internet usage (Center,

2017; Popovic-Citic et al., 2011), males seem more susceptible to cyberbullying (Festl & Quandt, 2016; Popovic-Citic et al., 2011; Zhou et al., 2013), violent threats (Nasi et al., 2015), and online identity theft (Reyns, 2013), while female users have been found more prone to mobile-phone bullying (Holt, Fitzgerald, et al., 2016), sexual harassment/solicitation online (Holt, Bossler, et al., 2016; Khurana et al., 2015; Nasi et al., 2015; Saha & Srivastava, 2014), romance scams (Saha & Srivastava, 2014), and other online offenses centered around intimacy and/or deep, emotional interaction (Marganski & Fauth, 2013; Saha & Srivastava, 2014).

Clarity on the influence of other demographic factors aside from age and gender becomes more problematic in light of current empirical evidence. Consider cybervictimization by race or ethnic classification. Compared to the relative consistency in measured effects for age and gender, accounting for one's racial classification in in cybervictimization patterns tends to vary greatly in empirical evidence. Demonstrative of the conflicting findings, while some studies report non-White audiences experience higher rates of cyberbullying (Hinduja & Patchin, 2010) and computer crime involving financial loss (Choi, 2010), others contend race is not a significant factor in cyberbullying (Hinduja & Patchin, 2007, 2008) or overall online harassment (Holt & Bossler, 2009).

In line with a recent proposition from Sobba and colleagues (2017), such shortcomings in the confirmation of variables like race and ethnicity as cybervictimization correlates may simply be a matter of inconsistencies in operationalization, low sample sizes, differing sample sources, or other issues related to the nature, method and history of data captured. Alternatively, as much as demographic traits matter in traditional victimization models, the actual online behavior of users may speak more to victimization risk when considering relative models in the digital world. Compared to terrestrial settings, victimization in digital settings appears to be more dependent upon *what* one does online rather than the demographic category one falls into. This idea is precisely captured from the multitude of studies applying *routine activities theory* to cybervictimization models, and is likely one of the reasons why the theory has gained much notoriety as a popular framework for victimization research among scholars of digital phenomena.(Sobba et al., 2017)

The Routine Activities Perspective of Cybervictimization

Among the preeminent theories attempting to explain victimization in digital settings[1], the general sentiment behind *routine activities theory* (Cohen & Felson, 1979) is that the interaction between motivated offenders, suitable targets, and available guardianship explains much of the victimization one could experience in such settings (Dodel & Mesch, 2017; Holt & Bossler, 2009; Kirwan et al., 2018):

1. *A suitable target*—A target can be a person or thing that has value. In the language of the theory, the target needs to be "suitable" for victimization. A new Mercedes is probably a more suitable target than a new Chevrolet because the Mercedes has more monetary value. Value can also be symbolic and contextual. Brand-new, high-profile sneakers in urban neighborhoods have greater symbolic value and thus are deemed suitable targets. Within a cybercrime context, computers that house large volumes of valuable information are suitable targets (Graham & Triplett, 2017). For this reason, when a new exploit is found—what are called

zero-day exploits—it is often reserved for computers that could yield the highest returns.

2. *The lack of a capable guardian*—A guardian is something or someone that can protect the target, and the theory dictates it must be "capable" of such protection. Bodyguards are capable guardians for celebrities. Car alarms are capable guardians for cars. In the digital environment, there are several ways of guarding a computer and the information it houses (e.g., firewalls, virus protection software, fingerprint scanners).

3. *A motivated offender*—Motivated offenders are assumed to always be present in routine activities theory. That is, the theory maintains there will always be someone in a space or environment willing to commit a crime. This is especially so in the digital environment where offenders can more readily victimize someone within close physical proximity or across great distances with relatively similar ease. One could also argue there is some measure of rational choice theory embedded within this aspect of routine activities, as the offender can be more motivated to target individuals presenting themselves as more suitable and where guardianship is lower (thus, the risk-rewards dynamic is more favorable to the offender).

Whether in a terrestrial or digital environment, the theory maintains victimization opportunities will be influenced by these three factors as so (see Figure 9.2).

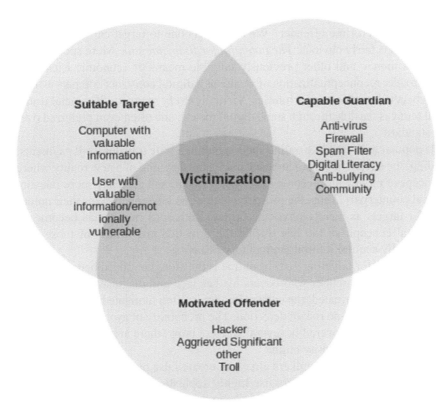

Figure 9.2 A Venn diagram illustrating digital victimization based upon the intersection between suitable targets, capable guardians, and motivated offenders (cyber-routine activities model).

Routine activities studies of cybercrime victimization focus on the interplay between motivated offenders, target suitability, and capable guardianship that influence victimization risk. Successful empirical applications of the theory have contributed much to its popularity throughout recent scholarly discourse, and offer an important pathway to understanding victimization paradigms in the digital world such that even the term *cyber-RAT* has begun to appear.

Featured most notably in the works of Majid Yar (2005), and Kyung-shick Choi (2008, 2010) not long after, cyber-RAT theory maintains that digital space serves as host to scores of suitable targets—online users connecting to the Internet with little-to-no concern for data precaution or computer security—and motivated offenders. When combined with a lack of capable guardianship, victimization in these environments tends to increase. Pivotal to the theory is an understanding that the nature of Internet access is such that the typical user transmits personal and valuable information from their various devices constantly, and prospective offenders (equipped with sufficient hardware and/or software for targeting such individuals) are drawn to seek out potential victims (Yar, 2005; Choi, 2008, 2010). Further empowered by the anonymity and range of worldwide access offered to offenders, particularly when employing higher-end technology, the Internet then becomes characterized by a constant presence of targets and offenders occupying the same space. Consider the first concept in the triumvirate: *Motivation*.

MOTIVATION

What motivates the cybercrime offender? What compels one to target entities in digital settings? One reason is fairly obvious: *The potential for financial gain*. More specifically, the digitization of money and other previously tangible means of economic exchange, along with the broader reconceptualization of wealth as a digital construct compels would-be thieves to cybervictimization opportunities. Virtually every manner of financial transaction relevant today is feasible through some digital means, and often even preferred over conventional standards.

Alongside popular activities like online auction bidding, wire transfers, bill payments, and stock trading, the advent of cryptocurrency marks the dawning of a new reality where the digital concept of money has become synonymous with, and arguably more relevant than, its physical counterpart. Thus, the prospective thief no longer perceives their potential prospects for targets as merely physical entities. Rather, as money has become an increasingly digital concept, so too has shifted the direction and efforts of those who would seek to illegally acquire it through predatory behavior.

Another motivation for targeting victims online is the aforementioned benefit of *anonymity*. Much like the bank robber who covers his/her face and disguises their voice to avoid having their identity revealed, the cyber-offender is often motivated by the fact that they can operate with little-to-no risk of detection. The probability of avoiding detection is a compelling motivation. As covered in several areas of book, there are numerous means by which one can mask their identity online.

Internet trollers, flamers, and stalkers alike can create false profiles to use in targeting their victims. Ransomware attackers use highly sophisticated software to mask IP addresses. Cyberpornography distributors often keep their illicit materials locked behind encrypted folders or hard drives—sometimes offsite in physically secured facilities;

this has also been a preferred tactic for purveyors of black-market goods on the darknet. Indeed, the reduced risk of detection is quite compelling to many cyber-offenders.

Still others may be compelled by a *sense of attraction* (however misguided) towards their victims. Most notably in cases of cyberstalking, the offender is drawn to their target via romantic urges that go unreciprocated. Whereas in the physical world, the stalker would face increased attention, likelihood of detection, rejection from the target of their attention and other considerable obstacles to acting on their urges, stalking facilitated online provides the aforementioned anonymity and safety in distance that emboldens the offender to engage in their deviance.

Then, there is the possible motivation of *ego*. The sheer sense of superiority one might feel in accomplishing a particularly dastardly and technologically complex type of victimization cannot be overlooked. A hacker might find it deeply gratifying to invade a highly structured and encrypted network such as Google's servers or Facebook's user database. Such feats could serve to boost such an offender's sense of self-confidence, as well as their reputation amongst like-minded deviant groups.

Last but not least, there is the potential motivation provided from the pursuit of an *emotional vendetta* or *revenge*; a cyberoffender could simply have an axe to grind against an individual or group of individuals in a personal sense. The college student failing at a particular institution might see fit to exact their frustration by hacking into the records of said institution and compromising important information such as grade records or financial aid data. Perhaps a group of disgruntled employees at a large corporation might initiate a flaming campaign against one or more of the corporation's senior executives. Either way, the personal satisfaction to be gained from seeking revenge is a palpable motivation.

TARGET SUITABILITY

Turning to the victims' side, what makes one more or less suitable to being targeted by a cybercriminal? What makes one a more likely "victim" of a cybercrime or act of digital deviance? For starters, being visible online—often synonymous with being heavily active—is a mainstay among risk factors for being targeted. Frequent social media usage, texting activity, and lengthy web browsing are often cited among factors raising digital victimization risk. Belonging to a demographic group highly susceptible to particular types of offending is another strong risk element for targeting. For instance, as mentioned at the outset of this chapter, young Internet users and elderly populations are highly coveted targets. Recalling also that female Internet users are likely targets for certain digital offenders, some scholars have found that romance scammers and other "relationship-oriented" cyber-offenders have been comparatively more successful with female targets (Halder & Jaishankar, 2011; Parkins, 2012; Saha & Srivastava, 2014).

Demographic and behavioral factors notwithstanding, perhaps the most consistent finding concerning target suitability in the digital world is that viable targets are nigh infinite. Suitable targets in the digital world can range from machines housing valuable data (e.g., healthcare records, corporate trade secrets, government intelligence, financial information) to individuals possessing precious information (e.g., passwords leading to banking information or access to a company's networks). A computer user who is emotionally or psychologically vulnerable can also be considered a suitable target. By design, the Internet connects all machines and users; those accessing the online world are not inherently isolated from digital presences at-large. Thus, there are limitless convergences online between suitable targets and motivated offenders.

GUARDIANSHIP

With respect to guardianship, the topic of digital victimization confronts the matter in two distinct ways. In one respect, guardianship is squarely a matter of what the end user does to safeguard his/her online experience. As Internet usage tends to be a highly personalized affair, the public at-large is expected to pursue a reasonable amount of precaution against the potential threats available online. Keeping important user credentials securely hidden, maintaining hardware and software integrity on one's devices (e.g., updating operating systems, antivirus software) and being aware of strangers in one's vicinity during online activity are just a few habits expected of the end user in the age of post-industrial awareness.

On the other hand, to the extent that guardianship is held as a responsibility of individual users, there is also an expectation that the architects and custodians of Internet content will practice due diligence in ensuring that the content made available online will minimize opportunities for victimization. Commercial and political entities alike have a vested interest and responsibility to providing adequate security measures for their online patrons. Financial institutions and social media entities are expected to provide a safe and secure environment for those individuals visiting their online spaces. Government organizations and political representatives are tasked with providing and enforcing guidelines in accordance with healthy online experiences.

A core precept of the routine activities perspective is that we are creatures of functional habit. We often driven by predetermined tasks as essential to our daily routines and consume ourselves with carrying out those tasks. Usually, we structure our interactions with others around these routines and the acts themselves take on certain predictability due to repetition. The extent to which we expose ourselves to positive and negative experiences is also rooted in these routines.

For example, consider the process we might engage in to start our work day. We wake up at certain times, dress a certain way based upon particular external factors (e.g., weather, type of occupation, expected duties for the day), prepare children for school (if they are present), eat certain things generally considered as "breakfast-fare," and depart our respective domiciles at certain times…all within a predictable pattern that can be carried out almost without thought. With respect to victimization risk, such pre-work routines might catch the attention of prospective thieves seeking easy targets to rob (i.e., homes where a physical presence is less likely during certain times), and thus increase our likelihood of victimization via burglary. Yet, that same predictability might also catch the attention of neighbors and/or local law enforcement aware that our home is vacant by a certain time every day. Thus, the presence of another individual near such a home during work hours might be more likely to raise suspicion and consequently decrease the risk of victimization. Either way, the routine becomes a critical correlate of victimization risk under the theory.

As our routines in terrestrial settings fall within certain bounds of predictability, so too have we become prone to routines in our digital lives. How we text and to whom is often consistent. Our browser histories are often saturated with multiple visits to a relatively

Table 9.1   Routine Activities: Terrestrial vs. Digital Settings

EXAMPLES OF...	... TERRESTRIAL SETTINGS	... DIGITAL SETTINGS
MOTIVATED OFFENDERS IN...	Home burglars, car thieves, bullies, pickpockets, kidnappers, sex traffickers, stalkers	Catfishers, bullies/cyberbullies, online phishing consortiums, credit card scammers, sex traffickers, trollers, cyberstalkers
SUITABLE TARGETS IN...	Any individual careless in securing their personal belongings (e.g., home, car, wallet, pocketbook)	Any individual careless in securing their digital belongings (e.g., e-mail address, browser history, user credentials on websites, laptops, mobile phones)
GUARDIANSHIP IN...	Home security systems, anti-theft automobile devices, local law enforcement, parents, neighbors, friends/family, security officers, electronic screening devices (e.g., metal detectors)	Parents, IT security professionals, federal/government-level watchdogs (i.e., FBI), friends/family, anti-virus software, password sophistication, WiFi firewalls, dual-factor authentication
POTENTIAL HARMS IN...	Emotional distress, financial loss, physical damage	Emotional distress, financial loss, physical harm (in response to the digital victimization experience)

narrow list of locations. We often use and reuse passwords for the various digital destinations we frequent, and we often conduct our digital affairs from the same IP addresses and accounts. Accordingly, under routine activities theory, our predictable digital behaviors contribute greatly to varying types and levels of potential harm (see Table 9.1).

Though our focus in this chapter, and generally this book, is the cybercrime investigative community, cybersecurity professionals may also find the insights from digital applications of routine activities theory of practical use. In effect, what cybersecurity professionals attempt to do is increase guardianship over computers, networks, and data, or reduce the suitability of those targets. Indeed, cybersecurity practices are based on the premise that there is something worth guarding (most commonly data), that there is a continuous supply of hackers attempting to access the data (motivated offender), and that their only option is to develop methods and technologies to protect the data (guardianship).

Cybervictimization Types

Long before applications to the digital world, early crime scholars have pondered the various groups crime victims might fall into. Among the originating theorists on this subject, criminologist Hans Von Hentig proposed thirteen victim types—six general demographic classes, six grounded in one's psychological state, and one transitional label (where the victim becomes the offender)—during the early development of victimology. Several decades later, attorney and "founding father of victimology" Benjamin Mendelsohn held victims generally fall into one of six distinct types: *The Completely Innocent Victim, the Victim with Minor Guilt, the Victim Who Is as Guilty as the Offender, the Victim More Guilty Than the Offender, the Most Guilty Victim,* and *the Imaginary Victim.* However, a slightly more simplified model proposed by Abdel Fattah offers perhaps the most ideal framework from traditional victimology for delineating contemporary cybervictimization types (Fattah, 1967).

Fattah summarized in *Towards a Criminological Classification of Victims* (1967) five victim types: Non-participating, latent/predisposed, provocative, participating, and false. For the *non-participating victim*, there are two distinguishing characteristics—an attitude of denial or repulsion towards the offense and the offender, and no contribution to the origin of the offense. Unfortunately, the prevailing literature and data on cybervictimization tells us that, while many victims would be inclined to deny or abhor being victimized in a digital environment, most fall short in avoiding contributing to their own victimization. Rather, we find cybercrime victims often knowingly or unknowingly contribute to victimization in a number of ways.

Beginning with the notion of a *latent or predisposed victim*—people who, because of peculiar predispositions or traits of character, are more liable than others to be victims of certain types of offenses—these victims are squarely covered under routine activities considerations of cybervictimization. An example could be the individual that regularly leaves their phone unlocked or tends to access sensitive, personal data in public settings; such an individual exposes him/herself to a higher risk of identity-related offenses. As long as the contributing precondition remains unaddressed, so too does the increased risk (perhaps even repeated targeting from the same or similar offenders). Again, such explanations have gained much traction in cybervictimization scholarship; thus, we can conclude that the latent/predisposed typology of cybervictimization is among the more popular at present.

Those victims that play a role by either inciting the criminal to commit a crime, or by creating or fostering a situation likely to lead to crime—the *provocative victim*—are not uncommon in spaces where certain acts of cyberviolence or cyberharassment thrive. For instance, consider the online gaming community and the act of *swatting*—calling in a false report of an emergency situation (i.e., bomb threat, hostage taking, gunshot victim) with the intent of inciting an aggressive response from public safety and/or law enforcement agencies. An increasingly common scenario is for the swatting offender/s to call in the false threat following either some negative exchange between themselves and the intended target in an online gaming environment, or in a practical joke attempt against an individual live-streaming to a large audience.

Such was the case when Joshua Peters of St. Cloud, Minnesota was swatted by an unknown prankster following a livestream of his gaming efforts in the online fantasy role-playing game, *Runescape*. During the stream, Peters paused the game to answer his front door while the webcam video of the stream continued running. The next series of events captured entailed the aggressive response from St. Cloud authorities raiding Peters' home under the false report of a shooting involving Peters' and his roommate. In this instance, the provocation was nothing more than the livestream itself and volume of audience members actively watching Peters' progress in the game. Unfortunately, the provocative victim may not have to engage in an act that is willfully antagonistic in order to become victimized. In Peters' case, the mere act of creating access to a large audience was all that was needed to incite the would-be offender.

A *participating victim* would be any such targeted individual that plays an active role in their victimization either by adopting a passive attitude towards their own security (thus, making the crime possible or easier) or else by assisting the criminal. Note that for the former defining quality—a passive attitude—this might already present itself under the latent victim category. The distinction, however, is if such an attitude exists *prior* to the victimization attempt. For instance, one who willfully engages in online bank transactions while logged into a public Wi-Fi hotspot, and especially while in an establishment of high-volume activity (i.e., Starbucks cafes) presents a number of risk opportunities and as such could be construed as playing a role in their victimization experience (participating victim). However, an argument could be made for labeling this victim as latent if their passive attitude towards data security predates the offender/s' efforts.

Nonetheless, ignoring such risks and willfully failing to engage in proper security measures in such instances (i.e., using a personal, encrypted hotspot, shielding one's screen from potential shoulder-surfing) would be characteristic of the participating victim. Similarly, giving out one's user credentials to personal websites for whatever reason opens one up to potential identity theft and cybertrespass attempts. Any ensuing victimization from sharing such credentials would be a failure associated with participating victimization.

Under the final category, the *false victim*, we would find those individuals that are not really victims at all of a crime committed by another person. They also include those who become victims of their own actions. As cybercrime becomes more ubiquitous and included among the general range of victimizations one could experience, we should expect to find fewer instances of false victimization. However, given the rapid pace at which technological innovations occur, it remains conceivable that user inexperience with emerging technology could result in negative experiences attributable solely to user errors. For similar reasons, it is also an ever-present challenge for the criminal justice community to keep crime definitions and legal statutes relevant with the various new deviance opportunities that emerge from new technology. An offense like cryptocurrency fraud might literally have been defined as false victimization barely ten years ago, for there would have been no specific legal code addressing fraud of that particular nature.

Outcomes of Cybervictimization

Few would contest that cybervictimization is a harmful experience. Victimization in the digital world is just as damaging as that which one could experience in a non-digital setting, and in some respects more so. Illustrating the range of such harm, Cross and colleagues (2016) noted in a study of online fraud victims:

> *Consistent with prior research…the overwhelming majority of participants in this study reported profound emotional and psychological impacts following their victimization. Participants described the fraud as 'devastating', 'soul-destroying', or as an event that 'changed [their] attitude to life'. One admitted having 'a bit of a nervous breakdown' following the fraud, and another claimed the impacts were such that 'it was the first thing I thought about when I woke up and the last thing I thought of before I went to sleep'. Participants described a number of (often interconnected) emotional responses following the fraud. The most common were shame or embarrassment, distress, sadness and anger. Others described stress, worry, shock and loneliness.*

> (Cross et al., 2016, 4)

Compounding such qualitative damage, recent data on the financial impact and nation-wide expanse of cybervictimization underscores the reality of harm experienced: (Cross et al., 2016).

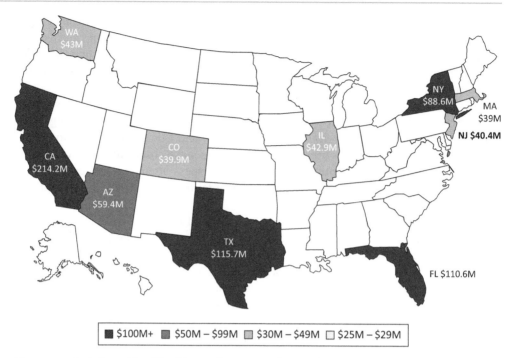

Figure 9.3   An infographic of Top 10 states by amount of money lost by victims. *Courtesy of the FBI ICC Center's 2017 Internet Crime Report.*

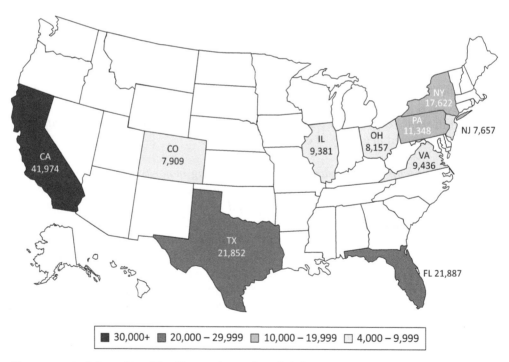

Figure 9.4   An infographic of Top 10 states by number of victims reporting cybercrime. *Courtesy of the FBI ICC Center's 2017 Internet Crime Report.*

Between 2010 and 2015, the U.S. Federal Bureau of Investigations (2017) averaged just over 288,000 complaints of Internet scams and recorded over one billion dollars in total loss in 2015 alone (Dutton et al., 2013). In 2017, these trends remained virtually the same, and as illustrated in Figures 9.3 and 9.4 (p. 180), the damage wrought stretches across the national landscape.

Cybervictimization results in a variety of direct negative impacts on digital identity, digital assets, software/hardware integrity and device performance (Dodel & Mesch, 2017). Subsequent indirect effects may take shape as well via stress induced from tracking down victimization culprits, closing down personal accounts, and managing financial losses suffered (Dodel & Mesch, 2017). Broader economic impacts such as decreased consumer confidence and spending activity in e-commerce destinations, which can have especially pernicious impacts in light of the post-industrial age of paperless spending, have also been recorded (Dodel & Mesch, 2017).

Online harassment has been proven to produce high levels of fear and distress, and notably among female audiences when the harassment stems from an intimate relationship (Lindsay et al., 2016). Within the context of dating, Schenk and Fremouw (2012) even note a differentiated set of responses to cybervictimization by gender; whereas males tended to resort to substance abuse as a coping mechanism, female victims were more likely avoid the technology altogether. Furthermore, while men tend to experience more instances of space violations online, female victims more often report feelings of distress and physical threat during such experiences (Lindsay et al., 2016; Schenk & Fremouw, 2012).

Perhaps nowhere are the vast and substantial damages associated with cybervictimization displayed more vividly that among the targets of cyberbullying. School-aged victims of cyberbullying experience a gamut of emotional and cognitive trauma, including depression, low-self-esteem, fear, and powerlessness (Kota et al., 2014; Wood Jr. & Graham, 2018). Suicidal thoughts and struggles with concentration are also common among cyberbullying victims (Lindsay et al., 2016; Schenk & Fremouw, 2012), as are lower grades and other signs of academic maladjustment (Kota et al., 2014).

Outwardly, the cyberbullied demonstrate greater hostility and proclivity towards delinquent—sometimes violent—behavior (i.e., school avoidance, weapon brandishing, alcohol consumption, sexual frequency) both in- and outside of school grounds (Hinduja & Patchin, 2007; Kota et al., 2014; Wood Jr. & Graham, 2018). The cyberbullied individual often expresses greater generalized fear of being victimized in digital environments, alongside those who've suffered from computer virus attacks, online scams and digital piracy infractions (Yu, 2014).

These insights notwithstanding, conclusions on the scope of cybervictimization outcomes must also be taken with some level of skepticism as the full reality of such victimization is not necessarily captured. Again, considering the example of cyberbullying, Sobba and colleagues (2017) found that while over 40% of teens in the United States reported experiencing some form of cyberbullying, only 25% tell their parents about their victimization. Their example illustrates the broader point that cybervictimization is difficult to track in some respects given that many cybercrimes go unreported, and victims of cybercrime tend to be reluctant to come forward for a variety of reasons.

Common among them include trivialization of the full impact of the crime itself by victims and law enforcement officials alike, and victims' own feelings of shame for falling victim to the offense committed against them (Cross et al., 2016; Halder & Jaishankar, 2011). This apprehension, along with an ever-fluctuating list of cybercrime definitions, and the general ease with which offenders can mask themselves behind a variety of identity-masking conventions, are key reasons victimization in the digital world tends to go underreported. This, in turn, leads to inaccuracies in the documentation of such crimes and causes greater difficulty in implementing proper safeguards since the full scope of the trends can rarely be ascertained.

Cybervictimization Restitution

"WHO IS THE VICTIM?"

From Richard Quinney's "Who Is The Victim?," published in *Criminology* (Volume 10, Issue 3, 1972):

The modern movement for compensation of victims also has its own conventional wisdom regarding the victim. The numerous proposals for victim compensation contain their own conceptions as to who is the victim. Moreover, these proposals are addressed to specific points regarding the victim, including ideas about the offender-victim relationship, responsibility, human nature, governmental functions, and the nature of society. "Who is the victim?" is not an innocent question.

Recognition of the need to compensate victims...is grounded on the notion that modern criminal law has evolved away from the victim's right to private redress. And since the state has taken upon itself the function of maintaining law and order, it is liable for the personal injuries of the victims of some forms of crime.

There are, of course, disclaimers to this notion of the victim and his right to be compensated. Some [writers] stress more emphatically the role of individual responsibility and question welfare programs by the government.

Those who argue against victim compensation or for extremely limited programs conceive of the victim as being responsible for his own victimization.

Another proposal...suggests the "functional responsibility" of both the victim and the offender...that the offender should compensate the victim when possible. Restitution to victims by offenders, it is suggested, would serve to rehabilitate the offender. Further, the victim is to prevent his own victimization and the offender is to account for his violation.

On the general matter of victim restitution, the preceding excerpt from Richard Quinney's *Who Is The Victim?* sets forth some key talking points to frame the discussion. What role should the state play in compensating victims of crime? To what extent should victims seek to address their recompense, particularly in light of the possibility that they may have contributed to their own victimization risk? And for that matter, what role should the offender have in compensating his her/victim? Albeit over 40 years removed from any notion of the cybervictimization concept we are confronted with today, questions and ideas Quinney proposed are no less relevant.

At least one piece of landmark legislation, *The Identity Theft Enforcement and Restitution Act of 2008 (ITER)*, sets a position on such questions in establishing the U.S. government's role in cybercrime victim compensation, as well as the respective responsibilities of victims and offenders alike. In essence, the ITER Act states that victims have the right to use the U.S. federal court system to the fullest extent possible in seeking restitution from entities associated with the theft and subsequent misuse of the victim's identity. Particularly, the ITER Act states:

- the victim may seek compensation for the time spent fixing problems ensuing from the theft. Specifically, the victim is allowed to receive a sum "equal to the value of the time reasonably spent by the victim in an attempt to remediate the intended or actual harm incurred by the victim from the offense."
- prosecutors may pursue offenders who threaten to take or release information from computers with the intent of cyberextortion
- prosecutors may pursue charges against cybercriminals with conspiracy to commit a cybercrime

The ITER Act further removed a previous restriction of having to show at least $5,000 in damages before filing charges associated with unauthorized computer access, and allows for federal prosecution even when parties reside within the same state (Doyle, 2014).

Since its inception, there has been one major federal ruling specifically invoking the ITER Act. The case, *United States of America v. Janosko (2011)*, ruled in favor of the plaintiff and subsequently ordered the defendant, Mr. Francis G. Janosko (Mass.) to pay restitution resulting from illegally accessing secured computer equipment and files housed within the Plymouth County Correctional Facility (where he was an inmate). Restitution was ordered as follows: $4,309 for the cost of purchasing elements of the system needed to replace those damaged by Mr. Janosko and retained as evidence, and $6,600 for the cost of monitoring credit records of the individuals who suffered the privacy violations and consequent risk of identity theft (*United States v. Janosko, 2011*).

Aside from the aforementioned ruling against Janosko, numerous other decisions in cybercrime court cases offer precedent for the awarding of compensation to cybercrime victims. The vast majority fall within the realm of infractions of cyberpornography, cybertrespass, or cyberdeception, and especially when a specific quantifiable amount of loss can be determined:

A SNAPSHOT OF FEDERAL CYBERCRIME COURT RULINGS RESULTING IN RESTITUTION

United States v. Watt (2010)

In 2010, Stephen Watt pled guilty to conspiracy, in violation of 18 U.S.C.S. § 371, based on his adaptation of software that enabled the principals of the conspiracy to steal credit and debit card information from certain companies. He was sentenced to 24 months incarceration, three years of supervised release, and ordered to pay **restitution of $171.5 million**.

United States v. Green (2010)

In 2010, Benjamin Green pled guilty to six counts of aggravated identity theft in violation of 18 U.S.C. §§ 1028 (a)(1) and (a)(4), six counts of fraud with an access device in violation of 18 U.S.C. § 1029(a)(2), and one count of bank fraud in violation of 18 U.S.C. § 1344. He was sentenced 84 months' imprisonment, five years of supervised release, and ordered to pay **restitution of $95,522.64,** along with a special assessment of $1,300.

United States v. Kearney (2012)

Patrick Kearney pled guilty (and later appealed) to 17 counts of transportation, distribution, and possession of child pornography, which he did through use of the Internet. As his appeal was denied, the original ruling that he pay **$3,800 in restitution** to the subject, "Vicky", depicted throughout the pornographic materials under 18 U.S.C.S. § 2259 was upheld. In the ruling, it was noted that restitution was calculated based upon Vicky's status as a minor during the time period of the offending behavior, as well as the expectation that she would require mental-health treatment following Mr. Kearney's conduct.

U.S. v. Benoit (2013)

In 2013, Joseph Benoit was convicted of receipt of child pornography in violation of 18 U.S.C.S. § 2252(a)(2) and (b)(1), and possession of child pornography in violation of 18 U.S.C.S. § 2252(a)(4)(B) and (b)(2). He was sentenced to concurrent terms of 125 and 120 months' imprisonment and **ordered to pay $11,466 in restitution**.

U.S. v. Gammon (2013)

William Gammon pled guilty to one count of possession of child pornography, in violation of 18 U.S.C.S. § 2252A(a)(5)(B) and (b)(2). Pursuant to 18 U.S.C.S. § 2259, the United States District Court for the Southern District of Texas ordered **restitution in the amount of $125,000 to each of three victims**.

Given what is now known about the variety of damage wrought from cybercrime offenses, few would argue that cybercrime victims are deserving of some recompense in cases such as the aforementioned. Yet, reconciliation of the harm committed against a target in the digital world may be the most troubling aspect of cybervictimization, and thus is still a matter of limited precedent at this time. Prominent among contributing factors to the complexity in awarding victim compensations for cybercrime offenses are: 1) dubious and/or unreliable methods for calculating proper compensation, 2) similarly questionable means of determining the total scope of victims/victimization resulting from the offense/s considered, and 3) inability of convicted defendants to produce victim compensation associated with their sentence.

Conclusion

In this chapter, we have discussed and considered the ramifications associated with cyber-victimization. Clearly, the subject has warranted and been paid much attention in recent scholarship and criminal justice legislation. By and large, the extant literature firmly settles on the notion that victimization in the digital world can be and usually is profoundly damaging. Accordingly, via such benchmark policy developments as the CFAA (see Chapter 2) and the ITER Act, federal court rulings, and some reinvention of the agency infrastructure in place to address victimization, the criminal justice community has responded in acknowledgment the various pains endured by those targeted in the cyberworld.

Yet, it is important to also remember that the discourse and treatment of victimization in the digital world is still developing and much remains to be explored and resolved. Paramount among such gray areas is the unawareness of and apathy towards the extent of potential damage from cybercrime still defining many academics, criminal justice practitioners, and the public at-large. The extent of underreporting from victims, along with conflicting notions concerning the very concept of what victimization means in a digital sense, remain confounding obstacles hampering progress in research and policy development on this subject.

CHAPTER 9 CURRENT EVENTS AND CRITICAL THINKING:

Did Reality TV and Social Media Cause Hana Kimura's Death?

Note—several references to the event described below can be found online. The authors note the following New York Times article among such references:

https://www.nytimes.com/2020/07/17/arts/television/terrace-house-suicide.html

On a popular reality TV show, *Terrace House*, Hana Kimura appeared alongside five other cast members during the show's fifth installment. Produced by Japan-based Fuji TV and the American streaming entertainment conglomerate, Netflix, the show was centered around six young strangers sharing a large, well-appointed home for the purpose of sharing their lives with one another for a period spanning several weeks to a few months. Though motives for each cast member varied, the general objective for each was to make friends and/or (potentially) find a love interest while inhabiting the home—all while being filmed and viewed by a panel of celebrity commentators in a separate studio. Viewers of the show were presented with episodes that appeared to be largely unscripted, and episodes of the current season appeared online even while the show was still filming. Thus, cast members can and often did watch previous episodes of a season they appeared in while still taping new episodes of that same season, and they could also read comments about those episodes posted by the viewing audience at-large.

In one such episode, Kimura (a professional wrestler by trade) expressed anger towards another housemate over a wrestling costume of hers being ruined while the housemate was doing laundry. Compared with most episodes of the show, where direct confrontations between housemates were rare and typically placid in tone, Kimura's outburst stood out. Kimura's aggressive reaction to the incident set off a wave of social media dialogue, not the least of which centered around whether Kimura was justified in her response to the other housemates over the incident. Kimura herself reported receiving much backlash afterwards on her own social media pages and several others affiliated with the show (notably, X/Twitter and Instagram), citing various instances of cyberbullying, flaming, and trolling following the airing of the episode.

Several months after her departure from the show, Kimura committed suicide. Various posts on her social media accounts, along with additional notes left behind, cited the emotional turmoil from her time on the show as a direct cause of her decision to take her own life. Instant message threads between Kimura and a close friend, shared posthumously by Kimura's mother with several media outlets, imply the argument between Kimura and the housemate was far more staged than the episode appeared. Within her messages, Kimura reported feeling pressured by the producers of *Terrace House* to behave more antagonistically towards the housemate—even suggesting that she slap him; this did occur in the episode. Representatives of the show refute the claims of coercion, but have also since canceled filming of the show. Despite its intense popularity and worldwide audience during its run, *Terrace House* has ceased filming as of this publication with no projected date of a reboot.

How would you explain the harm caused in this incident? Who is/are the victims? What is the nature of the victimization that occurred?

Under the "survivor" premise of cybervictimization, the individual who experiences a cybercrime event is empowered to overcome the experience (to see themselves quite literally as a survivor rather than a victim). What tools/resources from the preceding chapters, or any other content you've become aware of, might have helped Kimura address the cyberviolence she was subjected to?

NOTE

1 For a more comprehensive discussion of cybercrime theories, see Chapter 10—Cybercriminology.

REFERENCES

Alhaboby, Z., Barnes, J., Evans, H., & Short, E. (2023). Cybervictimization of adults with long-term conditions: Cross-sectional study. *Journal of Medical Internet Research, 25*, 23.

Bernat, F., & Godlove, N. (2012). Understanding 21st century cybercrime for the "common" victim. *89*, 2. https://www.crimeandjustice.org.uk/publications/cjm/article/understanding-21st-century-cybercrime-%E2%80%98common%E2%80%99-victim

Campbell, J., & Moore, R. (2011). Self-perceptions of stalking victimization and impacts on victim reporting. *Police Practice and Research, 12*(6), 13.

Center, Pew Research. (2017). *Internet and broadband fact sheet.* http://www.pewinternet.org/fact-sheet/internet-broadband/

Choi, K.-s. (2008). Computer crime victimization and integrated theory: An empirical assessment. *International Journal of Cyber Criminology, 2*(1), 308–333.

Choi, K.-s. (2010). *Risk factors in computer-crime victimization.* LFB Scholarly Publishing LLC.

Cohen, L. E., & Felson, M. (1979). Social change and crime rate trends: A routine activity approach. *American Sociological Review, 44*(4), 588-608.

Cross, C., Richards, K., & Smith, R. G. (2016). The reporting experiences and support needs of victims of online fraud. (*Trends and Issues in Crime and Criminal Justice,* Issue. https://aic.gov.au/publications/tandi/tandi518

Dodel, M., & Mesch, G. (2017). Cyber-victimization preventive behavior: A health belief model approach. *Computers in Human Behavior, 68*, 359-367.

Doyle, C. (2014). *Cybercrime: An overview of the Federal Computer Fraud and Abuse Statute and related federal criminal laws.* C. R. Service.

Dutton, W. H., Blank, G., & Groselj, D. (2013). Culture of the Internet: The Internet in Britain. *Oxford Internet Survey 2013,* Issue. University of Oxford.

Fattah, A. (1967). Towards a criminological classification of victims. *The International Journal of Criminal Police, 209*.

Festl, R., & Quandt, T. (2016). The role of online communication in long-term cyberbullying involvement among girls and boys. *Journal of Youth Adolescence, 45*(9), 14.

Graham, R., & Triplett, R. (2017). Capable guardians in the digital environment: The role of digital literacy in reducing phishing victimization. *Deviant Behavior, 38*(12), 1371–1382.

Halder, D., & Jaishankar, K. (2011). Cyber gender harassment and secondary victimization: A comparative analysis of the United States, the UK, and India. *Victims and Offenders, 4*(4), 13.

Henson, B., Reyns, B. W., & Fisher, B. S. (2011). Security in the 21st century: Examining the link between online social network activity, privacy, and interpersonal victimization. *Criminal Justice Review, 36*(3), 16.

Hinduja, S., & Patchin, J. W. (2007). Offline consequences of online victimization: School violence and delinquency. *Journal of School Violence, 6*(3), 89–112.

Hinduja, S., & Patchin, J. W. (2008). Personal information of adolescents on the Internet: A quantitative content analysis of Myspace. *Journal of Adolescence, 31,* 125–146.

Hinduja, S., & Patchin, J. W. (2010). Bullying, cyberbullying, and suicide. *Archives of Suicide Research, 14*(3), 17.

Holt, T. J., & Bossler, A. M. (2009). Examining the applicability of lifestyle-routine activities theory for cybercrime victimization. *Deviant Behavior, 30,* 1–25.

Holt, T. J., Bossler, A. M., Malinski, R., & May, D. C. (2016). Identifying predictors of unwanted online sexual conversations among youth using a low self-control and routine activity framework. *Journal of Contemporary Criminal Justice, 32*(2), 20.

Holt, T. J., Fitzgerald, S., Bossler, A., Chee, G., & Ng, E. (2016). Assessing the risk factors of cyber and mobile phone bullying victimization in a nationally representative sample of Singapore youth. *International Journal of Offender Therapy and Comparative Criminology, 60*(5), 598–615.

Investigations, Federal Bureau of. (2017). Internet crime report.

Jorna, P. (2016). The relationship between age and consumer fraud victimisation. *Trends & Issues in Crime and Criminal Justice, 17.* https://aic.gov.au/publications/tandi/tandi519

Khurana, A., Bleakley, A., Jordan, A. B., & Romer, D. (2015). The protective effects of parental monitoring and Internet restriction on adolescents' risk of online harassment. *Journal of Youth Adolescence, 44*(5), 8.

Kirwan, G. H., Fullwood, C., & Rooney, B. (2018). Risk factors for social networking site scam victimization among Malaysian students. *Cyberpsychology, Behavior, and Social Networking, 21*(2), 123–128.

Kota, R., Schoohs, S., Benson, M., & Moreno, M. A. (2014). Characterizing cyberbullying among college students: Hacking, dirty laundry, and mocking. *Societies, 4,* 549–560.

Lindsay, M., Booth, J. M., Messing, J. T., & Thaller, J. (2016). Experiences of online harassment among emerging adults: Emotional reactions and the mediating role of fear. *Journal of Interpersonal Violence, 31*(19), 3174–3195.

Luo, Q., Wu, N., & Huang, L. (2023). Cybervictimization and cyberbullying among college students: The chain of mediating effects of stress and rumination. *Frontiers in Psychology, 14,* 9.

Marganski, A., & Fauth, K. (2013). Socially interactive technology and contemporary dating: A cross-cultural exploration of deviant behaviors among young adults in the modern, evolving technological world. *International Criminal Justice Review, 23*(4), 20.

Nasi, M., Oksanen, A., Keipi, T., & Rasanen, P. (2015). Cybercrime victimization among young people: A multi-nation study. *Journal of Scandinavian Studies in Criminology and Crime Prevention, 16*(2), 8.

Parkins, R. (2012). Gender and emotional expressiveness: An analysis of prosodic features in emotional expression. *Griffith Working Papers in Pragmatics and Intercultural Communication, 5*(1), 9. Retrieved June 6, 2017, from https://cms-uat.itc.griffith.edu.au/__data/assets/pdf_file/0006/456459/Paper-6-Parkins-Gender-and-Emotional-Expressiveness_final.pdf

Popović-Ćitić, B., Djurić, S., & Cvetković, V. (2011). The prevalence of cyberbullying among adolescents: A case study of middle schools in Serbia. *School Psychology International, 32*(4), 12.

Quinney, R. (1972). Who is the victim? *Criminology, 10*(3), 314–323.

Reyns, B. W. (2013). Online routines and identity theft victimization: Further expanding routine activity theory beyond direct-contact offenses. *Journal of Research in Crime and Delinquency, 50*(2), 23.

Rodríguez-Enríquez, M., Bennasar-Veny, M., Leiva, A., Garaigordobil, M., & Yañez, A. (2019). Cybervictimization among secondary students: Social networking time, personality traits and parental education. *BMC Public Health, 19*(1499), 7.

Saha, T., & Srivastava, A. (2014). Indian women at risk in the cyber space: A conceptual model of reasons of victimization. *International Journal of Cyber Criminology, 8*(1), 12.

Sakellariou, T., Carroll, A., & Houghton, S. (2012). Rates of cyber victimization and bullying among male Australian primary and high school students. *School Psychology International, 33*(5), 16.

Schenk, A., & Fremouw, W. (2012). Prevalence, psychological impact, and coping of cyberbully victims among college students. *Journal of School Violence, 11*, 21–37.

Shirky, C. (2008). *Here comes everybody: The power of organizing without organizations*. The Penguin Press.

Sobba, K. N., Paez, R. A., & Bensel, T. t. (2017). Perceptions of cyberbullying: An assessment of perceived severity among college students. *Tech Trends, 61*, 570–579.

Williams, M. (2016). Guardians upon high: An application of routine activities theory to online identity theft in Europe at the country and individual level. *British Journal of Criminology, 56*, 29.

Wood Jr., F. R., & Graham, R. (2018). "Safe" and "at-risk": Cyberbullying victimization and deviant health risk behaviors in youth. *Youth & Society*, 1–20.

Yar, M. (2005). The novelty of 'cybercrime': An assessment in light of a routine activity theory. *European Journal of Criminology, 2*(4), 407–427.

Yu, S. (2014). Fear of cyber crime among college students in the United States: An exploratory study. *International Journal of Cyber Criminology, 8*(1), 36–46.

Zhou, Z., Tang, H., Tian, Y., Wei, H., Zhang, F., & Morrison, C. (2013). Cyberbullying and its risk factors among Chinese high school students. *School Psychology International, 34*(6), 17.

Chapter 10

Cybercriminology

Introduction

In the age of post-industrialism, data is king. Virtually every aspect of the human experience is rooted in or coincides with the existence of and access to information. This so-called "Petabyte Age" (Anderson, 2008) of human existence is defined by large amounts of data and advanced means of processing it. So much data now exists, in fact, that some thoughts have turned to the possibility of the scientific method being reimagined as a process increasingly less reliant upon traditional theory development, and more on formulaic, algorithm-driven calculations of new information and insight. While still debatable if traditional theory is indeed dying, concepts like AI, predictive policing, and Big Data analytics discussed in previous chapters underscore the notion that conventional theory building may be becoming obsolete, or at least reimagined as something quite different than what we once knew.

In this present reality, we do observe that people can be rather dismissive of theory. Many in society today would seem to lean towards decision-making grounded in facts as they exist in the real world—not projections of what may or may not be. Meanwhile, students often see theory as simply a course they need to take or block of ideas within a course, but not information that can be of use once they begin their lives in a professional setting. Alternatively, we maintain that the strength of theory is and always has been in its ability to explain in general terms how and why phenomena are connected and—hopefully—predict what will happen in the future.

For instance, when overseeing a murder trial, a judge is often tasked with weighing the multiple intervening variables that might have preceded a defendant's decision to take the life of another. Under a theory like differential association, such precedents could include exposure to models of deviant behavior or deviance justifications represented amongst the defendant's peers. A police officer may find a need to think about a wide array of variables when trying to prevent a rash of assaults along a dark path near a college campus. Ideas

DOI: 10.4324/9781003283256-10

from such theories as routine activities (e.g., the need for capable guardianship), while possibly too simplistic for the officer's immediate task, could serve as a starting point upon which to build more complex strategies for curtailing the assault trends. Moreover, even if the environment changes (e.g., the officer moves from a quiet, suburban college campus to a dense urban area), the officer can be confident that the general precepts asserted by routine activities theory will still hold.

Building upon our discussion of routine activities theories of cybervictimization in the preceding chapter, we will introduce several additional theories used to explain crime and deviance in the digital world. For each theory, the main assumptions are introduced, basic concepts relevant to the theory are explained, and its applicability to cybercrime is discussed. These theories are:

- Deterrence Theory
- Theories of Culture and Learning
- Social Learning Theory
- Labeling Theory
- Theories of Control
- Social Bonding Theory
- Self-Control Theory (A General Theory of Crime)
- Techniques of Neutralization
- Strain Theory
- Theories of Anonymity—Deindividuation and Disinhibition
- Crime Prevention Through Digital Design (CPTDD)

The list of theories presented here is neither exhaustive nor more important to explaining cybercrime than those not included. Rather, the exclusion of several traditional theories from this chapter is necessary for a few reasons. A major one is that, while some longstanding theories of crime like strain theory and self-control theory maintain general relevance in the current discourse, the empirical evidence supporting their applicability to offenses in the digital world is still developing. As the work of cybercrime scholars continues to advance, we believe chapters such as this one will transform to accommodate additional explanations.

Deterrence Theory

Deterrence theory argues that people will avoid criminal activity if the known punishments associated with the act outweigh any perceived benefit (Hua & Bapna, 2012; Shepherd & Mejias, 2016; Wrenn, 2012; Young & Zhang, 2007). This theory is grounded in the assumption that individuals are rational beings who weigh the costs and benefits of an action, and then make logical choices accordingly. A logical choice is one that maximizes their gain or positive outcome in any given situation. In the context of crime and deviance, this means that an individual considering a deviant or criminal act will consider the likelihood of being caught and the penalties they would incur. For policymakers and law enforcement personnel, the assumption of a rational actor also assumes that the criminal justice system can modify the punishments it administers to *deter* potential offenders—thus, deterrence theory.

There are three components to deterrence: celerity, certainty, and severity. *Celerity* is the time it takes for a punishment to be administered. A punishment that is received closer to the violating act is theoretically more effective at deterring future acts. A punishment that takes longer to administer—say, a sentence of death carried out several years after a guilty verdict—is less associated with the crime. *Certainty* is the freedom from doubt that, given a crime, a punishment will be meted out. An offender who believes that they will certainly be caught following the offending act will rationally avoid committing the act. *Severity* is the level of punishment, to include components like time spent in confinement, monetary fines, loss of privileges, and/or physical pain. Punishments that are more severe are theoretically more likely to deter crime.

There are two types of deterrence activities administered by states and other agents of authority: General and specific. *General deterrence* activities are undertaken to deter crime in the general population. A state levies a punishment on an offender to set an example, and the punishment is designed for public viewing. In medieval times, it was common for enemies of the state to be killed and have their heads placed on pikes for others to see as a warning. Public floggings were commonplace in colonial America. Modern societies are less violent and may use different methods of deterring criminal behavior. One example would be the "perp walk," where an offender must walk into a courthouse in full view of mass media and the viewing public.

Because of the relative newness of cybercrime, states may make an example out of someone if there is public concern that the crime is a harbinger of things to come. For example, Ross Ulbricht's punishment of life in prison without the possibility parole for his role in running the Silk Road online marketplace may be an example of general deterrence. It is questionable whether a life sentence was justified given than Ulbricht was only found guilty of creating and maintaining the site (not for directly selling any illicit goods or services through it). Nonetheless, the harshness of his sentence can be perceived as an attempt by the U.S. law enforcement community to convey a zero-tolerance message and agenda for such crimes.

Specific deterrence, on the other hand, is administered to prevent the individual from further criminal behavior. The "three strikes" laws, in which an individual will be given a life sentence if they commit three felonies, is designed to deter an offender from future offending. Specific deterrence may also come in the form of a tailored sentence, unique to that individual. For example, a person convicted of driving under the influence may be recommended to an alcohol recovery program. A famous example is that of Kevin Mitnick, who had committed so many hacking crimes he was sentenced to a psychological counseling program.[1]

Theories of Culture and Learning: Social Learning and Labeling

Another set of criminological theories focuses on the learned values, beliefs, and practices of offenders. These theories have a core assumption that criminal behavior, as with most social actions, is learned. Sociologists have traditionally argued that there are four influences, or *agents of socialization*, that teach people their cultures, values, and beliefs. A person's significant others (i.e., family, close intimate friends) are the first and arguably most important influence. A second influence is a person's peer group. For example, young people are influenced by their classmates and adults are influenced by their co-workers. A third influence is society's institutions (e.g., schools they attend, religious organizations, social clubs). A fourth influence is the media. People learn culture from what they see on television and movies, or read online. The theories discussed below—social learning, labeling theory, and techniques of neutralization—begin with these core assumptions and then develop along different paths.

SOCIAL LEARNING THEORY

Social learning theory rests on the premise that behavior that is positively reinforced is learned, while behavior that is negatively reinforced is not learned (Akers, 1996, 2009; Morris & Higgins, 2010). Modern social learning theory is composed of two strands of thought. The first strand is Edwin Sutherland's theory of *differential association*, which asserts that individuals learn culture (values, beliefs, attitudes, norms) from the people they associate with (Friedrichs, Schoultz, & Jordanoska, 2018). Sutherland identified nine characteristics of differential association:

1. Criminal behavior is learned
2. Criminal behavior is learned through communicating with others
3. Learning occurs primarily in intimate personal groups
4. When criminal behavior is learned, the learning includes (a) techniques of committing the crime and (b) the specific direction of motives and drives, rationalizations, and attitudes
5. The specific direction of motives and drives is learned from definitions of the legal codes as favorable or unfavorable
6. A person becomes delinquent because they learn more definitions favorable to crime than definitions unfavorable to crime
7. Differential association may vary in frequency, duration, priority, and intensity
8. The process of learning criminal behavior by association involves all the mechanisms in other forms of learning
9. Although criminal behavior is an expression of general needs and values, it is not explained by those general needs and values, because noncriminal behavior is an expression of the same needs and values

One drawback of Sutherland's work is that the processes that link differential association to learning are not specified. In other words, *how* does a person learn new behavior? Ronald Akers applied ideas from behavioral psychology to illuminate these processes (see Table 10.1; p. 193). Akers identifies four dimensions of social learning. Two of these are the aforementioned differential association and its definitions originally described by Sutherland. Akers adds *differential reinforcement* and *imitation*. These additions explain how a person comes to learn a new (criminal) behavior.

According to Akers' theory, a person experiencing associations that provide more definitions favorable to crime than definitions unfavorable to crime are only two components of the process. Those behaviors must also be differentially reinforced;the offender must be given rewards for certain behaviors and punished for others. Consider a person who is working at a company where corporate espionage (the theft and/or distribution of

Table 10.1 The Four Dimensions of Ronald Akers' Social Learning Theory

Differential Association	The process by which a person is exposed to definitions favorable or unfavorable to crime and deviance
Definitions	Individuals learn the attitudes, beliefs, and justifications that underpin any given behavior
Differential Reinforcement	When individuals are given rewards for behavior, they are more likely to continue that behavior. Conversely, if an individual is punished for behavior, they are more likely to stop that behavior
Imitation	Individuals learn behaviors after observing others

the company's or competitors) occurs. If many of that person's co-workers are involved in such illicit activity, they will likely avoid negative social sanctions and possibly even receive positive reinforcements for participating in similar behavior. These reinforcements might take the form of be being invited out for drinks after work or having their mistakes at work overlooked because they are a part of the "club."

Akers also identifies imitation as another component of the social learning process. Individuals need not have direct contact with another person to begin adopting deviant or criminal behaviors. It is possible to simply observe the behavior, and then imitate. Consider the college student that witnesses their fellow classmates using AI software like ChatGPT to write papers for college courses. Even if they do not interact with anyone directly engaged in such behavior, observing others committing the act without detection, and perhaps even receiving positive grades for such work could encourage the student to mimic the behavior as well.

The phenomenon of *swatting*—calling in a false report of an emergency (e.g., bomb threat, hostage taking, gunshot victim) with the intent of inciting an aggressive response from police and/or other agents of public safety—serves to further illustrate social learning theory. Swatting has become increasingly popular in recent years among deviant subgroups within online gaming communities. Offenders learn the technique of swatting via other gamers who have either swatted or been swatted. Particularly important in facilitating the act is the knowledge gained concerning the technologies needed and the tactics necessary to successfully incite an emergency response without revealing one's identity or location.

Similarly, the purveyors of child sexual abuse material represent another example of social learning theory. They are often involved in online communities where they learn the techniques necessary to find and share images while evading detection from law enforcement. In one of the largest formal crackdowns on such material, Operation Delego, offenders were identified and arrested via the online community, "Dreamboard." Members of Dreamboard had developed several techniques to evade law enforcement while trading in child sexual abuse material:

- Using aliases and screen names to avoid detection
- Links posted on Dreamboard were required to be encrypted
- Members accessed the board through a proxy server to hide their IP addresses
- Members were also encouraged to use encryption programs on their computers to encrypt their data

These techniques are not likely to be randomly distributed throughout a user population. Rather, prospective members of Dreamboard would have had to learn these techniques from others connected to the online community, and success in evading detection (and thus, criminal prosecution) and accessing the illicit material would have served as positive reinforcers.

LABELING THEORY

Labeling theory argues that deviance is socially constructed through the actions of an audience witnessing deviance, and not the individual who committed the act. Deviant behavior, according to proponents of the theory, does not exist until members in society define it as such. The location, the cultural context, and the characteristics of the offender and audience must be considered when trying to understand why some actions are defined as not deviant, mildly deviant, or severely deviant and worthy of strong negative sanctions.

Labeling theory is primarily understood as explaining deviance and crime at a micro-level, meaning the phenomena occur between individuals and in circumscribed, small group settings. *Micro-level phenomena* are contrasted with *macro-level phenomena*, which describe broad societal trends at the neighborhood or national level. For example, labeling theory may be used to explain why a group of kids in one setting smoking marijuana become seen as deviant, while in another setting the same behavior is ignored. It would not generally be used, however, to describe the national increase in marijuana usage.

Labeling requires power. Some groups and individuals have more ability to label an action as deviant than others. Consider the previous example of a group of youths smoking marijuana. Suppose the group is smoking on the school grounds after hours. The group will not only be disciplined through the formally written measures of the school, but the teacher may also tell other teachers and administrators about the observed behavior. This teacher may be so offended by what they saw that they describe the behavior in the worst possible terms. As a result, the group may become associated with deviance and bad behavior in the minds of the authority figures in the school. Words such as "weedheads," "potheads," and "stoners" may be used in association with the group.

Alternatively, imagine that the group gets caught by an unpopular student instead. The student may join in on the behavior in hopes of being accepted. In this case, the action is not even defined as deviant. Even if the student does not participate in the behavior, given their unpopularity, they will have less ability to influence how other students in the school think of the group. The labeling has less weight in the minds of others if it originates from the unpopular student.

Labeling theory asserts that the labels given to a person can cause further offending. The first acts of deviance are called *primary deviance*. Depending upon the context within which these first acts occur, a person may be labeled so severely and harshly that the label becomes a master status. A *master status* is a label that becomes the most important characteristic of the person. As a result of the label, the person may feel shame or embarrassment and commit further acts of deviance. Alternatively, they may embrace the label, which can also lead to committing further acts of deviance. This *secondary deviance* is progressively worse than the initial primary act. Labeling theorists argue that through the act of labeling early primary deviances, an individual may commit more serious secondary acts and embark on a career of deviance.

Importantly, the act of labeling is also an act of negotiation. It is not predetermined that an individual or group in power can define an action as deviant and the offender accepts the definition. Again, returning to the marijuana example, some of the offending youths may have home environments or personal connections that allow that youth to resist the label. If the youth is also involved in other activities—perhaps as a star on a softball team—then their other extracurricular activities may become more important alternate labels, and thus the label "pothead" is no longer associated with them.

As described in Chapter 2 on cybertrespass, the meaning of hacking has changed greatly over the past three decades. Hacking in the 1960s and 1970s was primarily done by students and academics to learn more about technology (Levy, 1984). The hack was about making technology work better. As a result, the hacking label was not associated with deviance. Instead, the label connoted intelligence and ingenuity. However, as more human activity has migrated into the digital environment, especially economic activity, the meaning of hacking has become more negative. Groups in power began to associate the tinkering with computer technology with the disruption of business operations. The hacker label is now primarily associated with deviance and criminality.

The negative connotations of hacking by journalists and people in law enforcement are resisted by hackers themselves. Turgeman-Goldschmidt (2008) interviewed a series of hackers in Israel, applying labeling theory to interpret their responses. Hackers, who were considered as "bad" hackers, described their hacking as a continuation of bad behaviors as children. In this sense, hacking is a type of secondary deviance. Moreover, these "bad" hackers rejected the labels they had been given, and used other terms or descriptions for themselves—preferring to see themselves as "wild" and "gifted" as opposed to immoral or criminal.

Control Theories: Social Bonding, Self-Control, and Techniques of Neutralization

Most of the theories discussed in this chapter focus on why people deviate from normative behavior. However, control theories ask a different question: Why don't we *all* commit crimes or act in deviant ways? Control theories begin with an assumption that people want to be deviant and require no special learning or motivation to do so. Moreover, this desire to break from normative behavior is consistent across individuals. The theories discussed now all assume that it is the controlling influences of society that prevent individuals from committing deviant acts.

SOCIAL BONDING THEORY

Social bonding theory asserts that crime and deviance result when an individual's bonds to conventional society are broken. There are, according to Hirschi (1969), four elements of the bond between the individual and society (see Table 10.2; p. 196). Individuals vary along each dimension, but the less an individual is attached, involved, committed, and believes in normative or conventional aspects of society, the more likely they are to act in their self-interest.

Social bonding theory would predict higher rates of deviance among people who are loners, unemployed, single, or not members of a religious organization. People who lack

Table 10.2 Hirschi's Elements of the Bond

Element	Explanation	Examples
Attachment	Emotional closeness to people	Friendships with schoolmates or workmates, favorable attitudes towards school and work, emotional bonds between children and parents, loving relationship with family
Involvement	The time invested in activities	Engaged in activities at work or school, attending religious services, participating as parent in child's school activities
Commitment	The willingness to conform to conventional behaviors	A desire to achieve or accomplish societal goals such as academic achievement, a desire to be seen in a positive light by one's peers
Belief	The ideas that support normative behaviors	An agreement with the laws that govern society, and a respect for authority figures such as police and teachers

these and other means of social integration are disconnected from normative goals and expectations. A person who is employed, for example, may become emotionally connected to their co-workers. They may care about how those co-workers view her and will embrace the norms shared by her co-workers.

The theory also explains the higher rates of offending among young people. Indeed, the theory originated as an explanation for juvenile delinquency. Young people, especially those who are not enrolled in high school or college, are often less integrated into society. They may not have started families. They are more transitory, especially males, and thus less likely to be integrated into a neighborhood. Moreover, they may experience unemployment or unstable employment.

Social bonding theory may explain how young men commit acts of domestic terrorism. On June 17, 2015, 21-year-old Dylan Roof shot and killed 9 African American worshippers and injured another at a church in Charleston, South Carolina. After a manhunt, Roof was arrested and is currently in prison. Dylan Roof appeared to lack social bonds. In the months after the shooting, the press asked about Roof to understand his motivations. Many people interviewed commented on his social isolation. A family member commented on Roof, "he was like 19 years old, he still didn't have a job, a driver's license or anything like that and he just stayed in his room a lot of the time."[2]

Social bonding theory can be applied to many types of cybercrime. One major application of the theory is in explaining extremist groups and the individuals who adopt extremist ideologies. Extremist groups use the digital environment to spread their message and recruit new members. A person who does not have strong social bonds in the physical environment to conventional norms may find the message of extremist groups in the digital environment appealing. In other words, they may become "radicalized" through content consumed online. Indeed, Roof was active on white supremacist websites the days and months before the shooting.[3]

In another example, cyberbullying, there is some notion that cyberbullies are characterized as being socially alienated from supportive networks. Discordant relationships with family members, minimal-to-no connections with social peers, and/or unhealthy relationships among co-workers can all serve as examples of the weakened social bonds that might contribute to deviance like cyberbullying. However, we also note here an inverse model between social bonding and cyberbullying in that the cyberbully can just as likely cause a fracturing of social bonds for their victims. *Denigration*—the act of making disparaging remarks about a target and distributing online—is a common activity of cyberbullies and often results in the fraying of social bonds between the intended target and his/her peers (Popovic-Citic et al., 2011).

SELF-CONTROL THEORY (A GENERAL THEORY OF CRIME)

Gottfredson and Hirschi (1990) argued that low self-control in individuals is a major predictor of crime and deviance. Individuals that lack self-control, according to their base theory:

- Prefer simple tasks
- Prefer physical activities rather than mental activities
- Are prone to emotional outbursts
- Are self-centered
- Prefer immediate gratifications

Gottfredson and Hirschi (1990) argue that children who receive inconsistent parenting are more likely to have low self-control as an adult. Inconsistent parenting includes not monitoring children, not recognizing behavior that is inappropriate given current social standards, and failure to discipline consistently. Individuals with low self-control are attracted to crime because crime and other deviant behaviors offer immediate gratification, are exciting and risky, and most crimes do not require a high degree of intellectual investment. As an example, armed robbery is more attractive to a person who has low self-control because there is an immediate monetary reward possible. The long-term effects of jail time and emotional damage to a victim are ignored. Moreover, individuals with low self-control are also more likely to engage in deviant behaviors such as excessive drinking, smoking, and risky sexual behavior. Again, this is for the same reasons of immediate gratification, excitement, and the disregard of long-term effects.

Self-control theory is meant to be a general theory of crime—meaning that it purports to explain all types of crime and deviance. As such, given the wide range of cybercrimes at present, applying the theory to such offenses offers a compelling challenge. On the one hand, many cybercrimes appear to require a person to have a high level of self-control. Learning the nuances of a coding language requires months-to-years of focused mental effort. The person who masters a coding language would likely not be the same type of person who prefers physical over mental activities. Similarly, a successful data breach may take months of planning and require several steps—from developing the exploit kit, to crafting a spear-phishing email, to successful exfiltration, to the monetizing of data stolen. The person involved in this type of activity is not the same as the person who prefers simple tasks and seeks immediate gratification. Even romance scams, which are not technically sophisticated, require months of grooming and a careful consideration of the words and symbols used to communicate to a victim.

On the other hand, many types of cybercrimes appear to be readily explainable through low self-control. Flaming, cyberbullying, and online shaming are all activities in which an individual can lash out immediately without regard for the emotions of those they hurt. The risky decision-making and behaviors often observed with young people exploited online are also key indicators of low self-control potentially characterizes offenders and/

or their victims. We note here the propensity for certain parents to presume the firmness of their control over the safety of their child's Internet activity merely because "they are in the room with me when online" or "they are using the apps I installed for them, so I know it is safe." Such thoughts are representative of the parenting inconsistency Gottfredson and Hirschi cited as harbingers of low self-control—albeit, in these cases, as explanations of *who* might become victims rather than who would commit the offense.

TECHNIQUES OF NEUTRALIZATION

Techniques of neutralization stem from the delinquency research of Gresham Sykes and David Matza (1957). The theory assumes that individuals in society—including members of subcultures—generally adhere to conventional social norms. An individual, the theory asserts, will commit a deviant or criminal act if they can neutralize the guilt associated with violating those norms. For Sykes and Matza, the male juvenile delinquents they observed held honest and law-abiding people in high regard. To commit acts of deviance, they argued, the juvenile delinquents developed mental techniques to make violations of normative behavior acceptable. They write:

> *Disapproval flowing from internalized norms and conforming to others in the social environment is neutralized, turned back, or deflected in advance. Social controls that serve to check or inhibit deviant motivational patterns are rendered inoperative, and the individual is freed to engage in delinquency without serious damage to his self-image.*
>
> (1957, 666–667)

Using these techniques before participating in a criminal or deviant act is an effort to neutralize guilt. These techniques can also be used after the crime is committed to *rationalize* the immoral behavior. For this reason, Sykes and Matza's theory has often been called *techniques of neutralization and rationalization*. It is also important to note that these techniques are used to excuse specific violations of social norms; they do not constitute wholesale rejections of a norm. For example, stealing is condemned by all groups in society. The techniques are used to excuse stealing under certain conditions.

Since its early roots in delinquency studies, scholars have successfully extended the neutralization concept to other types of offending. For instance, Coleman (2006) identified techniques used by white-collar criminals. One technique is the claim of normalcy, where crime is justified by asserting that everyone else is doing it. Another technique is entitlement, where the white-collar criminal justifies theft from an organization by arguing that they deserve something more for the hard (and inadequately compensated) work they have put into the organization.

Consistent across applications of the theory is some aspect of the five forms of neutralization Sykes and Matza initially surmised (see Table 10.3; p. 199). In listing these techniques, we have also given examples as to how they would relate to cybercrime.

The five listed above are the core neutralizations found in cybercrime. They can be understood even more so when framed from the perspective of the victimization target-offender dynamic presented in the preceding chapter. In denial of responsibility, the offender disconnects from the target by disassociating with the cybercrime activity they

Table 10.3 Techniques of Neutralization and Cybercrime Examples

Technique	*Example*
Denial of responsibility—someone else or external factors are the reason the crime was committed	"I am not responsible for the drugs sold on my website."
Denial of injury—asserting that no one was hurt during the crime, or nothing was damaged	"That man/woman is a billionaire. So what if I steal a couple hundred bucks worth of bitcoin from his/her account."
Denial of the victim—asserting that the victim was deserving	"Bank of America is a racist bank that denies loans to Hispanic people. The ransomware attack they got hit with was well-deserved."
Condemnation of the condemners—alleging that those doing the policing or disciplining are being hypocritical	"The US government has been spying on people in my country for years. That is why I am developing spyware to use against them."
Appeal to higher loyalties—the crime had to be committed because of an association with a gang or family	"I had to hack into my company's systems and steal PII. I need to make money for my family."

are directly or indirectly fostering. In denial of injury, the offender is unwilling or incapable of seeing harm experienced by the victim targeted. In denial of the victim, the offender has preconceived the victim targeted as being complicit in and/or deserving of the offense being inflicted. Often, the offender in this scenario has already concluded the target did or will do something that justifies the victimization inflicted upon them. Similarly, under condemnation of the condemners, the offender has determined the target is deserving of being targeted. However, the rationale is grounded in the perception that the target has already committed the same or similar offenses as what the offender is now committing. In appealing to higher loyalties, the offender is committed to serving an entity whose needs outweigh those of the target; thus, victimization of the target is justified if the needs of that entity are satisfied. Essentially, the victim targeted is perceived as standing in the way of a greater good.

Applications of neutralization techniques in cybercrime have been especially successful in studies of digital piracy (Ingram & Hinduja, 2008; Moore & McMullan, 2009). Smallridge and Roberts (2013) identified a new digital, piracy-specific neutralization called "DRM defiance." *Digital rights management*, or DRM, is the code embedded in digital content that manages how a person uses that content. For example, using DRM, a company may limit the number of devices a movie can be downloaded to. Smallridge and Roberts found that computer users who had adopted the belief that DRM should be defied were more willing to illegally download digital content.

Strain Theory

Strain theory, most associated with Robert Agnew (1992), asserts that the presence of unwanted stimuli, called strains, produces negative emotions. The effort to cope with these negative emotions can lead to deviant or criminal behavior. Agnew posited three categories of strains:

1. *Strain as the actual or anticipated failure to achieve positively valued goals*—When there is a disjunction between what we want or expect and what we achieve, we experience negative emotions. An example of this would be a person who values athletic prowess but finds that they cannot compete at a certain level. This creates a degree of disappointment and stress. Another example would be someone who values social status and prestige but finds that they cannot get respect from others
2. *Strain as the actual or anticipated removal of positively valued stimuli*—When something an individual likes or values is taken away or is threatened to be taken away, they will experience negative emotions. This could be the loss of income or a job, a child losing friends because of their parents' moving, or the death of a loved one. It could be a student learning that they may not graduate from college because they did not meet a certain requirement
3. *Strain as the actual or anticipated presentation of negatively valued stimuli*—The presence or threatened presence of noxious and unwelcome phenomena can cause stress in one's life. Cyberbullying falls into this category, as insults and slights are unwelcome. Punishments, especially if they are perceived as unjustified, also fall into this category. Poor grades are also a negatively valued stimulus

Strains often overlap. Consider the example above of a college student who may not graduate. The student may value academic achievement and expects to graduate in a certain amount of time, but for a number of reasons perceives they will not reach those goals (failure to achieve positively valued goals). Failing to receive the degree (the removal of positively valued stimuli) may result from a failing grade in a particular cybercrime class (the presentation of negatively valued stimuli).

In a later article, Agnew further specified strain theory by describing the types of strain most likely to lead to crime and deviance (2001). These strains are perceived as unjust and high in magnitude, are associated with low social control from authorities, and create an incentive for coping through criminal means. Bullying, Agnew argues, is a type of strain that can lead to crime and deviance. It is likely to be perceived as unjust because young people will think they are being treated unfairly. It is likely to be perceived as high in magnitude because peers are central to the lives of young people. It occurs in spaces where there are few authority figures present—bullying happens on playgrounds or in moments when teachers and adults are not monitoring. Finally, students who bully are often engaged in other deviant acts, thereby modeling to the offender forms of criminal coping. For this reason, strain theory has been most commonly linked to cyberbullying—both victimization and perpetration (see Figure 10.1; p. 201).

Several studies have explored the link between cyberbullying and strain. Hay, Meldrum, and Mann (2010) found that both physical bullying and cyberbullying are associated with delinquency. Both forms of bullying were positively associated with external acts of deviance towards others, and internal acts of self-harm. Jang, Song, and Kim (2014) link physical bullying to cyberbullying, with the former acting as a strain and the latter being a response. Keith (2017) found that being bullied was positively associated with two coping mechanisms, avoidance behavior and bringing a weapon to school. More recent studies continue to support the relevance of strain as both a catalyst for cyberbullying (Y. Lee et al., 2022; Lianos & McGrath, 2018; Wilson & Seigfried-Spellar, 2023) and an outcome of it (J. M. Lee et al., 2022).

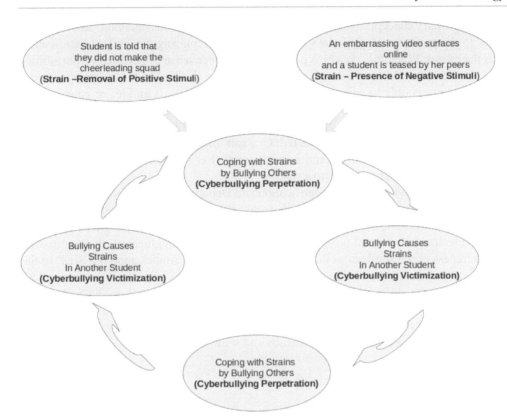

Figure 10.1   An infographic illustrating the links between strain, cyberbullying perpetration, and cyberbullying victimization.

Deindividuation and Disinhibition Theories

The theories of deindividuation and disinhibition attempt to explain the effects of anonymity online. *Anonymity*, in this case, means that individuals can develop their identities and behaviors free from social sanctions derived in the conventional offline world—as they can explore and interact online using screen names. It has also meant, however, that people are freer to commit certain deviant or criminal acts because they can avoid detection and negative sanctions. Someone can be rude or hostile, attempt to defraud another person, or consume child sexual abuse material under the veil of online anonymity.

DEINDIVIDUATION

Deindividuation theory has its foundation in Gustav LeBon's work *The Crowd: A Study of the Popular Mind* (2001). During LeBon's life, France had undergone waves of social unrest. He had experienced the Paris Commune in 1871—a radical populist takeover of the French government—and other smaller protests during the 1890s. LeBon's study was an attempt to explain the violence and irrationality exhibited in crowds.

Two primary concepts in LeBon's work are submergence and contagion. *Submergence* refers to the process of losing one's sense of self and replacing it with an identification with the crowd. When this occurs, a person loses his/her sense of personal responsibility and becomes susceptible to subconscious instincts and desires. In this submerged state, a person is susceptible to *contagion*. A contagion, for LeBon, is an idea or emotion that passes through a crowd. A random suggestion from someone could lead to the entire crowd advocating for that idea. In this way, a crowd is capable of considerable variation in mood swings and is easily manipulated. One can imagine a situation where a crowd of people are protesting at an event and someone says "Let's smash windows," and all of a sudden a peaceful protest turns into a riot.

Researchers who use Social Identification and Deindividuation Effects (SIDE) theory are applying LeBon's core concepts. SIDE argues that communication in the digital environment minimizes social comparison and self-awareness. Anonymity reduces the ability to individualize oneself and others in a group setting (deindividuation), thus increasing the awareness of the similarities that all in the group share. Studies applying SIDE to the digital environment have shown that Internet users who become deindividuated adopt behaviors that are more like the general norms of the group online (Lee, 2005; Postmes, Spears, Sakhel, & De Groot, 2001). These behaviors can indeed be positive—for example, showing support for someone in an addiction forum. Unfortunately, these behaviors can be negative, as when a group of users insults and shame someone.

DISINHIBITION

A second theory that attempts to explain the effects of anonymity is the online disinhibition effect (Suler, 2004). According to Suler, six factors lead to a change of behavior online. These are:

1. Dissociative anonymity—Behavior is compartmentalized, such that an individual can dissociate themselves from their online behavior
2. Invisibility—Individuals cannot see each other, giving people the courage to go places and do things they otherwise would not do
3. Asynchronicity—Because people do not interact with each other in real time, the normative aspects of continuous communication are lost. People can send an email or post to a discussion board and not get immediate feedback
4. Solipsistic introjection—Because of a lack of context cues, individuals may "feel that their mind has merged with the mind of the online companion" (Suler, 2004, 323)
5. Dissociative imagination—People may view their online experiences as not following the same rules and norms as their offline experiences—"they split or dissociate online fiction from offline fact" (Suler, 2004, 323)
6. Minimization of status and authority—In the physical environment, authority figures express their status and power in their dress, body language, and their environmental settings (e.g., an office space with a degree on the wall). This is missing in online environments

Taken together, these six factors create the conditions for an individual to act in ways they normally would not. They feel liberated from the norms that govern offline behavior.

The disinhibition effect can foster two types of behaviors. Positive behaviors, called *benign disinhibition*, include reaching out to others to resolve interpersonal conflicts, exploring new avenues of one's identity, and efforts to improve self-understanding. Negative behaviors, called *toxic disinhibition*, include rude, racist, and misogynistic language, as well as the acting out of socially reprehensible behaviors including consuming and sharing child pornography.

These ideas may offer better explanations for trolling and harassment than traditional criminological theories. In online forums, where a person can detach their online identity from their physical identity, a user may be more likely to commit acts that can be categorized as toxic disinhibition. They may be more likely to bait, antagonize, or hurl racist and sexist language at another person online. They may also be more likely to exhibit behaviors that are not a part of their in-person persona. For example, the 4chan discussion board "Politically Incorrect" (http://boards.4chan.org/pol/) has a norm of posting off-color and controversial topics. A computer user, while conforming to normative attitudes and behaviors about race, class, and gender in the physical world, may be more likely to offer deviant contributions to this board.

Crime Prevention Through Digital Design

Crime prevention through digital design, or CPTDD, connotes a variety of concepts developed separately, but linked by the overarching concept that digital technology and threats stemming from the design and usage of it can be understood through pre-existing theories of deviance control rooted in spatial criminology. For as much as features in a physical environment (e.g., the height of bushes in front yard, the frequency and brightness of streetlights in a neighborhood, availability of open, well-maintained recreational spaces with high visibility), and how people interact with and in that environment can impact the nature and frequency of deviant or criminal activity, so too can features of and interaction with spaces in a digital environment impact cybercrime offending patterns. CPTDD can be understood as a re-purposing of the classic CPTED model (Crime Prevention Through Environmental Design) pioneered through the activism of urban reformers like Jane Jacobs, and made famous through the advancement of scholarship in environmental criminology (Brantingham & Brantingham, 1981) and broken windows theory (Wilson & Kelling, 1982). Thus, a fair amount of relevant scholarship on the subject falls under labelling like *CPTED in digital environments*.

CPTDD has been shown to reduce hacking (Fisher et al., 2022) and the risk of various types of attacks on *cyber physical systems*[4] (Joo et al., 2018). As with the safeguarding of physical spaces under the CPTED philosophy, making online content and systems "defensible," along with target hardening are critical aspects of CPTDD (Phair, 2012). CPTDD further maintains natural surveillance and access control, along with territorial reinforcement and maintenance are all features of CPTED applicable to digital technology and the online spaces made accessible through them (Lim, 2021; Townsend, 2020).

Consider the personal laptop computer that a college student might use on and around campus. Certainly, such a device would be susceptible to a variety of threats both physical and digital in nature. Using a CPTDD framework, addressing the potential cybercrime threats presenting themselves to the student in this scenario might appear as follows:

1. Natural surveillance—The student is aware that the laptop is small enough to be easily stolen or compromised in some malicious way. Thus, they never leave it unattended or lend it out to anyone. They might even place a security lock on it or keep it in a locked room whenever closed and not in use for long periods of time
2. Access control—The student understands that unauthorized access to the laptop is just as likely via compromised access points (e.g., hacking a password). Thus, they regularly change their password and employ two-factor authentication standards. They might also employ a password manager to ensure minimal repetition in password usage across multiple devices and/or online accounts
3. Territorial reinforcement—The student knows that cybercrime threats not only exist on the laptop, but also via Wi-Fi networks the laptop regularly connects to. Thus, they employ a reputable firewall on any such networks they connect to and/or employ a virtual private network (VPN) on the laptop for added security
4. Maintenance—Knowing how common it is for cybercrime threats to target out-of-date hardware and software, the student performs regular updates on the laptop and the software it runs. They also recognize the important of physical maintenance (e.g., keeping the laptop free of dust and moisture) to reduce the risk of major malfunctions requiring additional parties to handle the laptop (e.g., tech support specialists)

Conclusion

In this chapter, we introduced theories to explain crime, deviance, and victimization. These theories come primarily from the discipline of criminology, with some contributions from sociology and psychology. We explored Deterrence Theory, Social Learning Theory, Labeling Theory, Social Bonding Theory, Self-Control Theory, Techniques of Neutralization, Strain Theory, Routine Activities Theory, two theories of Anonymity—Deindividuation and Disinhibition—and Crime Prevention through Digital Design. For each theory, the main assumptions were introduced, concepts relevant to the theory were explained, and its applicability to cybercrime and digital deviance was discussed.

A common discussion in the cybercrime literature is whether cybercrime is old wine in new bottles. Meaning, are we looking at new types of crime that require new theories? In this chapter, we highlighted several pieces of research and presented numerous case studies demonstrating that traditional theories could be used to explain cybercrime. After all, the actors and their motivations tend to be more similar than different regardless of whether the setting is physical or digital.

However, this does not imply that these theories cannot be improved or further specified. This is because, although the actors and motivations remain constant, the environment in which they operate has changed. Traditional theories may need to be adapted to take the new environment into account. A prime example of this is the extensions to traditional Techniques of Neutralization by Smallridge and Roberts (2013) discussed previously. Theoretical developments may move in this direction, where traditional theories explaining broad crime and deviance processes are modified and extended to account for the uniqueness of the digital environment.

CHAPTER 10 CURRENT EVENTS AND CRITICAL THINKING:

One Theory to Rule Them All?

Undergirding this chapter, and indeed much of this textbook, are some central questions: What causes a person to apply technology in the harming of another? Considering its humble, non-criminogenic origins, why has the Internet become such an attractive environment for criminal offending? How does one recognize, and ultimately reduce opportunities of victimization online and/or via digital technology?

Particularly, with so many theories attempting to address these questions and more, is there any one theory that better explains one or more of the cybercrime types addressed in the preceding chapters? Of the ones presented in this chapter, are there theories that seem outdated in the current reality of cybercrime and digital deviance? Explain.

NOTES

1 http://articles.latimes.com/1989-07-19/local/me-3886_1_hacker-kevin-mitnick
2 www.theguardian.com/world/2015/jun/18/dylann-roof-south-carolina-charleston-shooting-suspect
3 www.dailymail.co.uk/news/article-3136475/Dylann-Roof-active-white-supremacist-website-months-posting-comments-minorities-hate-filled-manifesto.html
4 Cyber Physical Systems = systems that connect cyberspace with physical space (i.e., traffic light systems, medical patient records terminals).

REFERENCES

Agnew, R. (1992). Foundation for a general strain theory of crime and delinquency. *Criminology, 30*(1), 47–88.

Agnew, R. (2001). Building on the foundation of general strain theory: Specifying the types of strain most likely to lead to crime and delinquency. *Journal of Research in Crime and Delinquency, 38*(4), 319–391.

Akers, R. L. (1996). Is differential association/social learning cultural deviance theory? *Criminology, 34*(2), 229–247.

Akers, R. L. (2009). *Social learning and social structure: A general theory of crime and deviance.* Transaction Publishers.

Anderson, C. (2008). The end of theory: The data deluge makes the scientific method obsolete. *Wired.* https://www.wired.com/2008/06/pb-theory/

Brantingham, P. J., & Brantingham, P. L. (1981). *Environmental criminology.* Sage Publications.

Coleman, J. W. (2006). *The criminal elite: Understanding white-collar crime* (6th edition). Worth Publishers.

Fisher, D., Maimon, D., & Berenblum, T. (2022). Examining the crime prevention claims of crime prevention through environmental design on system-trespassing behaviors: A randomized experiment. *Security Journal, 35*, 22.

Friedrichs, D. O., Schoultz, I., & Jordanoska, A. (2018). *Edwin H. Sutherland.* Routledge/Taylor & Francis Group.

Gottfredson, M. R., & Hirschi, T. (1990). *A general theory of crime.* Stanford, CA: Stanford University Press.

Hay, C., Meldrum, R., & Mann, K. (2010). Traditional bullying, cyber bullying, and deviance: A general strain theory approach. *Journal of Contemporary Criminal Justice, 26*(2), 130–147. doi:10.1177/1043986209359557

Hirschi, T. (1969). *Causes of delinquency.* University of California Press.

Hua, J., & Bapna, S. (2012). How can we deter cyber terrorism? *Information Security Journal: A Global Perspective, 21*(2), 102–114. doi:10.1080/19393555.2011.647250

Ingram, J. R., & Hinduja, S. (2008). Neutralizing music piracy: An empirical examination. *Deviant Behavior, 29*(4), 334–366. doi:10.1080/01639620701588131

Jang, H., Song, J., & Kim, R. (2014). Does the offline bully-victimization influence cyberbullying behavior among youths? Application of general strain theory. *Computers in Human Behavior, 31,* 85–93. doi:10.1016/j.chb.2013.10.007

Joo, M., Seo, J., Oh, J., Park, M., & Lee, K. (2018, 3–6 July 2018). Situational Awareness Framework for Cyber Crime Prevention Model in Cyber Physical System. 10th Annual Conference on Ubiquitous and Future Networks, Prague, Czech Republic.

Keith, S. (2017). How do traditional bullying and cyberbullying victimization affect fear and coping among students? An application of general strain theory. *American Journal of Criminal Justice, 43*(2), 67–84. doi:10.1007/s12103-017-9411-9

Le Bon, G. (2001). *The crowd: a study of the popular mind.* Dover Publications.

Lee, H. (2005). Behavioral strategies for dealing with flaming in an online forum. *Sociological Quarterly, 46*(2), 385–403.

Lee, J. M., Choi, H. H., Lee, H., Park, J., & Lee, J. (2022). The impact of cyberbullying victimization on psychosocial behaviors among college students during the Covid-19 pandemic: The indirect effect of a sense of purpose in life. *Journal of Aggression, Maltreatment & Trauma, 32*(9), 17.

Lee, Y., Kim, J., & Song, H. (2022). Do negative emotions matter? Paths from victimization to cyber and traditional bullying from a general strain theory perspective. *Crime & Delinquency, 68*(13–14), 25.

Levy, S. (1984). *Hackers: Heroes of the computer revolution* (1st edition). Anchor Press/Doubleday.

Lianos, H., & McGrath, A. (2018). Can the general theory of crime and general strain theory explain cyberbullying perpetration? *Crime & Delinquency, 64*(5), 26.

Lim, H.-W. (2021). A study on countermeasures against cyber infringement considering CPTED. *International Journal of Advanced Culture Technology, 9*(2), 11.

Moore, R., & McMullan, E. C. (2009). Neutralizations and rationalizations of digital piracy: A qualitative analysis of university students. *International Journal of Cyber Criminology, 3*(1), 441–451.

Morris, R. G., & Higgins, G. E. (2010). Criminological theory in the digital age: The case of social learning theory and digital piracy. *Journal of Criminal Justice, 38*(4), 470–480. doi:10.1016/j.jcrimjus.2010.04.016

Phair, N. (2012). Cutting cybercrime is a question of smart design. *The Conversation.* https://theconversation .com/cutting-cybercrime-is-a-question-of-smart-design-9013

Popović-Ćitić, B., Djurić, S., & Cvetković, V. (2011). The prevalence of cyberbullying among adolescents: A case study of middle schools in Serbia. *School Psychology International, 32*(4), 12.

Postmes, T., Spears, R., Sakhel, K., & De Groot, D. (2001). Social influence in computer-mediated communication: The effects of anonymity on group behavior. *Personality and Social Psychology Bulletin, 27*(10), 1243–1254.

Shepherd, M. M., & Mejias, R. J. (2016). Nontechnical deterrence effects of mild and severe Internet use policy reminders in reducing employee Internet abuse. *International Journal of Human-Computer Interaction, 32*(7), 557–567. doi:10.1080/10447318.2016.1183862

Smallridge, J. L., & Roberts, J. R. (2013). Crime specific neutralizations: An empirical examination of four types of digital piracy. *International Journal of Cyber Criminology, 7*(2), 125–140.

Suler, J. (2004). The online disinhibition effect. *CyberPsychology & Behavior, 7*(3), 321–326. doi: 10.1089/1094931041291295

Sykes, G. M., & Matza, D. (1957). Techniques of neutralization: A theory of delinquency. *American Sociological Review, 22*(6), 8. doi:10.2307/2089195

Townsend, K. (2020, July 22, 2020). Preventing cybercrime through environmental design. *Avast Blog.*

Turgeman-Goldschmidt, O. (2008). Meanings that hackers assign to their being a hacker. *International Journal of Cyber Criminology, 2*(2), 382.

Wilson, J. Q., & Kelling, G. (1982). Broken windows. *Atlantic Monthly,* (211), 29–38.

Wilson, N. C., & Seigfried-Spellar, K. C. (2023). Cybervictimization, social, and financial strains influence Internet trolling behaviors: A general Ssrain theory perspective. *Social Science Computer Review, 41*(3), 15.

Wrenn, C. F. (2012). *Strategic cyber deterrence.* Fletcher School of Law and Diplomacy (Tufts University). Retrieved from http://search.proquest.com/openview/2467c5b3016d7f027fc89d16acc6ffc1/1?pq-origsite=gscholar&cbl=18750&diss=y

Young, R., & Zhang, L. (2007). Illegal computer hacking: An assessment of factors that encourage and deter the behavior. *Journal of Information Privacy and Security, 3*(4), 33–52.

Index

Page numbers in *italics* refer to figures, those in **bold** indicate tables.

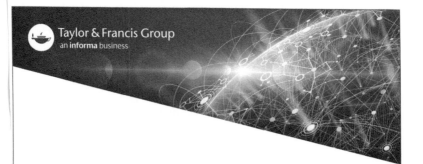